CHINA SINCE THE 'GANG OF FOUR'

CHINA

Since the

'GANG OF FOUR'

EDITED BY BILL BRUGGER

ST. MARTIN'S PRESS   NEW YORK

St. Martin's Press, Inc., 175 Fifth Avenue, New York, N.Y. 10010
Printed in Great Britain
First published in the United States in 1980

Library of Congress Cataloging in Publication Data

Main entry under title:

China since the "Gang of Four".

   Bibliography: p. 262.
   Includes index.
   1. China—History—1976—   —Addresses, essays, lectures.
I. Brugger, Bill.
DS779.2.C45 1980   951.05'7   80-10251
ISBN 0-312-13323-5

FE 12'82

Printed and bound in Great Britain

Contents

List of Tables

Acknowledgements

List of Abbreviations

Introduction   13

1. The Politics of Conflict and Compromise *Michael Sullivan*   20

2. Non-revolutionary Vanguard: Transformation of the
    Chinese Communist Party *Graham Young*   51

3. Industrial Development and the Four Modernisations
    Andrew Watson   88

4. Rural Policy *Bill Brugger*   135

5. The Blooming of a 'Hundred Flowers' and the
    Literature of the 'Wounded Generation'
    Sylvia Chan   174

6. Education — Why a Reversal? *Ronald F. Price*   202

7. China's Foreign Relations: The Reintegration of
    China into the World Economy *Greg O'Leary*   231

Bibliography   262

Contributors   275

Index   277

Tables

3.1 China's Economic Performance, 1969-78:
   Selected Commodities   129

4.1 The Three Sectors of Agriculture   152

4.2 The Collective and Private Sectors of Agriculture   153

4.3 Percentage of Income Generated in the 'Three Level'
   System of Ownership in Rural Communes   155

6.1 Student Numbers in Tertiary Schools, 1964-79   215

7.1 Chinese Trade, 1970-9   248

Acknowledgements

To Dennis Woodward and Steve Reglar for their advice on various chapters in this book. To Andrew Little for map work. To Suzanne Brugger for putting up with an editor who was even more ill-tempered than he was when he put together the previous book. To Marie Baker, Anne Gabb, Jenifer Jefferies and Linda Kelly for typing the manuscript. To Ron Slee for preparing the index and general editorial assistance.

Abbreviations

ASEAN	Association of South East Asian Nations
ANU	Australian National University
BR	*Beijing Review* (formerly *Peking Review*)
CB	*Current Background*
CC	Central Committee
CCP	Chinese Communist Party
CPSU	Communist Party of the Soviet Union
CQ	*The China Quarterly*
EEC	European Economic Community
FAO	Food and Agriculture Organisation
FBIS	*Foreign Broadcast Information Service*
FEER	*Far Eastern Economic Review*
FTD	Full-time Day (Schools)
GMRB	*Guangming Ribao*
GNP	Gross National Product
JPRS	*Joint Publications Research Service*
NATO	North Atlantic Treaty Organisation
NCNA	New China (Xinhua) News Agency
NPAD	National Programme for Agricultural Development
OECD	Organisation for Economic Co-operation and Development
PFLP	Peking Foreign Languages Press
PLA	People's Liberation Army
PR	*Peking Review*
RMRB	*Renmin Ribao*
SCMM	*Selections from China Mainland Magazines* (later *SPRCM*)
SCMP	*Survey of China Mainland Press* (later *SPRCP*)
SPRCM	*Selections from the People's Republic of China Magazines* (formerly *SCMM*)
SPRCP	*Survey of the People's Republic of China Press* (formerly *SCMP*)

Abbreviations

SW	*Selected Works*
SWB	*Summary of World Broadcasts* (British Broadcasting Corporation) *Pt 3 The Far East*
TPRC	*Translations from the People's Republic of China* (*JPRS*)
UNCTAD	United Nations Conference on Trade and Development
URI	Union Research Institute
US	United States
USSR	Union of the Soviet Socialist Republics

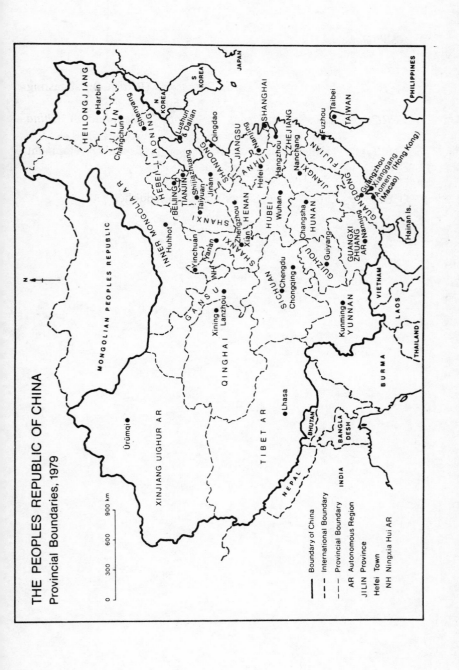

THE PEOPLES REPUBLIC OF CHINA
Provincial Boundaries, 1979

Introduction

BILL BRUGGER

Events in China, since the demise of the 'Gang of Four' in October 1976, have given rise to a debate amongst scholars as intense as that which accompanied the beginning of the Cultural Revolution in 1966. A host of questions has been asked. Has the Chinese commitment to revolution undergone a fundamental change or have China's leaders simply been reacting to the 'ultra-left idealism' generated in the Cultural Revolution? Since socialism may not be built in a state of generalised want, is the current stress on developing the productive forces the only possible socialist strategy? On the other hand, is such a stress an impermissible separation of means and ends? Was Trotsky right in seeing the development of the productive forces as a necessary precondition for ending bureaucratism or was Weber right in seeing such development as the very cause of bureaucratism? What, moreover, is the nature of that bureaucratism? Is it just a deformity, as Trotsky believed, or is it capable of generating new classes, as the 'Gang of Four' believed? If we accept the latter, then what was wrong with the strategy of the 'Gang'? Were they competent theoretically but incompetent politically or is it impossible to make such a separation? Is it true that the present leadership has rejected all of the 'Gang of Four's' arguments and, along with them, those of the late Chairman Mao or have certain leaders made merely a selective rejection? What, therefore, are the policy cleavages among those leaders? Perhaps the policy cleavages are not, in fact, very important and, for all the rejection of the 'Gang', we are merely seeing another version of the same strategy. If this is so, how may we best conceptualise the Chinese social system? Are concepts like 'Stalinism', 'totalitarianism', 'state capitalism' or even 'socialism' itself much use?

If we accept the 'Gang's' terminology and decide that policies currently pursued in China are 'revisionist', then how may we evaluate that 'revisionism'? When did it all begin? Was October

13

1976 a crucial date in the process or should we look to the aftermath of the Cultural Revolution, the early 1960s or even the 1950s? Perhaps the tendency towards 'revisionism' is inherent in the whole socialist project. If such is the case, is the socialist project doomed or can dialectics offer us an appropriate method for understanding the contradictions?

A basic principle of dialectics is that change is generated by internal contradictions. But may recent changes in China be explained solely according to internal causes? Is China responding to changes of a much greater magnitude in the international political economy? If so, then what is the relationship between internal and external factors? Could it be the case that 'right opportunist' tendencies have developed in China, because of the need to industrialise rapidly in the face of the Soviet threat, but that these tendencies do not constitute 'revisionism'? Or is it the case that the international crisis of capitalism required the incorporation of China and China has succumbed to international pressure? If so, to what extent has China succumbed? Does that country provide an inexhaustible market for Western exports? Can its vast resources be exploited for the benefit of multi-national corporations? All these questions have been raised and it will be a long time before we have adequate answers.

The contributors to this book only touch on a few of the above questions. But the contributions are more considered than some of the wild hopes and fears which have been entertained in recent publications on China. Four of the authors have lived and worked in China and witnessed the Cultural Revolution at first hand. All have visited China in recent years and have remained in close touch with recent events. Despite that, all have been perplexed by recent events and have undergone the painful, but perhaps salutary, experience of rethinking the framework with which to examine Chinese politics. This will be quite apparent if one examines the precursor of this volume, *China: The Impact of the Cultural Revolution*, in which five of the present contributors offered chapters.

The study of contemporary China suffers not only from the lack of an adequate conceptual framework. There is also a major problem of evidence. Official sources say one thing whilst indirect sources, which are said to derive from the same people but have come to us via Hong Kong, say something very different. Official sources are much less reluctant, nowadays, to talk about short-comings but the really major failings are leaked to the Hong Kong press. Are such sources accurate? Have they been distorted in the transmission? Indeed, could it be that the Hong Kong press has been used as a platform for members of the Chinese leadership to damn opponents who have presented far more sanguine a picture of economic and social achievements? One is not sure about the answers to such questions but the various chapters in this book will attempt to use such evidence as intelligently as possible.

Although this book is about contemporary events, it must also be about history. Throughout the last few years, events in the recent and distant past have been subject to reassessment and new and contradictory evidence has been produced to support current interpretations. The normal canons of scholarship demand that one rely exclusively on contemporary evidence and avoid *ex post facto* rationalisation. Yet what is one to do when current policy changes are expressed as a reinterpretation of history? What is one to do when documents appear, which purport to be productions of a certain period in the past but which had been suppressed by the then dominant faction? This book will not ignore such evidence but will handle it with due caution.

The use of the past as a mirror of the present is a very old practice in China. The Cultural Revolution, it will be remembered, started with a protracted debate about how to portray honest officials at the end of the Ming dynasty some four hundred years ago. The real issue, it was said, was the 1960s' assessment of the Great Leap Forward (1958-59) and the opposition to Mao Zedong's policies by the then Minister of Defence, Peng Dehuai. In the 1970s, attacks made by the 'Gang of Four' on Confucianism were taken as a covert way of protesting about what was felt to be Premier Zhou Enlai's reversal of the policies of the Cultural Revolution. The same was true for the positive reassessment, at that time, of the reign of the First Emperor of Qin in the third century BC. At first sight, it is not difficult to see why the use of historical analogy has been popular. It does, after all, allow leeway in interpretation and offers a fall-back position for those who fail to get majority support for a particular attack. On the other hand, precisely because of the latitude in interpretation, it is possible to damn anyone who engages in such debate and to attribute to that person the most sinister of motives. This is what China's present leadership has done with the 'Gang of Four' and yet one cannot ignore the fact that some of the 'Gang's' opponents also engaged in oblique historical polemics.

Attacks by historical analogy have continued after the demise of the 'Gang' but contemporary discussions tend to be more direct. The 'mistakes' made during the period after 1957 are now discussed much more openly. The policy of 'letting a hundred flowers bloom and a hundred schools of thought contend' has seen a wide variety of interpretations of the past and, by implication, arguments about the future. This Chinese 'hundred flowers' has, in turn, given rise to a 'hundred flowers' in Western Pekingology and article after article has appeared informing us as to who is really attacking whom. However distasteful, such Pekingology is unavoidable if one wishes to offer more than a depersonalised analysis of structural change. One always runs the danger, however, of being accused of barely substantiated speculation. To mitigate such a charge, Sullivan, in Chapter 1, attempts to locate policy differences within a broader ideological framework. Three views on the nature of socialist transition are considered — that of the 'Gang of Four', that of the no-nonsense 'modernisers' and that of people who condemn the specific methods of the 'Gang' but not Mao's theoretical perspective. Broadly, Sullivan divides the period since October 1976 into three. The first period (October 1976 to mid-1977) was characterised by behavioural attacks on the 'Gang' and an attempt to legitimise the position of the new Party Chairman, Hua Guofeng. The second period (mid-1977 to late 1978) saw a reiteration of Mao's position on socialist transition outlined in the mid-1950s. The final period (since December 1978) has seen a reaffirmation of policies, first mooted in China in the early 1960s but condemned during the Cultural Revolution. In this final period, there has been a liquidation of the Great Leap and the Cultural Revolution in all but name.

Not all contributors to this book accept Sullivan's periodisation. Watson, for example, argues that a decisive shift in industrial policy occurred as early as October 1976 and that 1977-78 was a period of gradual transition to policies of 'market socialism'. Nor do all contributors share Sullivan's view as to the policy positions attributed to various leaders. Yet there is agreement on one major point. No contributor denies that the leadership style of the 'Gang of Four' left much to be desired. But what was the origin of that leadership style? No one argues here that it stemmed merely from the 'evil' nature of the four people concerned. As Sullivan sees it, the élitist political style of the 'Gang' derived from a fundamental flaw in its theoretical position. While defending the 'Gang's' exploration of how to restrict 'bourgeois right' (the principle where equal rights were given to people made unequal by their economic position and capacity), Sullivan argues that no adequate theory was developed which linked Communist Party leadership to class struggle. If, as the 'Gang' claimed, class struggle in society at large was inevitably reflected in the Party, what were the implications for Party leadership? Who decided when the Party line was wrong?

Since October 1976, the Party has made some changes in the theoretical rationale behind its leadership and these Young explores in Chapter 2. The Party has shifted its focus to promoting 'modernisation', governed, it seems, by 'autonomous laws'. Thus, while returning to a more orthodox Leninist view of its 'vanguard' role, the Party may have adopted a very un-Leninist view of the role of theory. The theory, which guides the Party and of which the Party is supposed to be the embodiment, is to be found exclusively in 'practice'. This seemingly orthodox Marxist position has, however, been interpreted as the belief that, once relations of ownership have changed, what is valid is what works according to the value-free dictates of technology. Such a position has called into question the very rationale of the Party as the agent of theory-directed change.

In Chapters 3 and 4, Watson and I examine the specific details of 'modernisation' in the industrial and agricultural sectors. Though our assessments of policies in 1977 and 1978 are different, we both agree that, in 1979, there has been a return to the problematic of the early 1960s, when it was felt that the most efficient way to operate the economy was by methods of 'market socialism'. These implied far greater autonomy at the level of the productive unit, within a context of central control of key economic levers. There has also been a stress on profitability and investment funds have been channelled into areas which promise the greatest short-term return. Such a policy cannot but give rise to great disparities in wealth and income between regions. But will these disparities be greater than those which resulted from the old policies of 'self reliance'? Will, moreover, the revitalisation of the market and the private sector see a recrudescence of capitalism? There is no doubt that many Party theorists, in 1963, thought that it would and O'Leary makes much of the similarities between current Chinese policies and those criticised, at that time, in the famous essay 'Is Yugoslavia a Socialist Country?'

The parallels between China and Yugoslavia are, indeed, quite striking. Within the context of China's 'market socialism', one sees a renewed interest in industrial democracy. Such democracy, however, is defined in a *representative* sense rather than in the *participatory* sense promoted during the Cultural Revolution.

Which type of democracy is more appropriate in the present situation? How will such industrial democracy fit together with the new stress on discipline and neo-Taylorism? How, moreover, can one prevent 'market socialism' contributing to the atomisation of productive units and the concentration on the immediate benefit of one's own enterprise rather than the good of the whole?

A central issue in economic management is that of centralisation and decentralisation. The promotion of vertically integrated trusts and specialised operations will undoubtedly act as a centralising tendency. On the other hand, the principle of enterprise autonomy and the downward transfer of decision-making power to rural production teams and below is the very opposite. It is too early to say what these two tendencies will result in but, at least, Watson's and my own chapters suggest what one should look for.

In Chapter 4, I argue that, at the root of different strategies of rural development, has been the question of liberty and equality. The 'Gang', in pursuit of equality, sought to deny liberty to certain groups in society and to restrict the liberty enjoyed by economic enterprises to do as they wish. The present leadership has restored the liberty of many proscribed groups and has allowed much greater liberty in economic decision-making. In so doing, it has exacerbated 'bourgeois right'. This, the 'Gang' believed, could lead to the generation of new exploiting classes. Debates in China, in recent years, about the 'dictatorship of the proletariat' have been, in fact, debates about the contradiction between liberty and equality. Both are relative terms. The relationship between them is sometimes inverse, yet sometimes one is the precondition for the other. Here one confronts a basic question in political thought and one which is not capable of easy solution. It applies not only to economic relationships but also to fields such as art and literature. However much they might deny it intellectually, many writers and artists act as though there were such a thing as absolute artistic freedom and resent the imposition of limits on their creativity. This is true even in China where art and literature have for centuries been made explicitly subservient to politics. In Chapter 5, Chan explores the current 'blooming' of art and literature in China in the light of the history of the 'hundred flowers' policy since 1957. Not surprisingly, she finds that there is a contradiction between the injunction that art and literature should serve politics and that writers and artists should be free to depict what they like. Is this contradiction any nearer solution in the current situation or have we merely seen a change in the dimensions of current politics?

Chan is, of course, talking about the impact of recent policies on people associated with the élite. Education, moreover is now geared to selecting such an élite rather than its former prescribed role of creating the conditions for mass participation. But could the former policy ever have proved quick and effective enough to produce the specialists China needs? Price does not think so and, in Chapter 6, argues that, since the Cultural Revolution failed to produce specialists of the kind required by the new leaders, they turned back to the system which was familiar to them. As he sees it, the failure to produce an adequate Marxist theory of education was an important factor in what happened. But how may one develop an adequate Marxist theory of education and how would this relate to Party leadership?

Whatever we might feel about recent changes in China, there is no doubt that the debates of the last few years have raised vital questions about the nature of socialism, development theory, freedom of expression and the role of education. China's *rapprochement* with the capitalist West, which O'Leary examines in Chapter 7, has, moreover, contributed to a very important debate about the international economic system. It has raised questions also about the nature of the Chinese political process which was able to respond with such alacrity to the external economic environment. Discarding the naïveté of both left and right, which for many years dominated their field, many China scholars have begun to confront the above questions with fewer illusions. This book seeks to make a contribution to that task.

1   *The Politics of Conflict and Compromise*

MICHAEL SULLIVAN

The Cultural Revolution demonstrated that major ideological and policy differences exist within the Chinese Communist Party. It raised questions about the relationship between Party leadership and mass activism, between 'consolidating' the socialist material base and continuously transforming the socialist relations of production, and between the dictatorship of the proletariat and socialist democracy. But it did not provide ready-made answers and these questions were to plague the Party throughout the 1970s. They were at the centre of the debates which characterised the Party's preparations for the post-Mao Zedong, post-Zhou Enlai era. Furthermore, Hua Guofeng has recently implied that the Party has underestimated the effects of the Cultural Revolution when implementing its economic and social strategies. In addition, it has been made clear that a number of issues which have arisen in recent years cannot be resolved. These observations indicate that questions concerning the nature of socialist transition, which came to the fore during the Cultural Revolution, have, to a large extent, shaped the politics of the post-Mao era.

This chapter will analyse the Party's search for answers to these questions during the period between the Tenth Party Congress in August 1973 and the Second Session of the Fifth National People's Congress in 1979. It will outline three general views of socialist transition which have appeared in recent years and argue that each has important policy implications. These are the notion of 'continuous revolution', which was partially formulated by Mao in the mid-1960s and defended by the 'Gang of Four' in 1975-76, Mao's earlier notion of 'uninterrupted revolution', which was reformulated by Hua Guofeng in 1977-78, and finally the early 1960s' view of an 'advanced socialist system', which became salient once again in 1979. It will begin by charting the career of the 'Gang' from 1973-76.

Then, the post-Mao leadership will be examined in three general periods — from October 1976 to mid-1977, from mid-1977 to the last few months of 1978 and finally from that time to the present (June 1979). These periods overlap to a certain extent but such a division is useful in analysing contemporary events. Each of them was to see quite profound disagreements among the Communist Party leadership — disagreements which may be traced back to the heady days of the Cultural Revolution. Thus this chapter will focus on the recent struggles for political power in the Party and it will be pointed out that these struggles reflect a continuation of some of the ideological and policy disagreements which have marked much of the history of the Party in post-Liberation China.[1] Other contributors will discuss in more detail some of these differences in relation to the post-Mao era.

The 'Gang of Four'

Those subsequently identified as the 'Gang of Four' — Jiang Qing, Zhang Chunqiao, Yao Wenyuan and Wang Hongwen — rose to power in the Cultural Revolution of 1966-69. In the mid-1970s, two of their number — Yao Wenyuan and Zhang Chunqiao — achieved national prominence as the interpreters of Mao Zedong's theory of socialist transition. Their starting point was an interpretation of some remarks made by Mao Zedong, in the early 1960s, during the period of the great polemics with the Soviet Union. In particular, they developed ideas found in Mao's comments on a Soviet textbook on political economy[2] and clarified some of the scattered arguments put forward in the important document 'On Khrushchev's Phoney Communism and its Historical Lessons for the World' (1964).[3] Here, Mao developed the notion that class struggle was generated constantly throughout the whole period of socialist transition. It was just as much a consequence of the present situation as it was a result of remnants of the past. Such class struggle, Mao maintained, was reflected within the Communist Party itself as a conflict between opposing ideological and policy positions. A transitional process might be considered as socialist only if the dictatorship of the proletariat secured the progressive negation of the material base which generated class struggle. 'Taking the capitalist road', therefore, might be defined as anything which extended or institutionalised that material base. This position of Mao's, formulated in the early 1960s, was to supersede, to some extent, his view of the mid-1950s, whereby socialist transition consisted of a process of 'uninterrupted revolution' (*buduan geming*) in which social contradictions were progressively resolved. Other writers have pointed out the specific differences between 'uninterrupted revolution' and the new formulation — 'continuous revolution' (*jixu geming*).⁴ It is sufficient here to point out that not everyone in the Party was to accept the latter and that the interpretation of Mao Zedong Thought was to become increasingly divisive.

Different views on Mao's Thought were quite evident in the Party's reactions to post-Cultural Revolution policies of consolidation and in the aftermath of the still obscure Lin Biao affair of 1971.⁵ After the failure of Lin's alleged attempt at a coup d'état, there were debates in the Party concerning how to 'continue the revolution'. These debates were reflected in different emphases given in speeches to the Tenth Party Congress (1973) by Premier Zhou Enlai and the newly elected Party Vice-Chairman Wang Hongwen. Though both professed a commitment to 'continuing the revolution under the dictatorship of the proletariat', they drew different practical implications from such a commitment. As Zhou saw it, 'continuing the revolution' was a guide for the promotion of unity and stability after the turbulence of the late 1960s.⁶ Wang, however, stressed deepening class struggle and strengthening mass supervision as the basis of Party leadership.⁷ In distinguishing a 'revolutionary line' from 'revisionist deviation', Zhou argued that equal weight should be given to each of the three elements in Mao's famous slogan: 'practise Marxism and not revisionism, unite and don't split, be open and above-board and don't intrigue and conspire'.⁸ Yet Wang argued that the second and third principles were conditional on the first and thus implied that conspiratorial activities, carried on to promote the 'revolutionary line', were quite permissible.⁹ When it came to Mao's slogan that 'to go against the tide was a Marxist-Leninist principle', Zhou restricted its use to a situation where the Party had been overwhelmed by counter-revolutionary forces from without.¹⁰ Wang, however, persisted in the heterodox view, which had informed Mao on the eve of the Cultural Revolution in 1965, that the vanguard of the revolution might be transformed from within and could turn 'revisionist'. Rejecting the traditional Leninist view of Party discipline, Wang held that, if any policy directive was 'revisionist', any Party cadre had the right to resist it.¹¹

The above might be reading too much into what are perhaps no more than subtle differences of emphasis. After all, the focus of each speech was different. Zhou was reporting on politics since 1969 and

Wang was dealing with revisions to the Party Constitution. Differences might be explained in terms of the division of responsibilities within the Politburo. Nevertheless, it was not long after the Congress that Zhou Enlai and Wang Hongwen found themselves on different sides in a campaign to 'Criticise Lin Biao and Confucius'.[12]

The ostensible targets of the campaign of 1974 were the continuing influence of Lin Biao and traditional Confucian virtues. In fact, much of the campaign was about contemporary politics and historical analogy was used in much the same way as it had been in the prelude to the Cultural Revolution.[13] Though the campaign was launched by those subsequently identified as the 'Gang', both the 'Gang' and its opponents were sometimes the attackers and sometimes the targets.[14] When 'Lin's' alleged opposition to the Cultural Revolution and his desire to 'restore capitalism' were criticised, the target was clearly Zhou Enlai or the newly rehabilitated Vice Premier Deng Xiaoping.[15] On the other hand, when Lin was denounced for undermining stability and sabotaging production, the target was the 'Gang of Four'.[16] When that traditional paragon of Confucian virtues, the Duke of Zhou, was criticised for 'restoring the rites' and 'calling to office once again those aristocratic slave owners who had fallen', the target was Zhou Enlai who had rehabilitated victims of the Cultural Revolution.[17] On the other hand, the extolling of the virtues of Li Si, the First Minister of the First Emperor of Qin (third century BC), could be taken either as a defence of Zhou and Deng (for Li was a moderniser) or a defence of the 'Gang' (for Li was an advocate of the ruthless suppression of those who wished to restore the past).[18] The scope for confusion was immense and it is not difficult to see how the campaign soon became buried in a landslide of historical obscurantism.[19]

Undeniably, though, a fundamental issue of the campaign to 'Criticise Lin Biao and Confucius' was how to assess the Cultural Revolution. In a report to a central study class in January 1974, Wang Hongwen indicated just how divisive the Cultural Revolution continued to be:

> The problem is that some cadres in our ranks...still do not fully understand and do not effectively implement the Great Cultural Revolution as seriously and effectively as they did seven or eight years ago. Some even describe the Great Cultural Revolution as a dark night or as a raging flood or a savage beast. Still others say that their hair stands on end when one mentions the Great Cultural Revolution.[20]

Wang felt, in early 1974, that there was a danger that the general orientation of the struggle to criticise Lin Biao might develop into a 'liquidation of the Cultural Revolution'.[21] By the end of the year, however, what was being criticised was not the negation of the Cultural Revolution but attempts to split the Party.[22] The 'Gang', it would appear, was on the defensive. In an atmosphere of stability and unity, the Fourth National People's Congress met in Beijing in early 1975. Compromise seemed to be the order of the day and balance was stressed in the appointment at the congress of both Zhang Chunqiao and Deng Xiaoping as Vice-Premiers[23] and subsequently in their elevation to top positions in the People's Liberation Army.[24] The new spirit of compromise permeated the major speeches to the congress given by Zhou Enlai and Zhang Chunqiao[25] and it seemed as though the whole Party was about to rally behind the now famous call of Zhou Enlai to 'build China into a modern socialist state by the year 2000'. This was the origin of the current policy of 'four modernisations' (industry, agriculture, science and technology and national defence)[26] — a general policy with which no one, including the 'Gang of Four', had any major objection.[27]

When thoughts were given, however, as to how to translate Zhou's call for modernisation into practice, divisions within the Party became salient once again and the ensuing campaign to 'Study the Theory of the Dictatorship of the Proletariat' saw the recrudescence of polemic. During that campaign, two key articles were published which articulated most clearly the 'Gang's' perspective on modernisation. These were Yao Wenyuan's 'On the Social Basis of the Lin Biao Anti-Party Clique'[28] and Zhang Chunqiao's 'On Exercising All Round Dictatorship over the Bourgeoisie'.[29] It was argued that modernisation was not just a question of developing the productive forces. Any programme of socialist transition had simultaneously to pay due attention to the relations of production. Thus, the system of ownership, the nature of the distribution of the social product and the relations between people in the process of production had to be transformed in such a way as to restrict the material conditions for the generation of class struggle. Attention had to be given to the 'three major differences' (between town and country, worker and peasant and mental and manual labour) and to the principle of 'bourgeois right'. This principle rewarded people according to a capacity to labour which was necessarily unequal in the transitional economic structure. Unless restricted, the principle of 'bourgeois right' would provide the basis for the generation of new class differences.[30]

The 'Gang' held, therefore, that during socialist transition, the development of the productive forces only had meaning in terms of the transformation of the relations of production. It was the latter which dominated the former. Thus, socialism was not a particular configuration of the productive forces, nor even a synonym for state ownership. It was, in fact, the whole process whereby capitalism was negated and communism established.[31] In that process, the reflection of class struggle within the Party had important implications for the Party's vanguard role. The Party did not simply carry out dictatorship over 'class enemies'. Within the Party itself, it was necessary for the 'revolutionary line' to exercise dictatorship over the 'revisionist line'. Furthermore, to the extent that the Party was not articulating the interests of the proletariat, it must be 'taking the capitalist road'.[32] Such a state of affairs could only be changed by launching new 'cultural revolutions' in the same manner as Mao did in 1965. As far as the 'dictatorship of the proletariat' applied to society as a whole, it must apply to each and every level because *all* struggle was a reflection of class struggle. Now, class struggle was no longer seen just as the struggle against remnant landlord and comprador elements as it had been in the old notion of 'uninterrupted revolution'. Class struggle, in the new formulation, was intrinsic to the reproduction of structural inequalities. It was, moreover, manifested in the day-to-day conflict among workers, peasants, intellectuals and Party and state cadres. It resided even in those contradictions which had previously been considered 'among the people' and 'non-antagonistic'.[33]

From the above, one may see the importance the 'Gang' attached to the Cultural Revolution of 1966-69 as a symbol of 'continuous revolution'. Its members were concerned above all to stem the tide of reaction against the Cultural Revolution, which had begun in the early 1970s and which seemed just as serious in 1975. They were not, however, unconcerned with developing the productive forces. They did not ignore the constraints of existing material conditions. Nor is it accurate to say that they enjoyed no support from either Party or masses. Even if one makes allowances for the charge that the media under their control did not accurately reflect reality,[34] it is impossible to ignore the many examples cited in the press in 1975 of how the major theoretical arguments of the 'Gang' were related to specific material conditions[35] and how transforming the relations of production was related to increasing production and developing the productive forces.[36]

The negative policy of restricting 'bourgeois right' was coupled with what were felt to be the positive achievements of the Cultural Revolution. These were referred to as 'socialist new things'.[37] Together, these latter constitute much of what in the West has been referred to as the 'Maoist' approach to development.[38] They include 'self-reliance' in foreign economic relations and technical innovation, the modernisation of the army in the tradition of 'people's war', decentralisation of decision-making authority to local areas (Schurmann's Decentralisation II)[39] and within economic enterprises, the establishment of 'revolutionary committees' in units of government and production, the despatch of educated youth to the countryside, the participation of cadres in manual labour and the fusion of schools and society with the emphasis on breadth rather than depth.[40] Many of these policies will be discussed by other contributors to this book. It need only be noted that the 'socialist new things' which the 'Gang' defended were very real and did not just exist in people's heads. If the 'Gang's' proposals had not enjoyed much success, how might one explain the subsequent reactions to the reversal of policy? How also might one explain recent criticisms of cadres who are said still to be under the influence of the 'Gang of Four'?

But China was never the utopia which the press in 1975-76 made out; nor was it the chaotic mess which the current leadership would have us believe.[41] The problems of factionalism, resentment and recriminations remained and these were particularly serious at a time when China was preparing for the Fifth Five Year Plan (to begin in 1976). But are these negative effects of the Cultural Revolution sufficient to explain the ease with which the 'Gang' was arrested and the apparent joy at its demise? For an answer to this question, one needs to look at the sphere of political organisation. It would seem that the 'Gang' never articulated its view of class struggle to a theory of Party leadership; nor did it develop concrete measures for the implementation of that Party leadership. The 'Gang' thus became increasingly isolated from the rest of the Party and lacked the necessary organisational mechanisms to see that its policies were implemented.[42] Perhaps the development of an adequate theory was impossible, for how does one reconcile the need for vanguard leadership with the view that the Party is subject to the same kind of class struggle as that which pertains in the rest of society? Who, after all, is in a position to decide when the Party has become 'revisionist'? In the end, it could only be the 'Gang of Four' which decided and any opposition to its views was branded as 'revisionist'. The 'Gang' began to argue that everything which existed before the Cultural Revolution had been dominated by a 'sinister black line'[43] and any criticism of the Cultural Revolution became impossible. Nowhere was this more apparent than in the cultural sphere, dominated by Jiang Qing, as Chan will later discuss.

There was a failure too to analyse the practical implications of the notion of 'exercising all-round dictatorship over the bourgeoisie'. What does it mean to 'exercise all-round dictatorship' on the shop floor or in the wheat field? Once all struggle is held to reflect class struggle, is it possible to work out degrees of antagonism and specify, as Mao did, the differences between 'antagonistic' and 'non-antagonistic' contradictions? In such a situation, the Marxian notion of 'dictatorship' may degenerate into simple repression and the present leadership has made much of the replacement of discussion by dogmatic purity.[44] Calls for greater democracy and the implementation of the Mass Line did nothing to prevent struggles among the masses and the effect of such calls was only to exacerbate the factionalism left over by the Cultural Revolution. The result of all this was most ironic. The campaign to launch a new Cultural Revolution did not evoke much mass response.

The following outline of the struggles in 1975-76 will suggest that the potential for a compromise between the 'Gang of Four' and other sections of the Party may have existed in early 1975, though it is doubtful whether such a compromise was ever politically possible. The 'Gang' failed to 'unite with the majority' and consequently rejected the political style pioneered by Mao Zedong. Thus, Mao's personal criticisms of the 'Gang' focus, in the main, on its politics rather than its policies.[45] Yet, if one thinks back to Wang Hongwen's position at the Tenth Party Congress, when he suggested that it was correct to organise a split in the right cause, he was recalling exactly what Mao himself did at the beginning of the Cultural Revolution. Wasn't Mao then the only arbiter? The similarity between Mao on the eve of the Cultural Revolution and the 'Gang' in 1976 is striking!

The Struggles of 1975-76

The 'Gang of Four's' inability to 'unite with the majority' was nowhere more apparent than in its reaction to the policies put forward by the Party leadership in 1975 to implement the 'four modernisations'. To guide current work, in the spirit of the 'new course' charted by Zhou Enlai in the early 1970s, the State Council issued three documents which called for a reassessment of the policies carried out in the Cultural Revolution and criticism of the remnants of Lin Biao's 'ultra-left line'.[46] These documents ('On the General Programme for All Work of the (Whole) Party and the (Whole) Country', 'Some Problems in Speeding up Industrial Development' and 'Several Questions Concerning the Work of Science and Technology') were to be rejected by the 'Gang' as the 'three poisonous weeds designed to restore capitalism'.[47] There was, however, probably little disagreement as to the general goals articulated in the documents. It was planned to implement the modernisation proposals in two stages. In the first stage (up to 1980), the aim was to build 'an independent and relatively comprehensive industrial and economic system'. In the second stage (up to 2000), it was anticipated that the national economy would 'advance to the front ranks in the world'.[48] Throughout both stages, priority was given to agriculture in the spirit of Mao's seminal policy document of 1956, 'On the Ten Major Relationships'.[49] Much more contentious, however, was the fact that the modernisation strategy was predicated on policies of export-led growth. Large amounts of oil and coal were to be exported to pay for technological imports (and in particular the import of complete plants). To develop these resources, it was anticipated that China would have to seek foreign credit.[50]

We know now that the staunchest advocate of the modernisation plans of 1975 was Vice-Premier Deng Xiaoping and that the 'Gang of Four' rejected them. We are unsure, however, as to where other members of the Chinese leadership stood. Between Deng and the 'Gang', there was probably a broad intermediate position. It is also possible that some leaders accepted the modernisation proposals and yet still clung to the broad parameters of the theory of socialist transition put forward by the 'Gang'. This, one suspects, was the position of Hua Guofeng. Some scholars have argued that Hua was actively involved in formulating the strategy laid down in the documents of 1975[51] yet, if one looks at the speech given by Hua to the First National Conference on Learning from Dazhai in Agriculture in October 1975, one is presented with views not dissimilar from those of the 'Gang of Four'.[52] In his theoretical pronouncements, Hua faithfully echoed the position of the 'Gang' on 'bourgeois right':

> We must be aware...that in socialist society there are still classes
> and class struggle, and the three differences (between town and
> country, between worker and peasant and between mental and
> manual labour) still remain. *Our country at present practises a*
> *commodity system. The wage system is also unequal and so is the*
> *eight grade wage scale etc. Under the dictatorship of the prole-*
> *tariat such things can only be restricted.* New bourgeois elements,
> therefore, will invariably be engendered continuously. This is true
> of the countryside as well as the cities.[53]

It is highly unlikely, however, that Hua agreed with all of the
'Gang's' attacks on Deng. The 'Gang', it will be remembered, saw
the struggles of 1975-76 as the first stage of a new cultural revolution
directed at 'capitalist roaders' in the Party.[54] Hua, on the other
hand, described the polemics as simply a 'debate' and an example of
democracy.[55] Such comments might be seen as an opportunist
response to an unclear situation and it was Hua, more than anyone
else, who was to benefit from the downfall of Deng. The comments
may, on the other hand, simply reflect Hua's agreement with the
'Gang' on some points and with Deng on others. Whatever Hua's
position, it would seem that his attempt to combine elements of the
'Gang's' view of socialist transition with the 'four modernisations'
was insufficient to satisfy the purist 'Gang' and he was attacked for
'revisionism'.[56] As the 'Gang' saw it, Hua, who had worked closely
with the State Council since the Fourth National People's Congress
in early 1975, was guilty of a 'sell-out'.

The issue of 'selling out' or 'capitulationism' was to be a major
theme of a short-lived but significant campaign, launched by the
'Gang of Four' in late 1975, to criticise the Ming dynasty novel *The*
Water Margin (Shuihuzhuan).[57] This novel, which had enjoyed
considerable popularity in China during the past four hundred
years, portrayed the exploits of a band of Robin Hood-type outlaws
at the end of the Song dynasty. Like the campaign to criticise Lin
Biao and Confucius, this campaign was to see more criticisms of
current policies by historical analogy. The focus of the criticism was
the capitulation to the Imperial forces by the bandit leader Song
Jiang. On the one hand, the criticism was said to be a covert attack
on Zhou Enlai's policy of export-led growth (capitulating to foreign
countries)[58] and, on the other, it was an attack on new leading cadres
who were said to be 'selling out' to the veterans. Hua, it would seem,
was felt to have been 'selling out' the potential base of support for

the 'Gang' within the Party.[59] It was doubtless Hua's middle-of-the-road position which earned him the post of Acting Premier after the death of Zhou Enlai in January 1976 but, by then, any hope of a compromise between the various factions had probably evaporated and the 'Gang' renewed its attacks upon him.[60]

Evidence that all hope of compromise had evaporated before the end of 1975 was provided by the head of the Party's propaganda department, Zhang Pinghua, in July 1978, when he argued that plans may have been made to remove the 'Gang of Four' two or three months before the death of Zhou.[61] By the time of the now famous Tiananmen demonstrations in memory of Zhou Enlai in April 1976, the 'Gang' could only respond desperately by arresting demonstrators and attaching the blame for the disorder to the 'conspiracies' of Deng Xiaoping. With the removal of Deng Xiaoping from all his posts and the appointment of Hua Guofeng as substantive Premier after the suppression of the demonstrations, a campaign was launched openly to criticise Deng Xiaoping.[62] It was to be a lifeless affair which never had much effect at the grass roots level.[63] Though hampered by factionalism in many areas, the Party organisation, which the 'Gang' never succeeded in controlling, was able to limit the campaign and to produce a situation which was very far from the picture painted by the press that a new cultural revolution was about to erupt.[64] This is not to say, however, that all senior cadres boycotted the campaign. Indeed, some people, who were prominent in denouncing Deng, were to become equally prominent in the post-Mao leadership. Nor may one claim that the campaign gave rise to no debate. In the education sphere, in particular, there was to be a lively polemic about combating 'the right deviationist wind to reverse previously correct verdicts'.[65] In general, though, the 'Gang' found itself without an organisation to articulate its policy. Its political intransigence, moreover, had already deprived it of much institutional support.

It is when one considers the campaign to criticise Deng Xiaoping that the comparison between 1976 and the beginning of the Cultural Revolution is most instructive. Just as the Socialist Education Movement of 1963-66 had failed to live up to Mao's expectations, so the campaign against Deng failed to achieve the goals set for it by the 'Gang'. Both movements were seen as attempts to rectify the influence of a 'revisionist line' in the Party by means of mass activity. In the earlier movement, however, the Party machine insisted that rectification of the Party was an *internal* matter and was able to head off the criticism.[66] Similarly, in 1976, the Party closed ranks and modified the attacks against Deng. Yet the Socialist Education Movement developed, in 1966, into the Cultural Revolution. Why then was it that Mao was able to deal with Party obstruction in 1966 by successfully launching the largest mass movement in China's history, whereas the 'Gang', a decade later, was to fail?

One obvious reason was that the Party had learnt its lesson from the Cultural Revolution and knew how to pre-empt 'splittist activities'. Another explanation takes us beyond purely human factors. The awesome Tangshan earthquake in July 1976 was a major blow to the economy and did not augur well for policies which might damage production. Furthermore, the deaths of the three veteran leaders of the Chinese revolution — Zhou Enlai, Zhu De and Mao himself — within eight months of each other created an unprecedented situation. Perhaps most important of all, the 'Gang' did not command anything like the same ideological and personal respect enjoyed by Chairman Mao.

Examining the course of the campaign to criticise Deng in 1976, one wonders whether the 'Gang' had any inkling of the strength of the forces which were eventually to engulf it. By June, it would seem that at least one of its members — Zhang Chunqiao — realised that the contradictions between his views on Party leadership, 'all-round dictatorship', and increasing production might be exploited by his enemies. In a speech to a central study class in June 1976, whilst reaffirming his commitment to the new cultural revolution, Zhang went to great pains to separate the current campaign from the 'ultra-left' view which sought to denounce any cadre who had made any mistake.[67] Strong Party leadership was necessary, he declared, in order to combat anarchism and yet the roots of anarchism lay in the very 'adverse wind' which he advocated. This was the old problem of how to exercise Party leadership in a campaign which was directed against the Party. Belatedly, Zhang faced up to this problem and, in doing so, could only retreat to the old and unsatisfactory view that one must distinguish between 'antagonistic contradictions' and those 'among the people'.[68] He was also beginning to see the problems for production which stemmed from his particular inter-pretation of the primacy of politics. But it was too late! Production had already been disrupted. Anarchic behaviour was widespread and a wave of repression had resulted in the arrest of between 40,000 and 50,000 people in the wake of the Tiananmen demonstrations.[69]

One can only speculate on what might have happened had Zhang, the most articulate theorist of the 'Gang of Four', begun his re-evaluation a year previously. Within three months, Mao Zedong was dead and, on October 6th, the State Council guard unit 8341, under the command of Wang Dongxing, arrested the 'Gang' and ushered in a new period of Chinese history.[70]

Initial Disagreements Among the Post-Mao Leadership

The arrest of the 'Gang of Four' was immediately followed by a torrent of abuse and personal vilification which resembled the most vicious attacks made upon Liu Shaoqi during the Cultural Revolution.[71] It was alleged that Wang Hongwen was a typical 'new bourgeois element', Zhang Chunqiao was a Guomindang agent, Yao Wenyuan had been brought up in the family of a renegade and Jiang Qing had begun her counter-revolutionary career back in the 1930s.[72] It was claimed that the 'Gang' had sabotaged socialist construction, had opposed Mao Zedong, Zhou Enlai and large numbers of veteran cadres and had brought the economy to the brink of collapse.[73] For about eight months, the press piled accusation upon accusation to the point where it is possible to identify more than fifty policy areas in which the 'Gang's' 'pernicious influence' was said to have caused problems. Yet amid all this behavioural criticism, there was not much discussion of theory.

Why was it that basic ideological and policy issues were not discussed in the first half of 1977? Perhaps the most important reason was that, after the traumas of 1976, the Party leadership was unwilling to air differences which might split the Party and detract from the legitimacy of the new leadership. Faced with a degree of unrest in the provinces, the new leadership sought to build up the image of the new Party Chairman, Hua Guofeng, as Mao's lawful successor and the focus of unity.[74] Much also was made of the memory of Zhou Enlai as a rallying point around which the Party could focus people's emotions.[75] The appearance of unity, however, masked quite profound differences in policy. At one extreme stood the former Vice-Chairman of the Party, Chen Yun, an advocate of sound planning and management and a leading critic of the Great Leap Forward of 1958-59.[76] In early 1977, it is said, Chen demanded the immediate rehabilitation of Deng Xiaoping, a reversal of the verdict on the Tiananmen demonstrations of April 1976 and the posthumous rehabilitation of Peng Dehuai, the major critic of the

Great Leap Forward and the symbolic opponent of Mao's development strategy.[77] At the other extreme stood Wu De, the mayor of Beijing, who had played a mayor role in the suppression of the Tiananmen demonstrations and in the subsequent campaign to criticise Deng Xiaoping.[78] Between these two extremes stood the bulk of the Party leadership headed by Hua Guofeng and Ye Jianying, who was perhaps instrumental in keeping the post-Mao leadership together for many months.

As early as October 1976, Wu De attempted to seize the initiative. At a rally in Tiananmen Square on the 29th, Wu argued that, whilst denouncing the 'Gang of Four', there was a need to 'continue to criticise Deng and repulse the right deviationist attempt to reverse correct verdicts'.[79] Wu's comments were transmitted to the rest of the world by *Peking Review*. In December, however, the Party's theoretical journal *Hongqi (Red Flag)* announced that all of Mao's recent warnings about the danger of 'revisionism' had not really been directed against Deng but against the 'Gang'.[80] Thus, when Wu's October speech was published in the glossy English language publication *China Reconstructs* in January 1977, the references to continuing the struggle against Deng were omitted.[81] Had the Party changed its mind between October and December 1976 or did the issue of Deng Xiaoping continue to be the source of considerable disagreement? In the light of the poster campaign against Wu De in 1978 and his subsequent removal from office, one suspects that Wu was very reluctant to change his mind and accepted the authenticity of Mao's statement to the effect that Deng did not understand the importance of class struggle. Deng's view that 'it did not matter whether a cat was white or black so long as it caught mice' was felt to be a veiled repudiation of the difference between imperialism and Marxism.[82]

Reaction to Wu De's reluctance to revise the official verdict on Deng was revealed in a poster, appearing in Guangzhou in December 1976, which branded him an opportunist and 'bourgeois careerist'.[83] It was clear, moreover, that Wu was not alone in his reluctance and other posters indicated that the veteran military commander Chen Xilian and the commander of the State Council guard unit 8341, Wang Dongxing, who had arrested the 'Gang', had sought an assurance from Hua in October that the criticism of Deng would continue.[84] Such pressure was reflected in a speech by Hua Guofeng to rusticated youth attending a new conference to 'Learn from Dazhai in Agriculture' in December:

Very little reference has been made at this conference to the issue of criticising Deng. Some people, therefore, are in doubt, as to whether there will be a continuation of the movement to beat back the right deviationist wind...personally initiated and led by Chairman Mao... Despite the acute contradiction that once existed between Deng and the 'Gang of Four', they are actually no different from each other in terms of their revisionist nature... Our knocking down the 'Gang of Four' cannot be construed as an acquittal of Deng Xiaoping. However, at the present stage, the principle contradiction does not lie with him.[85]

The above quote may help us to understand why some poster writers, in January 1977, added Hua to the 'Gang' and referred to a 'Gang of Five'.[86] As Hua seemed to indicate, attacks on the 'Gang', if taken too far, might reflect on the position of Mao himself and it was through Mao that Hua claimed legitimacy. After all, Hua had just supervised the editing of the fifth volume of Mao's *Selected Works* and Mao's 1956 essay 'On the Ten Major Relationships' had just been published with much fanfare.[87]

In March 1977, however, Hua succumbed to pressure from the right and Deng was soon rehabilitated. Hua could only declare that the 'Gang' 'attacked and fabricated charges against Comrade Deng Xiaoping...all the slanders and unfounded charges made by the "Gang of Four" against Comrade Deng Xiaoping should be repudiated'.[88]

The Escalating Campaign Against the 'Gang'

The rehabilitation of Deng Xiaoping in mid-1977 was confirmed at the Eleventh Party Congress in August. Though the importance of Deng's 'three poisonous weeds' had enjoyed implicit recognition before the Congress, they were now explicitly referred to as 'fragrant flowers' and attempts were made to work out a new economic strategy based on the 1975 documents.[89] The Congress marked a distinct shift in emphasis in the campaign against the 'Gang of Four'. Previously, the stress had been on criticising the 'Gang's' behaviour and 'narrowing the focus of attack', especially at the organisational level. Now the focus of attack was widened and the campaign against the 'Gang' extended from a criticism of its behaviour to a denunciation of its *line* which was now linked to that of Lin Biao. Particular attention was devoted to those who sought to 'keep the lid on the struggle'.

By December 1977, the campaign had broadened to include the investigation, criticism and removal of 'hidden followers of the Gang'. All instances of factionalism were seen as manifestations of support for the 'Gang'. Such a charge was levelled, for example, at members of the Gansu Provincial Party Committee who apparently refused to implement the line of the Eleventh Congress.[90] In April 1978, in the city of Luda, 'followers of the Gang' opposed the activities of a work team which had been sent to investigate complaints at the Dalian Car Plant and engaged in a poster campaign. One of their number even went to the disgusting lengths of riding his bicycle round the plant, wearing short pants in broad daylight.[91] But, humour aside, there is much evidence of opposition to the extended campaign as people began to realise that criticism of the 'Gang' was developing into criticism of the Cultural Revolution and, by implication, Chairman Mao.[92]

Throughout late 1977 and 1978, prominence was given in the press to provincial and municipal Party committees who had successfully ferreted out 'followers of the Gang'. They were to be found all over the country — in Zhejiang, Heilongjiang, Hubei, Jinan, Tianjin and a host of other places.[93] Throughout, there were charges that Party committees were complacent, that they felt that the 'Gang' had been 'nipped in the bud' before it could cause any trouble and that the campaign did not really concern them.[94] Some cadres, it was said, were reluctant to link criticism of the 'Gang' with that of Lin Biao because they feared that the movement would be used to settle old scores and thus undermine the 'unity and stability' for which the Party had called.[95] It was pointed out, most forcefully, that a political repudiation of the 'Gang' was not the same as making a clean ideological break with it. Such a charge was, no doubt, levelled at Wu De but it might equally have applied to Hua Guofeng.[96]

In 1978, it was not at all clear just what the injunction to make a clean ideological break with the 'Gang' might mean. In such a situation, local Party branches were often cowed and fearful. They did not want to be held guilty of mistakes nor to 'lose face'.[97] But perhaps their fears resulted from the rather contradictory messages about the campaign which came from the Party centre. At the First Session of the Fifth National People's Congress in February 1978, Hua Guofeng announced that investigation of individuals and incidents associated with the 'Gang's' conspiracy had, in the main, been successfully concluded.[98] In July, he was to make the same point.[99] In August, however, Deng Xiaoping's close associate, Wei Guoqing, argued that some cadres had yet to be investigated[100] and the veteran military commander, Xu Shiyu, echoed this position, claiming that the 'Gang's' pernicious influence was both widespread and deep.[101] Since the Party centre appeared to be divided on the scope of the campaign, with some leaders more fearful of the consequences than others, is there any wonder that local cadres should also have been fearful?[102]

'Uninterrupted Revolution' and its Opponents

Divisions among the leaders of the Party, on the scope of the campaign to criticise the 'Gang of Four', must be seen in the context of much broader divisions concerning the nature of socialist transition. In Hua Guofeng's opinion, the 'four modernisations' had to be guided by Mao Zedong Thought and, in particular, his views on 'continuing the revolution'. What Hua meant by this, however, was not the same as what the 'Gang' meant in 1975. Hua's views were set firmly within the problematic of 'uninterrupted revolution' of the mid-1950s.[103] This, it will be remembered, saw the correct handling of social contradictions among the people as the motive force for development rather than class struggle. According to this view, class struggle was the result of remnant influences from the past and was not continually generated in socialist society. It was predicated upon the notion that there was a distinct social model identified as socialism and an implicit socialist mode of production.[104] Though Hua talked in language reminiscent of the 'Gang' to maintain continuity with the late Chairman Mao, his position was fundamentally different.

One might argue that the reason why Mao moved away from his mid-1950s' view of socialist transition to the problematic of class struggle was that the former was insufficiently dynamic. The point is, however, that Mao, in the mid-1950s, believed that his view of uninterrupted revolution was indeed dynamic and this view was shared by Hua in 1978. But Hua's view stopped short of a fully-fledged 'generative' view of class struggle. Hua accepted the view that class struggle was reflected in the Party and defended the Cultural Revolution as Mao's attempt to combat Liu Shaoqi's 'revisionist line'.[105] That revolution had, however, been sabotaged by Lin Biao and the 'Gang of Four' who had to bear the blame for all its shortcomings. The failures in the past, therefore, were due not to Mao but those people who were 'left in form and right in essence'.[106]

Returning to Mao's development strategy of the mid-1950s, Hua extolled the Great Leap slogan of 'self-reliance' and its subsequent re-interpretation in the Dazhai and Daqing models of economic development.[107] He upheld Mao's injunctions to 'grasp revolution and promote production', 'take steel and grain as the key link' and identified himself with a new Ten Year Plan.[108] This drew its inspiration from Mao's Twelve Year Plan of the mid-1950s, which was to inform the Great Leap Forward. Commenting on the plan, which Hua introduced to the First Session of the Fifth National People's Congress, articles drew explicit parallels between current policies and those of the Great Leap Forward[109] and there was constant reference to the 1958 General Line of 'going all out, aiming high to achieve greater, faster, better and more economical results in building socialism'.[110] After all, the Great Leap was the direct outcome of Mao's notion of 'uninterrupted revolution' and one should not be surprised that articles in the press spoke once again of the merits of 'imbalance' and 'wave-like development'.[111]

The Great Leap atmosphere, which accompanied the promulgation of ambitious production targets in early 1978, did not fit easily into the rehabilitation of the notion of export-led growth, despite Hua's attempts to combine the two in his outline of the National Plan. Nor did the new atmosphere promise 'great order across the land'. Indeed, there seemed to be a fundamental contradiction between the Great Leap scenario and the increasingly popular view that, once one had rejected the 'Gang's' position that socialism consisted simply in the negation of capitalism and adopted a distinct model of socialism, then 'building socialism' referred to policies of *consolidation* rather than imbalance.[112] The extent to which this consolidation might be achieved depended upon stability. The best way to develop the productive forces, therefore, was to promote efficiency, labour discipline, individual responsibility, scientific management, imports of technology and technical training.[113] According to this view, once one rejected the position of the 'Gang' that the relations of production dominated the productive forces, one had to maintain that the productive forces were relatively independent.[114] Such was the position of Hu Qiaomu who, in a speech to the State Council in July 1978, argued that the basic political task of the Party in the new stage of socialism was to understand the 'objective economic laws' of development.[115] Socialism was, in fact, threatened once politics and revolution *interfered* with the operation of these laws. Such interference had, moreover, been experienced in the bitter years after 1957 when 'more and more acute political movements came one after another'.[116]

The fundamental characteristic of socialism, Hu maintained, was planning in accord with the law of value, which operated in *all* economies. Socialist 'planned and proportional development' was made possible by the very essence of socialism — public ownership and socialised mass production.[117] There could be no more trenchant criticism of Hua's Great Leap scenario than that. Hu's view was, in fact, quite different both from that of the 'Gang' and that of Hua. Thus, 'imbalances' in the economy did not arise because of the regeneration of class struggle, as Mao in the 1960s and the 'Gang' in 1975 maintained. Nor did they arise because of the necessary existence of social contradictions, as Mao in the 1950s and Hua in 1978 maintained. They occurred when objective economic laws were violated — when people broke the law.[118] Hu's view, which was to become more and more influential in late 1978, had been vigorously criticised in the Cultural Revolution.[119] It can, moreover, be traced back to that of Chen Yun, who was to emerge at the end of the year as one of China's foremost policy makers.

As in all political movements in China in recent years, cleavages were manifest not only in political tactics and economic policy but also in the realm of philosophy. In September 1977, an article by Chen Yun appeared in the press entitled 'Keep to the Style of Seeking Truth from Facts',[120] though one is not clear whether this article had much impact at the time. A far more important document, 'A Fundamental Principle of Marxism', took up the same theme and has since been celebrated as a major statement of Deng Xiaoping's conception of the relationship of theory and practice. This article re-interpreted one of Mao's most influential essays 'On Practice' (and to a lesser extent his essay 'On Contradiction') in what may only be described as a positivistic and pragmatist way. It held that a theory was valid if it worked out in practice and 'practice' itself was defined as that which developed the productive forces.[121] The implication here was that the 'practice' of socialist transition existed independently of any guiding revolutionary theory. Thus, Mao Zedong Thought was seen as an historically specific corpus and no statement of Mao's might be taken out of its historical context.[122] The argument of the article is weakened somewhat by supporting quotes from Mao which are, in fact, taken out of context. Nevertheless, the implication was clear. Those parts of Mao's works which were considered obsolete might be discarded. Secondly, it was implied that facts were value-free and thus, once the facts were grasped, socialist modernisation would follow automatically. Thirdly, as Young will demonstrate later, the separation of theory and practice seriously weakened the role of the Party as the guide to theory-directed change.

The political import of the 'practice' criterion cannot be under-estimated. One of its primary functions was to justify the position that many of the ideas of the Cultural Revolution no longer accorded with reality.[123] Indeed, the 'practice' criterion became the rallying cry for all those who wished to reject the whole of Mao's post-1957 strategy from the Anti-rightist movement onwards. This group has, according to the Hong Kong press, been dubbed as the 'practice' faction (*shijianpai*).[124] Opposed to them was a varied group of people who have been labelled by their critics as the 'whatever faction' (*fanshipai*) because of their alleged adherence to 'whatever Mao Zedong thought or did'.[125]

In the light of the above discussion, it would be tempting to place Hua Guofeng at the head of the 'whatever' faction and Deng Xiaoping at the head of the 'practice' faction. Indeed, Hua had seemed eager to bring the campaign against the 'Gang' to a close whereas Deng seemed to symbolise those who wished to 'take the lid off the struggle'. In their speeches to the National Science Conference in March 1978,[126] to the National Education Conference in April[127] and to the Army Political Work Conference in May and June,[128] there are distinct differences in emphasis. Yet there are similarities in the position outlined by Hua at the National Finance and Trade Conference in July and that of the 'practice' faction.[129] When things came to a head at a month-and-a-half long Party Work Conference which preceded the Third Plenum of the Party Central Committee in December 1978, neither Hua nor Deng was a major protagonist.[130] The battle, it is said, was between Chen Yun (the 'practice' faction) and Wang Dongxing (the 'whatever' faction). With the victory of the 'practice' faction, Hua, for the sake of Party unity, even went so far as to make a self-criticism for having opposed Deng.[131]

The Aftermath of the Third Plenum

As all the contributors to this book will note, the Third Plenum marked a significant change in the policies pursued by the Chinese leadership. Policies on economic management, planned and proportional development, agriculture, industry and foreign economic relations were reformulated.[132] Emphasis was given to the role of the banks in regulating the economy.[133] The slogan 'grasp revolution, promote production' was abandoned.[134] Stress was laid on the low viability of the small rural production teams which were to be linked with other economic units by legally enforceable contracts.[135] A greater degree of private economic activity was encouraged and discussions were held on 'socialist market relations'.[136] As the position outlined by Hu Qiaomu on 'objective economic laws' became official policy, the Great Leap scenario was negated. Thus, when imports of technology were held back, it was usually not because of the kind of arguments put forward by the 'Gang' but because an overextended import policy might cause imbalance.

In early 1979, instead of a Great Leap atmosphere, one saw a strategy of retrenchment and readjustment. There was that odd mixture of economic centralisation and decentralisation (to economic units) which Schurmann saw as characteristic of Chen Yun and which was implemented in the early 1960s.[137] As the generalisation of the mid-1950s gave way to the generalisation of the early 1960s,[138] institutions set up at that time, such as the vertically integrated trusts, which had been abandoned in the Cultural Revolution, were given a new legitimacy.[139] As the Party switched its main focus to modernisation in early 1979, there was not only a return to the economic policies of the early 1960s but a return also to the official view on class struggle of that time. The Third Plenum had declared that 'large scale turbulent class struggles of a mass character had come to an end'.[140] This implied that inner-Party struggle might not necessarily be a reflection of class struggle in society at large. Problems in the Party since the Great Leap Forward were now explained simply as the result of a line no longer dubbed 'left in form but right in essence' but simply called 'ultra-leftist'.[141] Significantly, no longer was any attempt made to disassociate the late Chairman Mao from such a line.

Symbolically, the Third Plenum decided to implement the suggestion, allegedly made in early 1977 by Chen Yun, to rehabilitate the deceased Peng Dehuai.[142] The political import of this move was rammed home by Lu Dingyi, a prominent victim of the Cultural Revolution, who argued that it was 'left deviation' which had caused Peng's correct evaluation of the original Great Leap to be condemned.[143] Article after article went on to suggest that the Great Leap had been a leftist adventure[144] and even the play *Hai Rui Dismissed from Office*, which had sparked off the Cultural

Revolution, was positively assessed.[145] This play, written in the early 1960s by Wu Han, was considered in the Cultural Revolution to have been an attack on the Great Leap. The honest Ming dynasty official Hai Rui had protested when venal officials had taken land away from the peasants and, for his pains, had been dismissed by a senile emperor misled by flatterers. As Mao had seen it, Hai Rui was in fact Peng Dehuai, the seizure of land was the Great Leap Forward and the senile emperor was Mao himself. The reassessment, therefore, was a confirmation of Mao's senility. Similarly, a set of poems celebrating the Tiananmen incident of April 1976 rejoiced at the passing of the 'feudal rule of the First Emperor of Qin'.[146] Since Mao had willingly accepted his likeness to the First Emperor of Qin during the campaign to Criticise Lin Biao and Confucius, there could be no doubt that Mao was under attack.

The list of implicit criticisms of the late Chairman in 1979 is almost endless. The infamous 'Three Family Village' which satirised Mao in the 1960s was reassessed.[147] Peng Zhen, the first major target of the Cultural Revolution, was rehabilitated. Liu Shaoqi's wife, Wang Guangmei, reappeared.[148] The 'February Adverse Current' of 1967, which tried to moderate the Cultural Revolution, was defended[149] and Kang Sheng (Mao's close colleague over several decades) was attacked as the 'close advisor' of the 'Gang'.[150]

At a theoretical level, a most important rejection of Mao's position may be found in the rehabilitation, in a major theoretical journal, of the basic line of the Eighth Party Congress of 1956.[151] This held that the major contradiction in Chinese society was not a class contradiction but that between 'the advanced socialist system' and the 'backward productive forces'. This was a very different argument from the traditional Marxist one about the contradiction between the productive forces and the relations of production. It implied that an advanced socialist system was already in existence. It was, in fact, the managers of this system who would define just what constituted backwardness and indeed what social contradictions were. It is possible to argue that there was always an element of arbitrariness in Mao's 'On the Correct Handling of Contradictions Among the People'. Nevertheless, the adherents to the theory of 'uninterrupted revolution' always believed that social contradictions actually existed in society and were not the product of managerial decision. It is for this reason that they rejected the line of the Eighth Party Congress.[152] The new managerial conception of leadership, which echoed the position adopted by Stalin in 1936, implied that there were two kinds of contradiction in Chinese society. First there were *economic* contradictions resulting from the operation of 'objective economic laws' and secondly there were *social* contradictions. These latter were defined not in terms of the 'social relations of production' (the class structure) but according to the managerial prescriptions of those who controlled the 'advanced socialist system'.[153] Antagonistic social contradictions were, therefore, no more than violations of the law.[154] But, whose law?

One possible answer to that question was that law had to be seen as the law of the whole people.[155] Thus, major efforts were made in early 1979 to codify law and this process culminated in the promulgation by Peng Zhen, at the Second Session of the National People's Congress in June 1979, of laws governing social, political and economic activity.[156] These laws were to apply equally to all members of society and were to be administered equally by the state. The implications here for Party leadership were quite profound. Those who recall Mao's trenchant denunciation of Khrushchev's position in the 1960s will wonder whether China has not itself embraced the Khrushchevian notion of a 'state of the whole people'[157] and whether this much maligned term will soon be rehabilitated. But the bitterness of Sino-Soviet relations will, one suspects, preclude such an eventuality, just as those same relations prevented any official Chinese attempt, in the 1960s, to trace back the notion of a 'state of the whole people' to Stalin.

The equality before the law of people made unequal by their position in the productive process is, of course, one manifestation of 'bourgeois right'. Far from wishing to restrict the operation of this principle, the present leadership seeks rather to extend it in order to develop the productive forces.[158] This has resulted in the adoption of new positive and negative material incentives and systems of piecework.[159] Far from generating 'new bourgeois elements', such policies are expected to dissuade people from going outside 'the socialist system' and thus becoming 'new bourgeois elements'.[160] But what are the implications of this reformulation of 'bourgeois right'? As the 'Gang of Four' saw it, one could measure progress to the extent that 'bourgeois right' was restricted. However unsatisfactory this might have been as an indicator of social progress, one is now left with no potential indicator of progress save the development of the productive forces. How then does one know when one is heading towards communism or back to capitalism?

The above perspective, adopted by the Chinese Communist Party after the Third Plenum in December 1978, is strikingly different from that put forward by Hua Guofeng earlier in that year. This has led some people to conclude that Hua is now little more than a figurehead.[161] Such a view is too simplistic. The victory of the 'practice' faction, in late 1978, was not achieved without some degree of compromise on its part. Deng, it appears, has modified his position somewhat[162] and there are still elements within the Party which seem to have prevented any official criticism of Mao by name.[163] Furthermore, though some of the apparent critics of the reassessment of Mao's strategy — Wang Dongxing, Ji Dengkui, Zhang Pinghua, Chen Yonggui, Chen Xilian, Ni Zhifu and Wu De — have lost a great deal of power,[164] articles in the press in 1979 indicate that their influence has not been totally negated. Fearing, it would seem, a recurrence of the faction-fighting which characterised the final years of the 'Gang's' influence, the Party leadership has taken pains to present a picture of compromise.[165] Such compromise, however, is somewhat uneasy.

Undoubtedly, there continue to be disagreements in the Party leadership and one may only speculate on their dimensions. What, for example, is one to make of the reported criticism of Chen Yun's close associates, Hu Yaobang and Hu Qiaomu, by the State Council planner Yu Qiuli at a work conference in April?[166] Could it be that the State Council was worried that the decentralisation of decision-making power to economic units might weaken its own power? This, after all, had been a major fear in 1957.[167] What is one to make of the criticisms of the excessive import of technology? Sometimes one is told that such imports should be avoided because they cause imbalance, yet at other times one finds echoes of the 'Gang's' position that, along with the technology, one might import capitalism.[168] If it is the case that the readjustments of 1979 constitute a repudiation of the economic rationale which informed the plan of early 1978, then some of that repudiation must be aimed at Deng who, on his visits to Japan and the United States, was more than enthusiastic about the targets.[169] One should indeed be cautious before one places Deng in the ranks of the 'practice' faction. If, furthermore, it is the case that recent attacks on the 'cult of personality' and the insistence that all leaders should have the simple title 'comrade' is a criticism of Hua, then the same criticism might equally be aimed at Deng Xiaoping who was eulogised in the media in 1978.[170] Finally, how does one explain the continued injunctions to adhere to Mao Zedong Thought when the old Chairman's prestige has been so gravely shaken?[171] If the above questions do, in fact, suggest continued major disagreements then it will be difficult to move towards the Twelfth Party Congress (scheduled for the middle of 1982) without further political struggle. The dimensions of this struggle will reflect, in part, the extent that current policies exacerbate social and economic inequalities.[172] One thing is certain; we should beware of any conclusions to the effect that compromises amongst the Party leadership have resulted in fundamental unity. Commentators reached such a conclusion after the Fourth National People's Congress in 1975[173] and that congress took place on the eve of the greatest upheaval in Chinese politics since the Cultural Revolution.

Conclusion

Any assessment of the politics of the post-Mao leadership must be set against the rise and fall of the 'Gang of Four'. Contrary to the views of some Western commentators, who maintain that the 'Gang' had no theoretical position,[174] this chapter has argued that it did in fact have a quite coherent theory of socialist transition which was based upon the notion of 'continuous revolution' which Mao initiated in the 1960s. What the 'Gang' lacked was an appropriate leadership strategy and an organisation through which to implement that strategy. This is not to say, however, that its theory was not flawed and that its defensive dogmatism in 1976 was merely a behavioural problem.

For the first six months after the 'Gang's' downfall, there was very little discussion of theory in the Chinese press and the reader was entertained with a barrage of behavioural criticism. This was because of the desire to give the impression of unity, to legitimise the position of Hua Guofeng, and because the Party was undecided on the proper approach to be adopted towards the case of Deng Xiaoping. With the rehabilitation of Deng, however, the campaign to criticise the 'Gang of Four' expanded into a campaign to criticise the *line* of the 'Gang' and a major rectification movement engulfed Chinese society. Disagreements were to focus on how far this should go and on the theoretical issues which were now debated quite openly. Policies, in this second period, were to be set within the problematic of 'uninterrupted revolution', as developed by Mao in the mid-1950s and articulated most coherently in 1977-78 by Hua Guofeng. This problematic, however, was to subside in favour of a new generalisation of the early 1960s in which Mao's views on both

'uninterrupted revolution' and 'continuous revolution' were abandoned. The proponents of this final trend came to be known as the
'practice' faction and those who objected to the new course came to
be known as the 'whatever' faction. The discussions before and
during the Third Plenum in late 1978 were to result in the victory of
the 'practice' faction. This faction was able to criticise most of the
policies of Mao Zedong, pursued since 1957, and to articulate a view
of socialism very different from either the 'Gang' or Hua in 1978.
Yet the victory of the 'practice' faction was not unequivocal and disagreements still continue. In these disagreements, both Hua and
Deng seem to have adopted a position of compromise though one is
uncertain how long this may last. Other chapters in this book will
explore in detail the various policy changes sketched in this chapter.
It is hoped that what will emerge will be more than an exercise in
Pekingology and something will be added to our thinking on the
definition of socialism and the problems of socialist transition.

Notes

1. Contrast this with those who concentrate solely on analysing the factions which
struggled for political power. Domes (1977, pp. 474-8) is representative of this
approach. See also Domes 1978, pp. 2-16; Kuo 1978, p. 5; Ting Wang 1978, p. 46.
2. Mao Zedong 1960 (or 1961-2), *JPRS* 1974, pp. 247-313. This is discussed by
Levy 1975, pp. 95-117.
3. *PR* 29, 17 July 1964, pp. 7-28.
4. See, in particular, Young and Woodward 1978. For contrasting views, see Starr
1971; Schram 1971; Esherick, 1979.
5. Woodward 1978, pp. 80-8.
6. Zhou Enlai, PFLP 1973 (a), pp. 4 and 7.
7. Wang Hongwen, PFLP 1973 (a), p. 46.
8. Zhou Enlai, PFLP 1973 (a), p. 18.
9. Wang Hongwen, PFLP 1973 (a), p. 46.
10. Zhou Enlai, PFLP 1973 (a), pp. 19-20.
11. Wang Hongwen, PFLP 1973 (a), p. 54.
12. *Lishi Yanjiu* 1, 1977, *SPRCM* 921, p. 1; *Hongqi* 4, 1977, *SPRCM* 923, p. 53.
13. Especially in relation to the role of women in society. See *Chinese Sociology
and Anthropology*, Summer 1975, pp. 4-12; *Chinese Studies in History*, Summer
1974, pp. 92-6. For a discussion of other issues, see Price (ed.) 1977.
14. Compare Goldman 1975, p. 435 with Chang 1974, p. 875.
15. *RMRB* 7 August 1973, *SCMP* 5436, pp. 106-15.
16. *Hongqi* 4, 1974, *SPRCM* 773, pp. 13-22.
17. *Xuexi yu Pipan* 4, 1974, *SPRCM* 782, pp. 23-6.
18. Brugger (ed.) 1978, pp. 258-9.
19. E.g. *Hongqi* 1, 1975, *SPRCM* 807, pp. 39-44. For this reason, there was
hardly any mass mobilisation except in parts of industry. See Andors 1976, p. 42.
20. Wang Hongwen, 14 January 1974, *Issues and Studies*, Vol. XI, No. 2,

February 1975, p. 97. Text altered for stylistic reasons.
21. Ibid., p. 102.
22. *RMRB* 1 January 1975, *SPRCP* 5772, p. 58.
23. NCNA 18 January 1975, *SPRCP* 5783, p. 98.
24. *FBIS*-CHI-75-20-El.
25. Zhang Chunqiao, 13 January 1975, PFLP 1975, pp. 31-43; Zhou Enlai, 13 January 1975, PFLP 1975, pp. 45-65.
26. Zhou Enlai, 13 January 1975, PFLP 1975, p. 55.
27. *Hongqi* 1, 1976, *SPRCM* 856, p. 54.
28. Yao Wenyuan, *Hongqi* 3, 1975, *SPRCM* 814, pp. 16-26; *PR* 10, 7 March 1975, pp. 5-10 (references to this).
29. Zhang Chunqiao, *Hongqi* 4, 1975, *SPRCM* 819, pp. 2-11; *PR* 14, 4 April 1975, pp. 5-11 (references to this).
30. Zhang Chunqiao, *PR* 14, 4 April 1975, p. 7; Yao Wenyuan, *PR* 10, 7 March 1975, pp. 6 and 8. The initial discussion of 'bourgeois right' is in Marx 1875, pp. 18-19 and Lenin 1917, pp. 353-6. See also Cutler, Hindess, Hirst and Hussain, 1977, pp. 31-2.
31. *PR* 41, 10 October 1975, p. 20. For a general discussion of how the Party has viewed the relations of production and the productive forces, see Axilrod 1972, pp. 381-2.
32. Zhang Chunqiao, *PR* 14, 4 April 1975, pp. 8-9.
33. *Hongqi* 2, 1975, *SPRCM* 811, p. 4.
34. Han Suyin 1978, p. 449.
35. *PR* 22, 30 May 1975, pp. 18-21; *Xuexi yu Pipan* 4, 1975, *SPRCP* 321, p. 13.
36. *PR* 31, 1 August 1975, pp. 17, 18 and 23; NCNA 25 August 1975, *SPRCP* 5929, p. 130; *GMRB* 30 July 1975, *SPRCP* 5934, pp. 165-8.
37. E.g. *Hongqi* 3, 1975, *SPRCM* 814, p. 59; Bonavia 1978, pp. 178-93.
38. E.g. Gurley 1971, pp. 324-356; Gray 1973, pp. 109-57; Gurley 1976, pp. 198-229; Goodstadt 1972, pp. 201-32; Breth 1977, pp. 150-67.
39. Schurmann 1966, pp. 175-8, 188-94.
40. *PR* 24, 13 June 1975, pp. 12-15; *Xuexi yu Pipan* 12, 1975, *SPRCM* 854, pp. 2-3.
41. Hua Guofeng, 26 February 1978, *PR* 10, 10 March 1978, p. 12. some economists (e.g. Prybla, 1977, p. 1125) doubt this claim. On the basis of this claim, however, other commentators (e.g. Frolic 1978, p. 414) argue that the Chinese leadership has come to its senses and has implemented practical development policies to overcome the 'impractical Maoist approach'.
42. For an alternative point of view, see Smith n.p.d., p. 12. He argues that members of the 'Gang' were experts in political organisation and tactics in their desire to 'restore capitalism' and 'seize state power'. See also Dittmer 1978, pp. 28-9, 41 and 48.
43. *PR* 5, 3 February 1978, pp. 16-17; *PR* 17, 28 April 1978, pp. 7-11; *PR* 23, 9 June 1978, pp. 8-12.
44. *PR* 6, 10 February 1978, p. 6.
45. E.g. 'Don't appear in public too often, don't write comments on documents, don't form a cabinet whereby you (serve as the string-puller). You have offended too many people. Be sure to unite with the majority. These instructions are of utmost importance.' CCP.CC *Zhongfa* 24 (1976), *Issues and Studies*, Vol. XIII, No. 9, September 1977, p. 102.
46. Chi Hsin 1978, pp. 207-8.
47. Ibid., pp. 203-38, 239-76, 277-86 (references to this). Also in *Issues and Studies* Vol. XIII, No. 7, July 1977, pp. 90-113; No. 8, August 1977, pp. 77-99; No. 9, September 1977, pp. 63-70.
48. Chi Hsin 1978, p. 203.
49. Ibid., pp. 255-6.

50. Ibid., pp. 263-4.

51. Lieberthal 1978 (a), pp. 33-44.

52. *Shehuizhuyi Zhengzhi Jingji xue* 1975, p. 91. See also the discussion in Friedman 1978, pp. 873-9.

53. *RMRB* 21 October 1975, p. 2.

54. *RMRB* 18 February 1976, *SPRCP* 6044, p. 7.

55. Quoted in *Current Scene*, Vol. XV, No. 1, 1977, p. 12.

56. *Hongqi* 1 1977, *SPRCM* 910, pp. 115-23.

57. According to Starr (1976, pp. 472-5), the campaign was essentially about foreign policy. See *PR* 37, 12 September 1975, pp. 7-8.

58. *PR* 22, 23 June 1977, p. 22; *GMRB* 24 March 1977, *SPRCP* 6317, p. 7.

59. *PR* 14, 1 April 1977, p. 11; *GMRB* 24 March 1977, *SPRCP* 6317, p. 7.

60. *RMRB* 30 December 1976, *SPRCP* 6261, pp. 68-71.

61. *Issues and Studies*, Vol. XIV, No. 12, December 1978, pp. 92-4. We know that the Federation did meet at that time and that Zhang did deliver a speech. See *PR* 32, 11 August 1978, p. 12.

62. *Xuexi yu Pipan* 5, 1976, *SPRCM* 875, p. 3; ibid., p. 16.

63. Goodstadt, *FEER* 18 May 1976, p. 8; Brugger (ed.) 1978, pp. 267-8.

64. *PR* 35, 27 August 1976, p. 5.

65. See Starr 1976, p. 475; Zweig 1978 (a), p. 150; Gittings 1976, pp. 292-3; *GMRB* 19 December 1975, *SPRCP* 6005, p. 77; *Xuexi yu Pipan* 12, 1975, *SPRCM* 854, p. 15; *Xuexi yu Pipan* 12, 1975, *SPRCM* 855, p. 1.

66. Brugger (ed.) 1978, pp. 268-9.

67. *Issues and Studies*, Vol. XII, No. 12, December 1976, pp. 98-9.

68. Ibid., p. 107.

69. Ibid., p. 106.

70. There has been almost as much written abut the 'Gang's' downfall as has been written about the Cultural Revolution. See the major polemic in Bettelheim and Burton 1978. For a completely different perspective, see Evans 1978. For specific reactions, see Leys 1977, p. 21; Chang 1976, p. 1004; Goodman 1977, pp. 3-10, Moody 1977, pp. 712-14; Dittmer 1977, p. 62; Harding 1977, p. 8; Oksenberg 1977, p. 116; Onate 1975, pp. 540-65; Tsou 1977, pp. 498-527; Nolan 1978, pp. 29-38.

71. Mao was highly critical of this. See Esmein 1973, p. 161.

72. E.g. *Hongqi* 5, 1977, *SPRCM* 928, p. 98; *RMRB* 2 January 1977, *SPRCP* 6273, p. 132; *GMRB* 22 January 1977, *SPRCP* 6273, p. 121; NCNA 27 April 1977, *SPRCP* 6336, pp. 71-8.

73. E.g. NCNA 30 December 1976, *SPRCP* 6256, pp. 79-83; *GMRB* 18 July 1977, *SPRCP* 6395, pp. 152-5; *RMRB* 25 March 1977, *SPRCP* 6325 pp. 11-17; *RMRB* 26 March 1977, *SPRCP* 6329, pp. 233-6.

74. *GMRB* 2 November 1976, *SPRCP* 624, p. 146; NCNA 14 December 1976, *SPRCP* 6245, p. 115; *RMRB* 11 December 1976, *SPRCP* 6244, p. 55.

75. *RMRB* 9 January 1977, *SPRCP* 6264, p. 227; *PR* 3, 21 January 1977, p. 17.

76. Wheelwright and McFarlane 1970, p. 76.

77. *Issues and Studies*, Vol. XV, No. 2, February 1979, p. 88.

78. Zweig (1978 [a]) described the intervention of Wu Den at Beijing University. There the campaign against Deng amongst the teachers was progressing too slowly.

79. *PR* 44, 29 October 1976, pp. 13-14.

80. *Hongqi* 12, 1976, *SPRCM* 404, p. 18.

81. *China Reconstructs*, January 1977, p. 13.

82. *RMRB* 28 March 1976, *PR* 14, 2 April 1976, p. 5. This contrasts markedly with the argument in 1979 that Deng's statement was 'valid' and in accord with reality. *Gongren Ribao* 3 February 1979, *FBIS*-CHI-79-31-E7.

83. *Issues and Studies*, Vol. XIII, No. 5, May 1977, p. 106.

84. *Chinese Law and Government*, Vol. X, No. 1, Spring 1977, pp. 52-3.

85. Ibid., p. 67.

86. Ibid., pp. 70-1; *Issues and Studies*, Vol. XIII, No. 3, March 1977, pp. 112-13.

87. *PR* 1, 1 January 1977, pp. 10-25.

88. *PR* 31, 29 July 1977, pp. 9-10.

89. *PR* 33, 12 August 1977, pp. 28-32; *PR* 42, 14 October 1977, pp. 5-13; *PR* 44, 28 October 1977, pp. 5-8.

90. Lanzhou, Gansu Radio, 14 December 1977, *TPRC* 411, p. 3.

91. Luda Radio, 10 December 1977, *TPRC* 411, p. 8.

92. Shenyang, Liaoning Radio, 2 September 1978, *SWB* FE/5912/B11/11.

93. Hangzhou, Zhejiang Radio, 10 July 1978; Harbin, Heilongjiang Radio, 8 July 1978; Jinan, Shandong Radio, 5 July 1978; Tianjin Radio, 17 July 1978; Wuhan, Hubei Radio, 14 July 1978. All in *SWB* FE/5873/B11/8-9.

94. Taiyuan, Shanxi Radio, 18 November 1977, *TPRC* 410, p. 17; NCNA 19 July 1978, *SWB* FE/5875/B11/8.

95. Jinan, Shandong Radio, 18 February 1979, *SWB* FE/6055/B11/3.

96. *RMRB* 4 October 1978, *SWB* FE/5936/B11/3-4.

97. Liaoning Radio, 2 September 1978, *SWB* FE/5912/B11/11; *Jiefangjunbao* 25 July 1978, *SWB* FE/5878/B11/2.

98. Hua Guofeng, 26 February 1978, *PR* 10, 10 March 1978, p. 15.

99. Hua Guofeng, 7 July 1978, *PR* 30, 28 July 1978, p. 7.

100. Wei Guoqing, *Jiefangjunbao* 25 August 1978, *SWB* FE/5902/B11/8.

101. Xu Shiyu, *Hongqi* 9, 1978; *SWB* FE/5913/B11/4.

102. *RMRB* 27 August 1978, *SWB* FE/5906/B11/1-3; Ji Dengkui, NCNA 17 August 1978, *SWB* FE/5899/B11/7.

103. Hua Guofeng, *PR* 19, 6 May 1977; p. 16; *Hongqi* 6, 1977, *PR* 27, 1 July 1977, p. 6.

104. *PR* 36, 8 September 1978, p. 11.

105. Hua Guofeng, 12 August 1977, *PR* 35, 26 August 1988, p. 33.

106. *PR* 6, 10 February 1978; *Wuhan Daxue Xuebao* 3, 12 May 1978, *TPRC* 462, pp. 28-35.

107. Hua Guofeng, 25 December 1976, *PR* 1, 1 January 1977, pp. 32 and 41; Hua Guofeng, 9 May 1977, *PR* 21, 20 May 1977, pp. 7-14.

108. Hua Guofeng, 26 February 1978, *PR* 10, 10 March 1978, pp. 14, 20, 22 and 24. See also *PR* 9, 3 March 1978, pp. 13-14.

109. *Hongqi* 6, 1977, *PR* 27, 1 July 1977, p. 10; *PR* 20, 19 May 1978, pp. 7 and 9. See the discussion in Lieberthal 1978 (b), pp. 1-5; Prybla 1979, pp. 418-32.

110. Both of these notions are central to Mao's economic ideas which underpinned the Great Leap Forward. See Howe and Walker 1977, pp. 195-6.

111. *PR* 39, 29 September 1978, p. 17.

112. *PR* 27, 1 July 1977, pp. 6-7.

113. *RMRB* 4 October 1978, *SWB* FE/5936/B11/3-4.

114. This position represents one side of a general debate in Marxism. See Gartman 1978, pp. 98-9.

115. *RMRB* 6 October 1978, *SWB* FE/5939/B/11/1-20; *PR* 45, 10 November 1978, pp. 7-12; *PR* 46, 17 November 1978, pp. 15-23; *PR* 47, 24 November 1978, pp. 13-21. See also the discussion in *Monthly Review*, Vol. XXXI, No. 1, May 1978, pp. 1-19.

116. *RMRB* 9 March 1979, *SWB* FE/6065/B11/2.

117. *PR* 45, 10 November 1978, p. 9.

118. *PR* 52, 29 December 1979, p. 11.

119. See Mao Zedong 1960 (or 1961-2), *JPRS* 1974, p. 285; *PR* 44, 28 October 1966, p. 35.

120. *RMRB* 28 September 1977, *PR* 49, 2 December 1977, pp. 9-13.

121. *PR* 28, 14 July 1978, p. 12.

122. *Kunming, Yunnan Radio, 16 October 1978*, *SWB* FE/5949/B11/1-2.

123. *PR* 29, 21 July 1978, p. 12.

124. *Jingbao* (Hong Kong) 18, Special Supplement, 10 January 1979, *FBIS*-CHI-79-11-N1.

125. *Dongxiang* (Hong Kong) 4, 16 January 1979, pp. 14-17, *FBIS*-CHI-79-16-N3. An article in the official media which criticises the 'two whatevers' is in *Jiangxi Ribao* 1 June 1979, *SWB* FE/6137/B11/2.

126. Hua Guofeng, *PR* 13, 31 March 1978, p. 8; Deng Xiaoping, 18 March 1978, *PR* 12, 24 March 1978, p. 16.

127. Deng Xiaoping, 22 April 1978, *PR* 18, 5 May 1978, p. 7.

128. Hua Guofeng, 29 May 1978, *PR* 24, 16 June 1978, p. 10; Deng Xiaoping, 2 June 1978, *PR* 25, 23 June 1978, p. 15.

129. Hua Guofeng, *PR* 30, 28 July 1978, pp. 14-15.

130. *Qishi Niandai*, February 1977, *FBIS*-CHI-79-032-N1-2.

131. *Kyodo*, 2 February 1979 and *Kyodo*, 3 February 1979, *FBIS*-CHI-79-025-F2.

132. E.g. Fraser (1979, p. 11) argues that there are plans to close down over 25,000 unprofitable factories and small enterprises. This is suggested in *RMRB* 16 March 1979, *SWB* FE/6071/B11/10. See also Liu, *FEER* 16 March 1979 and Kulkarni, *The Christian Science Monitor*, 2 April 1979, p. B14.

133. Gu Mu, NCNA 11 April 1979, *SWB* FE/6092/B11/1; Gu Mu, NCNA 28 March 1979, *SWB* FE/6082/B11/1.

134. *RMRB* 9 March 1979, *SWB* FE/6065/B11/2.

135. Shenyang, Liaoning Radio, 18 December 1978, *SWB* FE/6013/B11/7.

136. *RMRB* 8 April 1979, *SWB* FE/6090/B11/2; *RMRB* 9 MArch 1979, *SWB* FE/6065/B11/5; Beijing Radio, 6 November 1978, *TPRC* 468, p. 19; *NCNA* 18 March 1979, *SWB* FE/6083/B11/17.

137. *RMRB* 16 March 1979, *SWB* FE/6071/B11/8. Hence imbalance was criticised in all areas. See NCNA 6 April 1979, *SWB* FE/6089/B11/11; Beijing Radio, 3 April 1979, *SWB* FE/6089/B11/13-15.

138. Schurmann 1966, pp. 197-8. Most of the policies were incorporated under the general heading of 'comprehensive balance'; see Jao 1968, p. 46.

139. *PR* 47, 24 November 1978, pp. 15-16; *RMRB* 15 June 1979, *SWB* FE/6149/C/5.

140. *PR* 52, 29 December 1978, p. 11.

141. *RMRB* 28 February 1979, *SWB* FE/6057/B11/1-3

142. *PR* 52, 29 December 1978, p. 14.

143. *RMRB* 8 March 1979, *SWB* FE/6065/B11/6. This goes against the resolution adopted by the Third plenum of the Tenth CC in July 1977, which described the struggle against the 'Gang' as the eleventh major struggle between the two lines in the history of the Party, *PR* 31, 29 July 1977, p. 7.

144. *RMRB* 30 March 1979, *SWB* FE/6089/B11/6-7; *RMRB* 11 January 1979, *SWB* FE/6017/B11/11; NCNA 22 March 1979, *SWB* FE/6082/B11/3-4.

145. *BR* 10, 9 March 1979, p. 6.

146. *RMBR* 21-22 November 1978, *PR* 48, 1 December 1978, p. 15.

147. *GMRB* 28 January 1979, *FBIS*-CHI-79-029-E8; *GMRB* 26 January 1979, *FBIS*-CHI-79-029-E7.

148. Peng's rehabilitation had been rumoured for many months. The first official indication came in January 1978. See *RMRB* 12 January 1978, *SWB* FE/6017/B11/5. See *BR* 5, 2 February 1979, p. 3. The first indication of Wang's rehabilitation was *BR* 5, 2 February 1979, p. 3. See also AFT 8 March 1979, *SWB* FE/6067/B11/4.

149. *RMRB* 26 February 1979, *SWB* FE/6056/B11/1-6.

150. *GMRB* 28 January 1979, *FBIS*-CHI-79-029-E10.

151. *Lishi Yanjiu* 4, 1979, *SWB* FE/6147/B11/6.

152. See e.g. *PFLP* 1973(a), pp. 26-8; Mao Zedong, 7 October 1957, *JPRS*, 1974, p. 75.

153. This is one implication of *RMRB* 9 March 1979, *SWB* FE/6065/B11/2-3.

154. Shanghai Radio, 5 April 1979, *SWB* FE/6087/B11/9.
155. *PR* 52, 29 December 1978, p. 14; *RMRB* 17 June 1979, *SWB* FE/6145/C/6.
156. For an outline of the laws, see *SWB* FE/6172/C/1-26. See also, *BR* 27, 6 July 1979, pp. 32-6; Peng Zhen, *BR* 28, 13 July 1979, pp. 8-16.
157. Even though articles continue to criticise this notion. See *BR* 2, 12 January 1979, p. 28; *BR* 9, 2 March 1979, p. 8.
158. *PR* 7, 17 February 1978, p. 8.
159. Beijing Radio, 3 April 1979, *SWB* FE/6089/B11/12; *PR* 16, 21 April 1978, pp. 6-7.
160. *PR* 7, 17 February 1978, p. 8.
161. Some people argue that this dates from Deng's rehabilitation. See Lieberthal 1978 (b) pp. 10-11.
162. It is claimed that he is the supporter of the 'four principles to guide socialist modernisation'. These are (1) the socialist path, (2) the 'dictatorship of the proletariat', (3) CCP leadership and (4) Marxism Leninism Mao Zedong Thought. See *The Economist*, 9-15 June 1979, p. 63; Zorza, *The Guardian Weekly*, 4 February 1979, p. 7; *GMRB* 6 April, 1979, *SWB* FE/6089/B11/8; *Wenhuibao* 4 April 1979, *SWB* FE/6089/B11/11.
163. This is one aspect of the injunction not to dwell on the past but look at the future. *RMRB* 1 April 1979, *SWB* FE/6084/B11/1-11.
164. *Mingbao* (Hong Kong), 12 January 1979, p. 3, *FBIS*-CHI-79-12-E1.
165. Hua Guofeng, 18 June 1979, NCNA 18 June 1979, *SWB* FE/6146/C/3.
166. *The Economist* 9-15 June 1977, p. 63. The report does not mention names. Both are mentioned in *AFP* 11 June 1979, *SWB* FE/6141/B11/18. The reason given in this report is that they had given too much support to the 'democracy campaign', which started in November 1978.
167. Schurmann 1966, p. 197.
168. *Jiefangjunbao* 7 April 1979, *SWB* FE/6090/B11/5; *GMRB* 6 April 1979, *SWB* FE/6089/B11/8. This is also reflected in an emphasis on 'self-reliance', *Gongren Ribao* 7 April 1979, *SWB* FE/6091/B11/17; *Gongren Ribao* 22 March 1979, *SWB* FE/6075/B11/2; Beijing Radio, 19 April 1979, *FBIS*-CHI-79-087-L12.
169. *Round Table* (273, January 1979, p. 5) argues that the four modernisations are usually associated with Deng.
170. E.g. Deng gave numerous press conferences to Western journalists. See *PR* 44, 3 November 1978, pp. 14-17; *PR* 48, 1 December 1978, p. 3; *PR* 7, 16 February 1979, pp. 17-20. See *Time* (1 January 1979, pp. 4-21) in which Deng was named 'man of the year'.
171. *GMRB* 6 April 1979, *SWB* FE/6089/B11/8.
172. For a manifestation of the kind of tensions which are created, see Beijing Radio, 14 March 1979, *SWB* FE/6071/B11/9. For an example of some of the policies promoted, see Fuzhou, Fujian Radio, 13 March 1979, *SWB* FE/6073/B11/10-11.
173. *FEER, Asia Yearbook*, 1976, p. 138.
174. Fitzgerald 1978, p. 112; Chi Hsin 1978, pp. 44-5; Terrill (1978, pp. 94, 96, 127-8) argues that the 'Gang' and Mao did have a conception of 'continuing the revolution', but dismisses it out of hand. Two of the few works to discuss their theories seriously, and from opposing viewpoints, are Tsou 1977, pp. 498-527 and Nolan 1978, pp. 29-38.

2 Non-revolutionary Vanguard: Transformation of the Chinese Communist Party

GRAHAM YOUNG

The Third Plenum of the Eleventh Central Committee of the Chinese Communist Party, in December 1978, will rank as one of the most significant milestones in the Party's history. Its influence appears likely to equal, and perhaps in the long run transcend, other crucial turning-points, such as the Zunyi meeting of January 1935, or the Central endorsement of the Cultural Revolution at the Eleventh Plenum of the Eighth Central Committee in August 1966. For it was the Third Plenum which announced the basic re-orientation of the Party away from its former role of promoting and guiding revolutionary change in Chinese society, culminating and giving new impetus to a process which had been in train since the downfall of the so-called 'Gang of Four'. This chapter will consider the major contours of this transformation through analysis of the changes in the prescribed relationship between Party and revolution, the role of revolutionary theory and ideological leadership, the operations of Party organisations, cadre policy, and the Party's leadership of the masses.

The Party and Revolution

From the beginning of the attacks upon the 'Gang of Four', one principal focus was the relationship between revolution and economic development, discussed in greater detail by other contributors to this volume. It was this orientation which eventually led to the major change in the conception of the Party consummated at the Third Plenum. Initially, there was sustained repudiation of many of the formulations concerning revolution, class struggle, and the dictatorship of the proletariat with which Zhang Chunqiao and Yao Wenyuan in particular had been associated. Hua Guofeng

51

himself sometimes made statements such as that revolution meant liberating the productive forces.[1] But Hua's Political Report to the Eleventh Congress paid great attention to his interpretation of the theory of continuous revolution. Thus, while rejecting the 'Gang's' supposedly mistaken analysis, Hua still maintained the centrality and persistence of class struggle in socialist society, which he saw as not inconsistent with the promotion of stability and unity. While announcing the victorious conclusion of the Cultural Revolution, Hua asserted that such political revolutions would occur many times in the future, an assurance which was included in the General Programme of the new Party Constitution.[2]

After the Congress, however, the emphasis gradually shifted in the discussion of the relationship between politics and economics in the Party's tasks. This involved several thrusts. First, there was the separation of politics from economics, with the view that each had its own laws. While revolution had to be 'in command' of production, it could not be used as a substitute for production, which had to be governed by 'objective' economic laws.[3] Thus, people had to be both 'red' and 'expert', but there should be no intrusion of political standards in the development of production. Secondly, there was the growing tendency to define the Party's political work in terms of the development of production. At the Eleventh Congress, Deng Xiaoping had called for 'less empty talk', a phrase which was increasingly associated with what had formerly been central aspects of the Party's political tasks. Political work had to 'serve the economic base and guarantee the accomplishment of economic work', and any kind of 'abstract "revolutionary work" ' was useless.[4]

Deng's own speech at the opening of the National Science Conference in March 1978 argued that, since the main task of scientific research institutes was the production of scientific results and the training of competent people, the main criterion for assessing the work of Party committees in such institutes had to be the fulfilment of this task. If not, 'putting politics in command will remain mere empty talk'.[5] Another sign of this trend was the argument that the general task of any period was politically the most important thing. With the four modernisations as the general task, their realisation was the most important political objective, crucial to the interests of the Party and the people and to the success or failure of the revolution.[6] Thus, not only should politics not interfere with the operation of 'objective' economic laws, but the content of political work was to facilitate the development of production. Similarly, revolution itself was defined in terms of increasing production. So long as political power was in the hands of the proletariat, every development of production was a 'material force' for the consolidation of the dictatorship of the proletariat and the prevention of capitalist restoration.[7]

Finally, the definition of revolution in terms of increasing production was reinforced by the argument that only a greatly expanded material base could ensure the achievement of long-term revolutionary goals such as the elimination of class struggle and the three major differences. Thus, it was argued that Marx and Mao considered revolution only a 'motive force', promoting historical development at crucial stages, and not as an 'ultimate cause'. While class struggle might be the 'motive force' of social development, production was the base of society, determining all other activities, including class struggle. Capitalist restoration would become impossible when the socialist system had created higher productivity than that achievable by the capitalist system. The triumph of socialism over capitalism was ensured because socialism could create higher labour productivity![8] Hence, in the short term, revolution was defined as the increase in economic production, and in the long term, growth in production was not only necessary for but would inevitably bring about the realisation of revolutionary objectives.

All of these discussions of the Party's tasks in revolution and production culminated in the explicit 'shift in focus' of the Party's work to the four modernisations. Deng had prefigured this shift in March 1978, when he argued that the new tasks confronting the Party demanded 'changes in the centre of gravity for Party work and in the Party's work style'. While the Party had concentrated on political revolution during the Cultural Revolution, it now had to wage 'a great political and economic revolution and a great scientific and technical revolution' — the 'new content' of continuous revolution.[9] The communiqué of the Third Plenum claimed that socialist modernisation is 'a profound and extensive revolution'. As well as growth in the productive forces, it requires 'changes in those aspects of the relations of production and the superstructure not in harmony with the growth of the productive forces' and 'changes in all methods of management, actions and thinking which stand in the way of such growth'. Although there were still class enemies who would oppose socialist modernisation, 'the large-scale turbulent class struggles of a mass character have in the main come to an end', and anything which damaged 'the political stability and unity required for socialist modernisation' could not be permitted.[10]

Despite that part of the Party Constitution's General Programme which asserted that political revolutions like the Cultural Revolution would occur many times in the future, the aftermath of the Third Plenum made it clear that such political activity was to cease.

> From now on, so long as there is no large-scale invasion by external enemies, modernisation is the central task of the whole Party. All other work, including the Party's political work, revolves around and serves this central task. There can be no more 'political movements' and 'class struggle' departing from this central task and harming modernisation.[11]

Achieving the four modernisations was identified as the means of grasping the essence of Marxism and upholding the banner of Mao Zedong Thought. And the definition of the correct political direction in terms of economic performance was now complete.

> The four modernisations will not come about through empty talk; we must certainly refrain from empty talk and firmly give substance to politics in production, vocational and technical work. Those on various fronts must see that every kind of work we are now doing is in the service of realising the four modernisations and has the utmost political significance. From this perspective we can say that extracting more oil is the politics of the petroleum industry, producing more coal is the politics of coal-miners, growing more grain is the politics of peasants, defending the frontier is the politics of soldiers, and working hard in study is the politics of students. 'The only criterion for the results of political education is the utility in improving the economic situation.' We must persist in taking practice as the sole criterion of testing truth, and actual results in work and the situation of work as the criterion for the political level of all units and individuals.[12]

Except to the extent to which it was defined in terms of increasing economic production, revolutionary politics was to be of no real concern to the political party of the proletariat.

Revolutionary Theory and Ideological Leadership

The former conception of vanguard leadership rested on the basic rationale that the Party must lead the revolutionary movement because of its grasp of revolutionary direction gained through its superior understanding of revolutionary theory. While many of the substantive theoretical revisions which have occurred in the last few years have already been discussed by Sullivan and require no further elaboration here, the changes in the relationship of theory to Party leadership and in the notion of the Party's ideological tasks — changes which are closely related to the emergent focus on modernisation — are important in understanding the transformation of the Party.

One of the major emphases in Party building in the aftermath of the Cultural Revolution had been the re-assertion of the Party's theoretical superiority, which had been severely eroded by the attacks on revisionism and by the arguments that revolutionary direction could be provided by the *direct* integration of Mao Zedong Thought with the mass movement. Many of the same concerns with the preservation of the Party's ideological leadership, and many of the same methods towards that end, re-emerged after the downfall of the 'Gang of Four'. As Hua noted in December 1976, it was necessary to encourage greater study of Marxist-Leninist works in the Party, not only in order to refute the theoretical positions advocated by the 'Gang of Four', but also with the more general aim of building 'a powerful Marxist theoretical contingent'.[13] The intention to reinforce the Party's ideological dominance was shown by the re-establishment of Party schools at various levels which was announced in a Central Committee decision of October 1977 and which emphasised the need for cadres to have a longer period of systematic theoretical study.[14] Thus, ideological leadership was more closely related to the Party organisational structure and was to be strengthened by an exclusively inner-Party form. On the other hand, the 'simple class feelings' held by the masses of the people, while valuable, were distinctly inferior to the 'scientific knowledge of communism' gained by the Party membership.[15]

While insistence on the Party's ideological leadership has been maintained consistently, it has nevertheless also become increasingly less relevant with the shift from social revolution to economic modernisation. This was linked to the emphasis on the Party's tradition of 'seeking truth from facts', which was contrasted with mere 'empty talk'.[16] Certainly, it was accurate to point to this principle as a major part of the Party's tradition, and one which Mao himself had been important in formulating. And the need to overcome political posturing which took no account of existing realities was heavily emphasised. But the notion that 'the sole criterion of truth is practice'[17] provided a very one-sided interpretation of the linkage of theory and practice which had been central to Mao's writings and to the previous conception of Party leadership. In particular, it indicated an exclusive stress on the methodological aspects of investigation and study, while ignoring the notion that revolutionary practice had to be theory-directed.

This treatment of revolutionary theory was very useful in shifting the focus to economic modernisation. It implied that any type of theory which did not have direct relevance to the immediate needs of economic construction was 'empty talk'. One criticism of the 'Gang' was that its fragmentary treatment of Marxism had isolated class struggle from the complete body of Marxist theory and ignored that production was the basis of society.[18] When it was again classified as 'ultra-left', the 'Gang' was accused of opposing socialism through its brand of communism and of negating objective economic laws through exaggerating the dynamic role of ideology, while ignoring material constraints imposed by existing conditions.[19] The criticism of Lin Biao and the 'Gang' also dealt with their treatment of Mao, with the rejection of notions such as 'absolute authority' and 'every sentence is truth' and the claim that they had attempted to turn Mao Zedong Thought into a dogma and had promoted the 'theory of genius'.[20] This facilitated the revision of many policies formerly associated with Mao Zedong Thought, without explicitly repudiating Mao. Further justification derived from the arguments that solutions devised by revolutionary leaders to deal with one set of circumstances could not be applied 'mechanically' in a different context, and that, although revolutionary leaders might be more far-sighted, they also had to learn from practice and could not have been expected to prescribe policies in advance.[21]

Finding solutions for problems which the revolutionary classics could not be expected to confront was seen as one of the tasks of theoretical work after the shift of focus at the Third Plenum. While such theory had to be based completely on practical experience, it had to be universal and systematic rather than relying only on local or more limited practice.[22] Thus, the Party's theoretical work was to be concerned with providing general guidelines for realising the four modernisations. The change in the notion of Party ideological leadership was reflected in a speech by Hu Yaobang, Director of the Propaganda Department of the Central Committee, to a meeting of heads of provincial-level Party committee propaganda departments. As Hu listed them, the basic tasks of propaganda work were:

> Closely link the universal truth of Marxism-Leninism-Mao Zedong Thought to the great practice of the four modernisations, study and solve new problems, do our best to ensure that ideological and theoretical work moves ahead of practical work, push Mao Zedong Thought forward and accelerate the pace of socialist modernisation.[23]

As the *Renmin Ribao* editorial on this meeting made clear, a large part of this work involved getting people to accept the new focus. Thus, propaganda departments had to combat the theoretical positions associated with the 'Gang' and Lin because many people, especially the young, erred in taking their 'counter-revolutionary revisionism' as Marxism. Propaganda departments also had to deal with people's views concerning the changes from past practices and to overcome whatever did not conform to the actual situation in those practices, clearing up the harm which Lin and the 'Gang' had caused for over a decade.[24]

A similar orientation is evident in another editorial discussion of the Party's ideological and political work. This asserted: 'Whatever we members of the Communist Party are doing, we always persist in one thing, that is, paying attention to ideological education and raising people's consciousness. Without revolutionary theory there can be no revolutionary movement.' And it sought to reinforce this apparent continuity with the Party's former orientation in ideological leadership by reference to the four 'fundamental principles' which could never be abandoned: the socialist road, the dictatorship of the proletariat, Party leadership, and Marxism-Leninism-Mao Zedong Thought. Such assurances appear to have been necessary to counter suggestions that there was no longer any role for the Party's ideological work:

> Now, however, when the centre of gravity of the Party's work is shifting, there are some comrades who think that, since from now on the building up of production will be the central task and there will be no more political movements, ideological and political work is not that important, and even that we can either have it or not. And they think that, since from now on we emphasise doing things according to economic laws and using economic measures

to govern the economy, ideological and political work has no role.

But, it was argued, the shift in focus and the four modernisations would demand changes in the superstructure and in 'all the inappropriate ways of management, activities and thinking'. Such changes would involve every individual and every aspect of social life. Thus, the major task of the Party's ideological work was to deal with problems arising with these changes and to achieve popular acceptance of whatever was necessary for realising the four modernisations. The masses had to be helped to understand that the four modernisations represented the interests of the people of the whole country, and that a prolonged period of stability and unity was necessary for their realisation.

A second major task of ideological work was to encourage people to work hard. They not only had to be made to understand the need for the four modernisations, but also to be fired with 'revolutionary spirit' and to receive the 'spiritual strength' imparted by ideology. For example, while it was necessary to rely on material incentives, this did not mean ignoring the motivating force of ideology, which encouraged awareness of the overall situation and long-term interests. Hence, the major thrust of this part of ideological work was the need to get people to exert greater efforts for the four modernisations, a position consistent with the tendency to define political virtue in terms of economic output. Lastly, ideological work had to deal with the growth of bourgeois ideologies, especially with the danger of contamination from greater contact with foreign countries.[25]

Thus, the major orientation of the Party's ideological leadership after the Third Plenum has been that ideology and theory have to be at the service of increasing production. The Party has to show people the benefits of the four modernisations, eliminate the vestigial influences of the Party's former political orientation, and get people to accept whatever changes are now considered necessary. The Party certainly has not relinquished its position as the locus of political and ideological authority. Indeed, the present leadership has countered tendencies deriving from the Cultural Revolution which challenged that position. Nevertheless, the change in the nature of political and ideological work has been more fundamental than a mere change of content. Little is left of the Party's former role of defining and maintaining the direction of a process of revolutionary social transformation through the integration of theory and practice. Now the direction of change is clearly defined in almost exclusively economic terms, and the Party's theoretical and ideological leadership must be subordinated to these external dictates, serving to facilitate and encourage the four modernisations.

The Party Organisation

Since the fall of the 'Gang of Four', there have been continuing efforts to strengthen the Party organisation, ensure adherence to operational procedures, and revive the Party's traditional style of work. There have been several objectives involved here. In the first place, these efforts should be taken seriously at face value. The Party organisation had been decimated in the Cultural Revolution and, according to the evidence presented since 1976, had never regained its former strength, despite the emphasis on Party organisational leadership since 1970.[26] As Teiwes shows, there had been an even longer process of erosion of inner-Party norms,[27] and this had certainly been exacerbated in the Cultural Revolution and its aftermath. Thus, there has undoubtedly been a desire to cure these diseases which have long affected the Party organisation. Secondly, and following from this, is the attempt to re-establish regularity and predictability in the Party organisation. Thirdly, the strengthening of the Party and its procedures has been closely linked to the Party's shift towards a focus on the four modernisations. While the revival of traditions may have reflected a genuine desire to cure a long-standing disease, the traditions have also been interpreted in such a way as to make them useful in shifting the Party's focus, in making the Party organisation a more suitable means of achieving economic goals.

The early criticisms of the 'Gang' concentrated on its supposedly flagrant breaches of the Party's organisational structure. It was accused of paralysing Party organisations, interrupting communication lines, establishing secret 'liaison posts' and its own intelligence system, attempting to cut off links between the Central Committee and the higher levels, encouraging lower levels to report directly to the 'Gang' and to accept its orders, and so on.[28] The 'Gang' was also indicted for the ideas which had helped to undermine the Party organisation in the Cultural Revolution. Thus, it was accused of spreading the notion that the leadership of Party organisations could be ignored on the grounds of resisting erroneous leadership, of fidelity to Mao Zedong Thought and of obeying only the Central Committee.[29] Certainly, these notions had enjoyed wide currency during the Cultural Revolution. Although they had been vigorously repudiated from 1970 onwards, the re-fighting of such Cultural Revolution battles suggests that these efforts had not been entirely effective. There was thus renewed stress on the basic tenet that correct political direction could be achieved only through the Party as an integrated organisational system.

This was also evident in Ye Jianying's criticism, at the Eleventh Congress, of people who were addicted to anarchism and factionalism and 'who prefer to remain free from constraint by the Party organisation and the leadership'.[30] Nevertheless, this insistence on organisational obedience was not unequivocal. Ye himself congratulated those who had dared to 'go against the tide' in resisting the 'Gang',[31] ignoring the fact that the 'Gang' had been in leading positions within the Party organisation. Conversely, there was a general criticism of cadres who had shown a lack of political principle by not resisting the 'Gang'. Those who accused the 'Gang' of severing the connection between the correct political direction and the Party organisational system tended to do the same whenever it was expedient.

A major stress in strengthening the Party organisation concerned the staffing of leading bodies. One of the eight tasks listed by Hua at the Eleventh Congress was to 'do a good job of consolidating and building up our Party's leading bodies at all levels'.[32] As Yu Qiuli claimed with respect to consolidating Party organisations in industrial enterprises, provincial-level Party committees had to make sure that they solved the problems of leading bodies in their jurisdiction, concentrating on the two top people in Party organisations of key enterprises.[33] And in June 1978, at the Army Political Work Conference, Deng emphasised that 'straightening things out' meant primarily straightening out leading bodies and rectifying work style. He reminded his listeners that he had urged this as long ago as 1975, with the criticism of 'leading bodies which were weak, lazy and lacking in unity'. And the main reason why problems remained was that leading bodies had not really been reorganised well.[34]

A significant factor in the reorganisation of leading bodies and the implementation of cadre policy was the attempt to strengthen Party organisation departments. It was claimed that the 'Gang of Four' had usurped the leadership of organisation departments, suppressing cadres who opposed it and covering up the problems of its own followers. Thus, it was a necessary first step in implementing cadre policy to investigate cadres in organisation departments and readjust the membership, making sure that only cadres of the highest political virtue were included.[35] For example, in Anhui, an important measure for solving problems in the implementation of cadre policy was that the Provincial Party Committee first solved the problems of its own organisation department and then set about readjusting the departments at lower levels.[36] But as well as the 'Gang's' supposed interference, a more general problem seems to have been that the work of organisation departments had often been in disarray since the Cultural Revolution. As a group of veteran cadres remarked, in previous periods cadres had seen going to the organisation department 'as returning to their own home' because it took good care of them, listened to their opinions and handled their problems. But this tradition had been disrupted and organisation departments had refused to fulfil their responsibilities to the Party.[37]

The strengthening of the Party organisation system is also evident in the restitution of a system of Party control, which had not been used since the Cultural Revolution. The significance of this is difficult to assess at the moment because the information provided so far has been very scanty. But it is possible to make some speculations on the basis of previous experiences of Party control.[38] The Constitution adopted at the Eleventh Congress provided that the Central Committee and local Party committees at *xian* level and above (and regimental level and above in the Army) should set up 'commissions for inspecting discipline'. These were to be elected by the Party Committees at the respective levels, and 'under their leadership, should strengthen Party members' education on discipline, be responsible for checking on the observance of discipline by Party members and Party cadres and struggle against all breaches of Party discipline'.[39]

The name of these new bodies suggests a similarity to the discipline-inspection committees established from 1949-1955. These were also creations of Party committees, in contrast to the vertically-integrated system of Party control established to replace them in 1955. Thus, this early-1950s precedent suggests that there would be no direct relationship between commissions at various levels and that all contact would have to be mediated through Party committees. It remained unclear, however, to what extent the activities of *xian* level commissions would extend to Party organisations at lower levels.

The new commissions were also similar in objectives to their

1950s ancestors, which, as well as dealing with immediate problems of enforcing Party discipline, also had a more general role of encouraging the proper work-style and of combating the pervasive danger of 'bureaucratism'. In a similar vein, Ye's explanation of the establishment of the new commissions, as well as stressing the need to ensure the adherence to Party discipline, also saw them as a means of safeguarding the system of democratic centralism within the Party and of preventing all actions which might damage relations between the Party and the masses.[40]

There was little further reference to Party control until the Third Plenum, which established a Central Commission for Inspecting Discipline, consisting of 100 members and headed by Chen Yun. Chen's elevation to the position of Party Vice-Chairman indicates that the Commission was to be an important body. Also, the Second and Third Secretaries, Deng Yingchao and Hu Yaobang, were elected to the Politburo, and the Permanent Secretary, Huang Kecheng, was added to the Central Committee.[41]

The Commission held its first plenary session in January 1979 although, oddly enough, much of the reporting of this meeting was delayed until March. These reports confirm the impression that the Commission was concerned with far more than discipline defined in a narrow way.[42] As the Third Plenum had announced, the Commission's tasks related to the needs of strengthening democracy in Party life and the political life of the state, making explicit the Party's political line, and strengthening the Party's leading organs, all of which were necessary for achieving the four modernisations. The Commission's plenum saw its role in overcoming 'abnormalities' in the Party's life in areas such as democratic centralism, in preventing arrogance among Party members (and particularly among leading cadres) which caused them to place themselves above Party organisations, and in preventing estrangement from the masses. Much of the discussion indicates that the commissions were to take over many of the responsibilities normally vested in Party organisation departments. Thus, they had to carry out education in Party discipline and work-style among the Party members (especially those admitted since the Cultural Revolution), to deal with rehabilitation and the handling of cadre cases, and to promote and monitor the proper style of work within the Party organisation. But they were also to play a major role in the handling of relations between the Party and the masses. They were to be a channel for dealing with complaints and appeals from the masses, and had to uphold people's democratic rights and the socialist legal system, launching struggles against those who suppressed criticism, retaliated or abused their powers and bullied people.

Clearly, one of the main concerns in the strengthening of this control system was the desire to combat Party bureaucratism, which was seen as a danger to the realisation of the four modernisations. And, in this regard, the general guidelines for the new commissions show a real awareness of problems besetting earlier forms of control. In particular, the Control Committee before the Cultural Revolution, rather than combating bureaucratism within the Party, had tended itself to become a rigid vertical bureaucracy, with control defined almost completely in top-down terms. The stress on opening channels with the masses suggests an attempt to prevent this emerging. On the other hand, the discipline-inspection committees of the early 1950s, which were completely subordinate to Party committees, were often not treated seriously and rendered ineffective. The increase in the prestige of the Central Commission after the Third Plenum may have been designed to counteract this, without establishing a separate vertical structure of control. It was, however, not entirely clear what sort of network of discipline-inspection commissions it was intended to provide. It was stated that the commissions must 'help Party committees at all levels' in fulfilling various tasks,[43] without mentioning the Constitution's provision for the commissions' subordination to Party committees (although this was recognised in the recapitulation of the history of Party control earlier in the Central Commission's announcement, and in the accompanying *Renmin Ribao* editorial), and ignoring the provision that they were not to be created 'at all levels' but only at *xian* level and above. Nevertheless, although the organisational arrangements are not entirely clear, the greater stress on discipline-inspection commissions does indicate another means of strengthening the Party organisational system and of orienting it towards the tasks of the four modernisations.

The concern for the operation of the Party organisation was also shown in the attempts to overcome various 'abnormalities' in the Party's life. Initially this was linked directly to the criticism of the 'Gang's' supposed crimes of engaging in intrigues and conspiracies, 'splittist' and 'sectarian' activities. These activities were compared to those of Trotsky, the Hu Feng clique, the Gao-Rao clique and practically every other 'bourgeois careerist' in the histories of the Chinese Communist Party and the Communist Party of the Soviet Union.[44] The stress on obeying the rules and adhering to the proper procedures did not, of course, deal with the extraordinary way in which the coup against the 'Gang' itself was carried out, since it would be entirely impossible to reconcile this with the Party's rules.

Nevertheless, there was, almost from the beginning of the period after the 'Gang's' downfall, a concentrated effort to revive or restore the Party's traditions which had atrophied over a long period. The three most emphasised were 'seeking truth from facts', the Mass Line, and, most important in the operations of the Party organisation, democratic centralism. Apart from the genuine desire to eliminate the 'abnormalities' which had prevailed in Party life, the stress on traditions was also intended to eliminate insecurity within the Party and to restore regularity and predictability. Thus, one of the major criticisms of the 'Gang' was that it had run 'steel' and 'cap' factories within the Party — that is, it had resorted to pinning political labels on those with whom it disagreed. This had resulted in fear of being accused of political crimes and had, therefore, undermined the processes of discussion and criticism within the Party. Towards the end of 1978, this criticism was extended to a more significant attempt to reduce the political stakes involved in inner-Party discussions. In yet another reversal of Cultural Revolution notions, it was argued that the whole history of the Party could not be seen in terms of 'two-line struggle'. Line struggle was one aspect of the Party's history and one manifestation of contradictions within the Party. Inner Party struggle should not be elevated to the level of line struggle and should not be treated as the battle against enemies, but should be considered as a normal process of criticism and self-criticism within the Party.[45] And another *Renmin Ribao* article in early 1979 argued that even line struggles within the Party had to be distinguished from counter-revolutionary activities. So long as matters were handled by discussion and criticism within the Party, no dispute over line should be considered as involving a contradiction with the enemy.[46] Thus, there was an attempt to encourage discussion and criticism in the Party by assuring members that it would not lead to accusations of serious political crimes.

An increasing emphasis, in all the discussions of reviving traditions, was the need to get the Party's work closer to the practical situation. This was most evident in the stress on 'seeking truth from facts'. It was also related to the view that too great an emphasis on political correctness had led to a political strait-jacket being placed on Party organisations, with consequent bureaucratic and inefficient work. For example, the 'Gang' was accused of encouraging 'formalism', which meant that cadres were afraid of saying or doing anything without an authoritative source to justify themselves and merely followed the prescribed form set by the prevailing political line. To overcome this, it was demanded that leading cadres should pay more attention to doing concrete work, that they concentrate on the efficiency with which actual problems were solved, and that they never indulge in 'empty talk'.[47] At the same time, leading cadres were warned not to get bogged down in trivial affairs, lose sight of the overall situation while concentrating on specific tasks, and ignore the long term by concentrating on the immediate.[48]

The need to link the Party's work more closely to the practical situation was also evident in the discussions of democratic centralism. As Ye argued at the Eleventh Congress, the practice of democracy was vital for stimulating the initiative of Party members and cadres. He related this to the principle of collective leadership and the pooling of the wisdom of the collective.[49] A similar view emerged from Nie Rongzhen's discussion of the Party's traditions; without democracy there could be no exchange of views, nor summing up experience, and no correct centralism.[50] A further stimulus towards the promotion of democracy was the publication of Mao's 1962 speech on democratic centralism. This speech was useful because it rejected the 'abnormal' democratic life within the Party prior to 1962, and because it used the metaphor of the Party organisation as a processing plant. People like Deng Xiaoping delighted in using Mao's works in this way to reinforce the Party's orientation towards practice.[51]

The Third Plenum led to an even greater emphasis on such organisational rules as democratic centralism, collective leadership, criticism and self-criticism. With respect to democratic centralism, the Plenum communiqué asserted that the strict implementation of rules and regulations was crucial for the realisation of modernisation, but that this could be achieved only on the basis of full democracy. In the past, the relationship between democracy and centralism was severed, and there was too little democracy.[52] This applied not only within the Party but also among the people. The press took up this theme, celebrating the Plenum and the Work Conference which preceded it for their restitution of full democracy within the Party. This was specifically linked to the Party's shift in focus, with the view that for realising the four modernisations, 'politically, the urgent task is to strive for a healthy democratic life within the Party, to develop fully socialist democracy'. In particular, the promotion of democracy within the Party was vital for democracy in all Chinese political life, and within the Party the most crucial factor was democracy within the Central Committee.[53] Similarly, the lessons of the Plenum's promotion of democracy were also seen to apply to other Party organisational procedures, such as the system of collective leadership and the roles of Party committee secretaries.[54]

Finally, the new emphasis on democracy and collective leadership in the Central Committee was applied to the position of individual leaders. The Plenum announced that people in the Party should not address each other by official titles, that no personal view was to be known as an 'instruction', and that all should be open to criticism.[55] Chen Yun stated that the practice of applauding leaders should stop.[56] There was stern criticism of the flattery of leaders, let alone deification.[57] Although Hua himself was said to have proposed these rules, clearly he was the one most affected by them. It contrasted strongly with the attempts to boost Hua's legitimacy and authority as Party leader immediately after the fall of the 'Gang'. At that time, numerous pamphlets were published celebrating Hua's revolutionary activities at various times and places. In a way somewhat similar to the stress on the 'great leader' in 1970, it had been argued that defending the status of the leader and his revolutionary authority was a major part of every two-line struggle. The revolutionary leader had to represent the fundamental interests, will and aspirations of the people, to get them united and organised, and so on.[58] Thus, it was a reason for great joy that the Party again had its own 'wise leader'. This was reinforced by the continual assertion that Mao had personally chosen and trained Hua to be his successor, a claim made by both Hua and Ye at the Eleventh Congress.

The embryonic cult of Hua was difficult to reconcile with the new stress on the Party's traditions. In particular, the Party's proper procedures were difficult to defend in a situation where the prime justification for the position of the Party Chairman was that he had been personally selected by his predecessor. Thus, there may have been good reason for Hua to insist that he should no longer be called 'wise leader' and that the stress on individuals should be removed. At the same time, however, it would seem that the Party leadership was intent to ensure that there could be no repetition of the situation in which Mao was able to use his own authority and position to undermine the Party organisation.

Party and Masses

As well as attempting to straighten out the situation within Party organisations, the period after the fall of the 'Gang' saw considerable attention devoted to strengthening the leadership of Party organisations over the mass movement. This involved another clear example of the refighting of Cultural Revolution battles. The 'Gang' was accused of diverting the mass movement from Party leadership by claiming that the mass movement is always rational, of attempting to replace the Communist Party with mass organisations, of using the slogan of supporting 'new things' in order to free those organisations under its control from subordination to Party committees, of inciting people to disobey Party committees and of paralysing Party organisations.[59] Against these activities it was asserted, as in the immediate aftermath of the Cultural Revolution, 'in fact, strengthening Party leadership is completely in uniformity with following the Mass Line. Any mass movement can have the correct direction only under the unified leadership of the Party, otherwise it will go astray.'[60]

This principle was maintained with respect to the campaign for criticising the 'Gang'. The mass activities had to be under the leadership of Party committees and it was forbidden to establish ties or organise fighting groups independent of Party committees.[61] As it was argued in a *Hongqi* article in 1978, it was necessary to mobilise the masses to criticise those who exercised 'revisionist' leadership, but only under the direct leadership of a Party committee at a higher level and in conformity with Party policies. It was forbidden that anyone should ignore Party leadership, let alone resort to 'anarchist' tactics such as instigating work stoppages and disrupting order.[62]

The Mass Line was an important component in the revival of Party traditions. As Nie explained it, the Mass Line was 'the source not only of our strength but also of the correct thought of leadership'. It was a necessary means for the Party to understand the complexity of the practical situation. Party members had to be pupils of the masses, to avoid alienation, and always to serve mass interests. And there had to be large-scale mass movements in handling matters concerning the majority of the people.[63] Many press discussions dwelt on problems of Party members being aloof from the masses, acting in a commandist fashion and not accepting mass criticism. Especially from the middle of 1978, there were many illustrations of mass responsiveness — such as the masses helping

Party committees in rectifying work-style, Party officials accepting mass criticism, or the serious attention paid to letters from the masses.[64] There was also increasing emphasis on the institutionalisation of mass political activity, especially through the three major mass organisations, the trade unions, the Women's Federation and the Youth League. Nevertheless, this was not much of a departure from the notion of the Mass Line, since it was always emphasised that such organisations had to be under the leadership of the Party and to operate as channels of communication between the Party and the masses.[65]

The discussions of socialist democracy, democratic rights and the legal system from the end of 1978 did, however, suggest a challenge to the previous conception of the Mass Line as a method of Party leadership. Just as in the discussion of democratic centralism within the Party, it was suggested that the promotion of democracy among the people was crucial for realising the four modernisations, since this could be done only by mobilising the enthusiasm and initiative of all the people.[66] Socialist democracy was seen not as a mere hope but as 'an objective requirement of the socialist economic base'. The Party needed democratic discussion and criticism so that it was not deceived by falsehoods and carried away by empty talk.[67] This was also explained in terms of the need to learn from mass practice in solving problems encountered in modernisation, summing up experience, and discovering people of ability.[68]

While this indicated a continuation of the Mass Line — although now restricted to economic modernisation rather than the broader scope of revolutionary activity — the discussions of democratic rights and the socialist legal system developed the position that the relationship with the Party was not the crucial element concerning mass political participation. This was suggested by the definition of democracy in terms of mass elections of officials at the lower levels and to people's congresses. But a more significant point was that suggested by a *Zhongguo Qingnian* (*China Youth*) article which argued that the people's 'will' as well as their 'rights' should be protected by the Constitution, the legal system and the judiciary.[69] The former conception of the Mass Line had insisted that popular will had to be mediated through the Party organisation, where it could be integrated with the broader strategy and objectives of the revolutionary movement. 'Uniting the general with the particular' derived from the Party's role as vanguard. To suggest that the people's will could be articulated or protected by other institutional means undercut a central basis of the Party's exclusive claim of leadership over the mass movement. Similarly, the Third Plenum communiqué announced: 'in order to safeguard people's democracy, it is imperative to strengthen the socialist legal system so that democracy is systematised and written into law in such a way as to ensure the stability, continuity and full authority of this democratic system and these laws'.[70] This again had the effect of defining mass participation by means other than the masses' relations with the Party. It was linked to codified law and an 'independent judiciary', rather than following the direction provided by Party policy.

It should be emphasised that these were tendencies only. Certainly there was no denial of the continuing need for Party leadership of the mass movement. And the discussions of socialist democracy included such points as that democracy among the masses would have to be 'guided' by the Party.[71] It was also argued that socialist democracy could be fully developed only with the development of socialist mass production, since, before such development, it would be inhibited by the continuation of contrary ideological traits. Also, although the people's enjoyment of democratic rights was the major distinction between a socialist and a capitalist country, they would have to delegate those rights to the politically and culturally more advanced among them because of the limited levels of social production and culture. The Party's duty, therefore, was to educate the masses with democratic ideas and to lead them in striving for democratic rights, although success could not be final so long as there was a backward economy.[72]

Some of the most serious implicit threats to the notion of Party vanguard leadership emerged in the celebration of the Tiananmen Incident and the linking of this to people's democracy. The incident was praised as a popular demonstration of opposition to the 'Gang of Four' and of support for the four modernisations. One very long *Renmin Ribao* article argued that only the Party could lead the people in their struggle for democracy, and that without Party leadership the people are prone to anarchism and ultra-democracy. The intrusion of enemies into the Party and the growth of bureaucracy could not be prevented without Party leadership. Nevertheless, it also asserted: 'with respect to conscious revolutionary action in the form of this kind of spontaneous struggle by the masses of the people, we revolutionaries and Marxists should raise our hands in exaltation, enthusiastically welcome it and firmly support it'. And it argued that, if the people had been able to choose the leaders of government organisations 'according to their interests and will', the 'Gang' would not have been able to gain its high position. Similarly, if the people really had been able to exercise the democratic rights stipulated in the Constitution, the 'Gang' would not have been able to carry out suppression of the masses. The article also suggested that people must have the right to dismiss communists or government cadres who have become alienated from them. The legal system, moreover, was vital in safeguarding the people's democratic rights, since Lin Biao and the 'Gang' could emerge only because they managed to find loopholes in the legal and judicial systems.[73]

While this article tends to see the main dimensions of mass political participation in terms other than the masses' relationship with the Party, perhaps the most surprising aspect is the implicit support for spontaneous mass activity, outside of the leadership by Party organisations, in correcting mistakes in the Party leadership. Although obviously very different in target and intention, this is similar to the 'Gang's' supposed support for mass spontaneity in the Cultural Revolution, which had of course been vigorously condemned. The same point applies to the *Renmin Ribao* editorial commemorating the third anniversary of the Tiananmen Incident in April 1979. The editorial admitted that the mass movement was not 'under direct Party leadership', and could thus be seen as a 'spontaneous revolutionary mass movement'.

> But comrades who took part in the April Fifth movement had all received education by our Party for many years; very many of the backbone forces were Communist Party members and cadres, Communist Youth League members and outstanding young people, and many Party organisations supported and directly organised the masses' struggle; seen from this perspective, the April Fifth movement could not have developed such gigantic force if it had departed from Party leadership. Party leadership depends mainly upon the correctness of the Party's line, principles and policies, and on the Party members' exemplary role.

Thus, it was inappropriate to see just the spontaneity of the movement and overlook the signs of Party leadership. The editorial went on to criticise those who wanted to reject Party leadership and to define democracy as doing what one pleases. They were reminded that socialist democracy could be achieved only under the leadership of the Party.[74]

Nevertheless, none of these rationalisations can disguise the fact that the object of praise was a mass movement outside of Party organisational leadership. In particular, the notion that Party leadership is embodied mainly in the correctness of the line is very significant, since it is a repetition of one of the faults for which the 'Gang' had been heavily criticised. This was the Cultural Revolution notion that Party leadership could be equated with the correct ideological direction as defined by Mao Zedong Thought, a notion which had been used in justifying attacks on Party organisations. A major thrust of Party building after 1970, and of the later criticism of the 'Gang', had been that there could be no separation of the correct political line from the role of Party organisations. Nevertheless, this editorial, in its attempts to reconcile the Tiananmen Incident with the concept of Party leadership, was willing to repeat this kind of notion, which had at other times proven its potential for undermining Party leadership over the mass movement.

Despite the repeated affirmations of the role of the Party as vanguard, these discussions also imply a fundamental challenge to the conception of vanguard leadership. Not only do they posit alternative means of articulating popular 'will', but they even see the 'interests' of the people independently of definition by the Party. The core of the former conception of vanguard leadership was that only the Party could define the interests of the class because of its superior understanding of the guiding revolutionary theory. Significantly, current discussions refer to the 'interests' of the people rather than those of the proletariat; even the class basis for the vanguard is diminished. If the people can recognise their own interests, and have the institutions through which to realise their will, then the rationale for the Party's role as vanguard disappears. At the Second Session of the Fifth National People's Congress, Hua identified 'the supreme interest of our country' as the realisation of the four modernisations.[75] The Party's role had formerly been predicated on the need for ideological leadership in the process of revolutionary social change. With the shift in emphasis away from such change to an exclusive focus on the four modernisations, that rationale for Party leadership became far less relevant and other conceptions of proper mass political activity became more appropriate.

Party Membership and Cadres

In many stages of the development of the Chinese Communist Party, there have been problems concerning the relations between new and old cadres — for example, with the influx of people into the Yan'an base areas in the 1940s and with the expansion and reorientation of the Party's activities after Liberation.[76] The Cultural Revolution produced one of the most dramatic generational cleavages within the Party membership and among Party cadres in particular. The cadre ranks tended to be divided between those who had gained positions of authority in the Cultural Revolution and those who, while being the targets of attack, had managed to retain their positions or were rehabilitated after demotion. Within the Cultural Revolution itself there were consistent attempts to lessen the mutual resentment, suspicion and intolerance between these two groups, but this remained a persistent source of conflict throughout the 1970s.[77]

This conflict remained crucial after the fall of the 'Gang'. In the initial period, it was linked to the criticisms of the 'Gang's' conspiratorial activities and attempts to usurp power. The 'Gang' was accused of inciting splits between new and old cadres, of infringing the official assessment of the political reliability of the overwhelming majority of cadres in the Cultural Revolution, of attempting in 1976 to generate a movement for overthrowing people in all leading organs, of opposing the rehabilitation of cadres after the Cultural Revolution and using this as a means of attacking Zhou Enlai.[78] In particular, it was argued that the 'Gang' had focused its attacks on the veteran cadres who had been the main obstacles to its conspiratorial activities.[79] This was linked to the repudiation of the 'Gang's' supposed equation of veteran cadres with capitalist-roaders, a charge against which the veterans were stoutly defended.[80] Rather than confronting the conflict between new and old cadres according to the dividing line of the Cultural Revolution, this suggested a far starker and simpler conflict: that between the 'Gang', defined by its unacceptable political behaviour, and the veteran cadres, defined by their prestige and authority gained through long experience in the revolutionary movement, especially before Liberation. Although this implied a more favourable attitude to old than to new cadres, it did not involve a direct attack on the latter. Rather, the criticism tended to be limited to the 'Gang's' direct use of Party membership and official position in recruiting people for its plots.[81]

Before long, however, it became clear that there was to be vigorous affirmation of the merits of the old cadres and increasing pressure on the new. This was shown particularly in the rehabilitation of cadres who had been criticised or punished in earlier political movements. As in the early 1970s, the return of Deng Xiaoping became a symbol of the return of cadres at all levels.[82] Certainly, after Deng's return, the focus shifted from an examination of cases involving fabrications or mistakes by the 'Gang' to a wide-ranging reassessment of all cases of cadres who had suffered in earlier political movements. It was assumed that no previous verdicts could be trusted, and that the re-examination would have to be all-encompassing. In this, the process was similar to the movement for 'cleaning the class ranks' from 1968 onwards. But the intention was quite the opposite; whereas the movement for cleaning class ranks had focused on the removal of people found to be unsuitable, the new examination of cadres focused on the restoration of those who had been wrongly treated.

This thoroughness was evident in the scope of the periods for which mistaken verdicts would be reconsidered. Obviously, it included the treatment of people who had suffered because of the 'Gang's' activities since the Cultural Revolution, especially in 1976. It also included the reversal of charges made against people in the Cultural Revolution. This was highlighted at the Third Plenum, with the rehabilitation of such Cultural Revolution targets as Tao Zhu, Bo Yibo and Yang Shangkun. But while it was stated that emphasis had to be on 'concoctions' of Lin Biao and the 'Gang', it was also recognised that mistakes made before the Cultural Revolution had to be corrected.[83] In this spirit, the Third Plenum announced the posthumous rehabilitation of Peng Dehuai.

As this shows, rehabilitation applied even to people who had been dead for many years. It extended to the family members and other associates of victims. There were also many people who had come under a political cloud in the Cultural Revolution or after whose cases had not been properly resolved. It was now intended that all such cases should be concluded as quickly as possible. And one of the most significant aspects of the entire policy was that cadres should be assigned suitable positions as soon as possible, and that those who had been given unsuitable positions should have them readjusted.[84]

Almost all reports of the process of rehabilitation include the injunction that verdicts found to have been correct should not be reversed. Other types of caution were suggested — for example, that it was important not to act with undue haste, otherwise people might resort to deceit or make rash decisions.[85] Yet the major emphasis was not on caution but on accelerating the process of re-examination and rehabilitation. The press was filled with articles heralding the successful re-examination of large numbers of cadres at all levels. But these were complemented by the statements that, although there may have been great achievements in overcoming past mistakes, there was still much work to be done. There were also several suggestions of deadlines at various levels. From the end of 1977 through 1978, there were frequent complaints that some units and areas were not doing their best to accelerate the process of rehabilitation.

These calls for acceleration suggested several types of inhibition of resistance. Causes included people's fears of admitting their own mistakes in previous treatment of cadres and the fear of retribution by rehabilitated cadres. This was linked to continuing political insecurity, with some people responsible for rehabilitation work preferring not to act decisively in case the political wind changed again.[86] And there was a strong rebuttal of the idea that it was wrong to point to the mistakes of the previous leadership. All mistakes had to be corrected, no matter who was associated with their commission. By the end of 1978, it was made clear that this applied even to those cases with which Mao himself had been associated.[87] Finally, there were frequent references to the fear of being accused of rightist deviations and of 'negating' the Cultural Revolution.[88] Many of these are the same as the objections raised against the 'liberation' of cadres from 1969 onwards. Undoubtedly, the charge of negating the Cultural Revolution would have far more force now: the earlier 'liberation' implied that the cadres had corrected the mistakes discovered in the Cultural Revolution, whereas the present rehabilitation implied that the mistakes were in the Cultural Revolution itself.[89] It is impossible to assess to what extent this continued difficulty indicates feelings of political insecurity and to what extent it indicates resistance to the current political direction and a desire actually to protect the Cultural Revolution policies which were in fact being negated.

While the old cadres were given greater praise and welcomed back into leadership positions, the reverse process applied to those who had gained Party membership, and especially those who had achieved leading positions, since the Cultural Revolution. The magnitude of this problem is shown by the figures quoted by Ye at the Eleventh Congress: nearly half of the more than 35 million members of the Party had been recruited since the Cultural Revolution and more than seven million since the Tenth Congress in

1973.[90] Initially, suspicion was directed at those new members and cadres who could be considered part of the 'Gang's' conspiracy. But as the focus moved away from the 'Gang' exclusively and began to encompass more wide-ranging problems throughout the Party, the legitimacy of the positions of all new Party members and cadres was called into question.

It was claimed that recruitment and promotion since the Cultural Revolution had infringed both explicit Party rules and long standing traditions. Much of this was associated with 'rush recruitment' and 'rush promotion'. This involved the setting of time limits for the admission of whole batches of Party members, in violation of the Party's rules on the individual testing and admission of applicants, and the wholesale incorporation of new people into leading Party bodies. It also included falsification of individuals' dossiers and use of threats of physical violence in forcing Party organisations to admit or promote individuals. When applicants could not gain acceptance by a Party branch, there were tactics such as getting them accepted by another branch ('flying across the sea' to join the Party) and even setting up a new branch in which they would be accepted. And some people were given the titles of 'secretary' or 'committee member' even before they were formally admitted into the Party.[91] The documents on Party building from 1968 onwards had stressed the prevention of all abuses such as these, even in Shanghai under Zhang and Yao.[92] But the renewed emphasis after 1976 suggests that they had not been prevented and that the Party's integrity and operational rules had been severely strained.

Many other faults, ascribed to the former procedures of admission and promotion, were not so much violations of explicit Party rules as infringements of standards. In opposition to Mao's five criteria for 'revolutionary successors', which were supposed to be the basis for promoting cadres, other principles had been used; including that those promoted should be 'rebels' and 'fighters going against the tide', that they should be 'familiar to the leadership' and have 'popular support'.[93] Again, much of this was linked directly to the 'Gang's' conspiratorial activities, with its encouragement of favouritism rather than merit and its use of loyalty to itself as the criterion for assessing cadres.[94] But it was easily generalised beyond those who might be directly implicated with the 'Gang'. It threw doubt on all those whose admission or promotion had been based on their political activism during or after the Cultural Revolution. For example, there was a two-pronged attack on the support for 'rebels'.

First, it was argued that this negated the distinction between the masses and the advanced elements of the proletariat. While rebels might include advanced elements, they also might be ordinary people or even counter-revolutionaries. Secondly, it was argued that the rebels whom the 'Gang' supported were those guilty of forming factions, engaging in violence, and disrupting Party and state.[95] Thus, not only was this not a relevant criterion for admission or promotion in the Party, but it also suggested the reverse — the reward of behaviour which should have been punished. Added to this was the doubt thrown on all sudden appointments:

> Every cadre must have a process of maturing; for some people it is fast, for others slow, but whether fast or slow, each cadre must be tempered and tested through practical struggles and prove ability to cope with a certain aspect of work before being promoted. That is, we must not look at only one period or one matter in a cadre's work, but look at his whole history and work, and, in selecting and training successors, examine and assess cadres in a long period of mass struggle.[96]

Thus, while there were still some instances of token support for the 'good' new members in the Party since the Cultural Revolution, the main emphasis severely undermined the legitimacy of their position. They had benefited from irrelevant or wrong standards, whether or not they were directly associated with the 'Gang'; and, with respect to cadres, they did not have the appropriate experience and training which could justify their leading positions.

While the increasing support for old cadres was reflected in the process of rehabilitation, the increasing suspicion of new Party members and cadres related more to the calls for rectification and even purge. It was not, of course, explicitly stated that this was directed against the new. Indeed, there was some criticism of a small number of cases concerning 'veteran' cadres who had degenerated and fallen in with the 'Gang'.[97] But there can be no doubt that the new members and cadres were those most directly affected by this trend. In general, the early period after the fall of the 'Gang' saw an emphasis on restricting the attack to only a few people who could be identified as direct folowers of the 'Gang', while conducting ideological education of those who made mistakes under its influence. This was evident in Hua's speech at the Second Conference on Learning from Dazhai in Agriculture in December

1976.[98] Chen Yonggui's speech at the Conference emphasised the same principle, while making it clear that one of the aims was to avoid too great an instability in the cadre ranks at the basic levels.[99] Such an orientation was almost invariably justified by reference to the Party's tradition of rectification in opposition to the 'Gang's' supposedly more ruthless methods. People who had made mistakes were to be subjected to severe ideological criticism, but the scope of punishment had to be kept narrow. This theme was kept alive by Hua in particular. He made a point of it in his exegesis of Volume V of Mao's *Selected Works*.[100] In his report to the Eleventh Congress, he repeated the view that only a few were 'absolutely unrepentant' people whose cases involved contradictions with the enemy.[101] Later in the report Hua, while asserting the need for investigation of individuals and incidents involved with the 'Gang's' conspiracy, still stressed the policies of distinguishing two different types of contradictions and narrowing the target of attack. He explained that the focus had to be on the 'Gang's' 'bourgeois factional set-up', which meant the 'Gang' itself and those 'backbone elements' who took part in its conspiratorial activities. But only a handful who had some role in the activities could be considered part of the factional set-up, and the attack was not to be directed against those who merely made mistakes and those who were implicated because they had been used by the 'Gang'. Even among the backbone elements, it was necessary to distinguish between those who refused to yield and those who had expressed their repentance after October 1976.[102] In a similar vein, Ye's report on the revision of the Party Constitution asserted that only a few people needed to be cleared out of the Party, but that many new members lacked an adequate understanding of the Party and its traditions and would, therefore, have to receive greater education.[103]

By the time of the Eleventh Congress, however, it was already apparent that there were mounting pressures to lessen the restrictions of the purge. While there was still emphasis on the tradition of rectification and on the various types of distinctions concerning culpability in the 'Gang's' plots, there were several signs of a widening focus of attack. One was the repeated claim that the overthrow of the 'Gang' did not mean the destruction of the factional set-up. With renewed stress on the investigation of all individuals and incidents which might be involved with the 'Gang', it was made clear that the factional set-up did not include only those who might be directly associated with the 'Gang'. Thus, it was claimed that the 'Gang' extended its tentacles everywhere, recruiting followers and agents, and that investigations would, therefore, have to cover every organisation at every level.[104] Furthermore, despite the continued emphasis on ideological education, the intention to use organisational punishment also became more evident. The work of investigation was directly related to 'the purity and consolidation of our Party and our revolutionary ranks organisationally'.[105] Those who were involved in rush recruitment and promotion had to be subjected to strict investigation in accordance with the stipulations of the new Party Constitution, and all bad elements had to be removed.[106] The 'Gang's' influence could not be underestimated, nor should there be any soft-heartedness towards its followers.

Similarly, there was a decided shift away from the narrow focus on the 'Gang's' conspiratorial activities to the inclusion of a much greater variety of political faults. *Jiefangjunbao* (*Liberation Army Daily*), in particular, was vigorous in condemning those who attempted to 'slip away' without making self-criticism or attempting to correct their mistakes, who had shifted the blame to others and pretended to have been deceived. It also condemned the 'wind faction' (those who did not adhere to the Party's standards but followed the prevailing political wind) and the 'earthquake faction' (those who sought to gain personal advantage from political disturbances).[107] This, in particular, implied renewed attention to political mistakes committed in the Cultural Revolution. While in August 1977 it was still asserted that it was necessary to distinguish the 'Gang's' factional set-up from those who were merely guilty of factionalism,[108] by 1978 some of the harshest criticism was being directed at faults most easily associated with the Cultural Revolution — factionalism, creating political 'earthquakes', becoming 'smash-and-grabbers', and so on.

There were some differences concerning the period which the investigations should cover. The usual position was that those who had corrected their mistakes after the Eleventh Congress were to be forgiven, while those who refused were not to be tolerated.[109] One Jiangxi report stated that the stress should be on investigation of the period since the Tenth Congress so as not to 'get entangled in old accounts of history'.[110] But a Jilin report only two months later, while agreeing that it was wrong to squabble over old scores such as the differences between mass organisations in the Cultural Revolution, warned that such a prohibition could not be used as an excuse for preventing criticism, and that people who had committed serious crimes had to be punished no matter how long ago they had occurred.[111] Deng Xiaoping, for his part, asserted that the focus should be on the period since the struggle against Lin Biao, and that it was necessary to 'deal severely' with those who had made mistakes after that time.[112] Such variation indicates that there was something of a free rein in defining the scope of those to be subjected to attack. What is clear is that the narrow target, which was stressed until the Eleventh Congress, was soon abandoned and that the examination of political faults became far more inclusive.

This complex situation does indicate disagreements within the leadership, of the type discussed by Sullivan, concerning the scope and intensity of the purge. As noted above, Hua in particular was most consistent in emphasising ideological rectification and restriction of targets. In his speech at the First Session of the Fifth National People's Congress, he recognised the need for organisational measures where necessary, but insisted that the target had to be narrow. While there had to be 'resolute blows' directed against unrepentant followers of the 'Gang', even those 'backbone elements' who were willing to repent should be treated leniently, and those who had made serious mistakes should not be subjected to continuing attacks.[113] The more general trend, however, was towards a token recognition of the priority of ideological education, with the greater stress given to organisational measures. Similarly, there were several announcements that the process of investigation had been completed in the main for the majority of areas and units.[114] But these were followed by criticisms of those who attempted to 'keep the lid on the struggle' and of the 'cover-up faction', consisting of people who used their power to cover up their mistakes, either for self-protection or to bide their time until they could create 'earthquakes' when any disturbance arose.[115] And those who were dragging their feet in the implementation of cadre policy faced the danger of accusations of being part of the 'Gang's' factional set-up, of being guilty of factionalism, or of adopting a bureaucratic attitude: everything connected with the 'Gang' had to be 'thoroughly destroyed politically, ideologically and organisationally'.[116]

Towards the end of 1978, however, it was evident that the campaign against political deviants was diminishing. *Jiefangjunbao* announced, in December, that the criticism of the 'Gang' would finish in most Army units at the end of the year. With the shift in focus announced at the Third Plenum, the examination of political errors became a far less important part of the Party's work. The declining significance of political standards had already been reflected in the calls for Party members (and especially leading Party cadres) to concentrate on acquiring technical and managerial skills, and in the admission of those with such skills into the Party.[117] Indeed, much seems to have been achieved in the implementation of cadre policy in 1977/8. The initial calls for stability and unity, immediately after the downfall of the 'Gang', had not, in fact, stabilised the situation for long. Some sections of the leadership were clearly anxious to spread the campaign against political deviants even at the expense of stability in the short term and in order to create a new basis to be stabilised. As a *Renmin Ribao* commentary in January 1979 indicated, this new basis had been achieved; the victory over the 'Gang' and Lin Biao had provided the stable political situation required for the development of the economy and culture, and the prime need was for stronger unity.[118]

The 'Gang of Four' had been accused of exacerbating conflicts between new and old cadres after the Cultural Revolution. In fact, the period after 1976 brought this conflict into far sharper focus, with a decisive shift in favour of the old cadres and against the new. The old were objects of veneration, vindication and rehabilitation, the new of suspicion, objurgation and possible purge. Certainly, one major reason for this was lingering resentment at the injustices suffered by many of the old cadres from the Cultural Revolution onwards and at the dubious backgrounds and behaviour of the new. The revival of Party traditions, moreover, inevitably reinforced the position of the veteran cadres. They were seen as the 'embodiment and guardians' of the traditions,[119] whereas younger Party members had been recruited and promoted in an environment in which the traditions had been undermined. But the treatment of cadres was of enormous importance in the eventual shift in the Party's focus of work. From the beginning, the qualities of the old cadres which were emphasised included their experience and ability in organisation, and it had been noted that their rehabilitation was essential for encouraging enthusiasm for the four modernisations. Conversely, it was also stated that the investigation of people and individuals connected with the 'Gang' was 'the essential political basis' for the four modernisations.[120]

It is, of course, impossible to judge the severity of purges in the Party from scattered reports of particular instances. But it is clear that the focus was not so much on removing people from Party membership as on removing them from positions of authority. Just as the younger cadres were to become less prominent in Party leading organs, so they would make way for older cadres who had been rehabilitated or who would experience a readjustment of their work assignments. This would, thereby, eliminate from important positions those who might create obstacles to the shift in the Party's orientation — through outright opposition, through a different political outlook because of experiences in the Cultural Revolution, or simply through inexperience or incompetence in the work being demanded. Thus, the rehabilitations, the widening of the scope of attack, and the insistence on organisational readjustment (and not just ideological education) had been necessary to create the types of Party organisations necessary for the shift to the four modernisations as the focus of the Party's work.

Conclusion

In the period since 1976, there have been major changes in all aspects of the position of the Chinese Communist Party. Many of these changes have been directed towards remedying the problems which beset the Party since the Cultural Revolution. They continued earlier efforts at Party building from 1968 onwards, although the focus on problems occurring throughout the 1970s suggests that these earlier efforts had not been successful. For that reason, the post-1976 régime has devoted considerable attention to restoring the Party's political dominance. It has insisted on the Party's ideological superiority and on the strengthening of the Party's organisational structure both internally and in its relations with the mass movement. Similarly, there have been attempts to revitalise the traditions and norms of inner-Party procedures which had long been under considerable strain. And one of the most prominent emphases was on dealing with perceived injustices and mistakes in the treatment of Party members and cadres in earlier political movements. In sum, therefore, this has been a period in which the Party addressed itself to overcoming what were seen as 'abnormalities' in its internal structure and procedures and in its external role. The leadership has claimed to have restored long-standing principles and methods of Party leadership after a protracted period of aberration.

These curative efforts have, however, masked a major transformation of the nature and role of the Party, which has been closely associated with the shift in focus of the Party's work to realising the four modernisations. Most fundamentally, this has involved a complete reformulation of the notion that the Party has to provide revolutionary leadership. Although the Party's explicit superiority in the understanding of the guiding Marxist-Leninist theory has been reaffirmed, the significance of this superiority has been undermined. Truth has to be verified through practice, and the criterion for successful practice has been defined increasingly as growth in economic production. This has eroded the most central rationale of vanguard leadership which formerly justified the leading position of the Chinese Communist Party — the need for a Party superior both theoretically and organisationally which could thereby guide the process of theory-directed revolutionary change. The Party's theoretical superiority may be established, but this has little relevance when the focus is exclusively on production increases, and all other questions concerning socialist transition are either defined in these terms or ignored. Similarly, the present régime has sought to restore the inviolability of the Party's political and ideological leadership. But politics have been redefined in terms of professional proficiency and economic productivity. And the focus of the Party's ideological work has become that of persuading people of the need for the four modernisations, getting them to accept whatever changes these might entail and encouraging them to work hard for their realisation. Rather than political and ideological work deriving from the Party's guidance of a process of socialist transition, they are in the service of goals defined according to 'objective' economic criteria.

This reorientation has inevitably been reflected in areas such as Party organisation, membership, and relations with the masses. Certainly there have been concerted attempts to strengthen the Party organisation, to enforce discipline as well as to promote discussion and criticism as the proper internal procedures. But while these attempts were undoubtedly motivated by the desire to overcome Cultural Revolution legacies, they have also been related to the emergent focus on the four modernisations. Party organisations have to become reliable instruments for the realisation of economic goals, obedient to higher levels, competent and able to adapt to prevailing conditions. Contrary to the former conception of political leadership, the integrative and cohesive functions of Party organisations are defined in terms of competent administration rather than in terms of discovering and implementing a 'correct' political direction. The repudiation of the notion of 'two-line struggle' as the dynamic of the operations of Party organisations has gone beyond the rejection of arbitrary political labelling, supposedly utilised by the 'Gang of Four', to the elimination of political questions as the centre of organisational activity. The strengthening of the Party organisation has been at the expense of those characteristics which distinguished it from and justified its dominance over all other organisations.

This change has been facilitated by the readjustment of personnel in leading positions in Party organisations through the processes of rehabilitation and purge. The leadership of Party organisations can thus be in the hands of those who find the pronounced reorientation of the Party more congenial and who have the experience and competence considered necessary to bring it into effect. Those who might be inclined to maintain the importance of political standards, especially those deriving from the period since the Cultural Revolution, can be removed or silenced. Despite the emphasis on stability and unity, there was a major campaign to discover and punish political deviants throughout the latter half of 1977 and 1978. Clearly, some sections of the Party leadership were concerned with the basis upon which stability was to stand, and were prepared to countenance further disturbance until that preferred basis was achieved.

Finally, one of the most crucial of the Party's traditions to be revived has been that of the Mass Line. The encouragement of mass initiative and enthusiasm is seen as vital for the realisation of the four modernisations. Thus, there must be increased democracy in all aspects of political life and the Party's alienation from the masses must be remedied. At the same time, it has been emphasised that the Mass Line must be seen in terms of the leadership by Party organisations over mass activity. There have been, however, other tendencies contrary to the former conception of the Mass Line. Many of the analyses of democracy and the 'socialist legal system' have defined mass political activity in terms independent of the Party's relations with the masses. It is often implicitly assumed that the masses themselves can define not only their will but even their interests independently of the Party, again undermining a crucial pillar of the notion of vanguard leadership. This has even been extended to the celebration of spontaneous mass activity outside of Party organisational leadership, relying on arguments similar to those for which the 'Gang of Four' had been criticised. These tendencies have been countered by the unremitting insistence that mass activities must be subordinated to Party leadership. But they are symptomatic of the increasing irrelevance of the theoretical and political leadership which was formerly crucial to the role of the Party.

Rather than being merely reactions to problems generated since the Cultural Revolution, these various post-1976 changes are closely connected parts of an overall design to redefine the Party's role according to the redirection of the whole of Chinese political life best summarised by the 'shift in focus' at the Third Plenum. As Sullivan has shown, the path towards this redirection has been tortuous; the Third Plenum itself and the Work Conference which preceded it were scenes of major disagreements and these have continued in the period since. Despite this, the transformation of the Party has been as rapid and dramatic as at any other time in the Party's history. While the period since 1976 may have seen the revival of many traditions, this has been at the expense of the *revolutionary* tradition according to which the Party had formerly baen defined.

Notes

1. *PR* 1, 1 January 1977, p. 41.
2. *PR* 35, 26 August 1977, pp. 32, 39 and 49; *PR* 36, 2 September 1977, p. 17. See Hua's discussion of class struggle at the 2nd session of the 5th National People's Congress in June 1979, *BR* 27, 6 July 1979, pp. 9-10.
3. *RMRB* 12 September 1977, p. 2; *RMRB* 22 April 1978, p. 1. See also Hua's assertion, at the National Finance and Trade Conference on Learning from Daqing and Dazhai, that emphasising 'objective economic laws' did not negate 'politics in command', *PR* 30, 28 July 1978, pp. 14-15.
4. *RMRB* 12 September 1977, pp. 1-2.
5. *PR* 12, 24 March 1978, p. 17.
6. *PR* 36, 8 September 1978, pp. 10-11.
7. *RMRB* 22 April 1978, p. 1. See also the argument that, if politics were not to be 'empty talk', the correct political orientation would have to be manifested in the success of production and 'vocational work'. Thus, a worker who applied himself to his work thereby showed his commitment to socialism and his correct political orientation, *PR* 43, 27 October 1978, pp. 15-17.
8. *RMRB* 16 January 1978, p. 2; *PR* 6, 10 February 1978, p. 7.
9. *PR* 12, 24 March 1978, p. 16.
10. *PR* 52, 29 December 1978, p. 11. Parts of this formulation echo phrases of Mao in the 1950s, although, as Sullivan notes, they are used in a very different theoretical context.
11. *RMRB* 25 December 1978, p. 4.
12. *RMRB* 11 April 1979, p. 1.
13. *PR* 1, 1 January 1977, p. 43.
14. *PR* 43, 21 October 1977, pp. 6-7. As Zweig (1978 (b) p. 91, n. 20) notes, Party schools enable the central leadership to monitor access into leading positions and to ensure a more uniform line in the Party.
15. *RMRB* 13 July 1977, p. 2.

16. Nie Rongzhen, *Hongqi* 9, 1977, pp. 68-71. See also Chen Yun's article tracing the tradition back into CCP history, *RMRB* 28 September 1977, pp. 1-2.
17. *RMRB* 24 June 1978, pp. 1 and 3; *RMRB* 19 September 1978, p. 2.
18. *PR* 6, 10 February 1978, pp. 7-8.
19. *RMRB* 16 February 1979, p. 3.
20. E.g. *RMRB* 29 August 1978, p. 2; *BR* 5, 2 February 1979, pp. 16-18; *RMRB* 30 October 1978, p. 2. Meanwhile, Yang Chengwu, who had been most associated with the notion of 'absolute authority of Mao Zedong Thought' in 1967, remained in the CC, free of criticism.
21. *RMRB* 22 September 1978, p. 2; *RMRB* 14 October 1978, p. 3.
22. *RMRB* 22 December 1978, pp. 1-2.
23. *BR* 4, 26 January 1979, p. 3; *RMRB* 16 January 1979, pp. 1 and 4.
24. *RMRB* 16 January 1979, p. 1.
25. *RMRB* 19 April 1979, pp. 1 and 4. The redirection of ideology has been applauded by many Western commentators. E.g. 'It has become increasingly clear, both to China's leaders and to the outside world, that what the country needs is better organisation and motivation, and less ideology. This does not mean that ideology is to be abandoned: it will remain the framework within which all policy decisions are justified. But in this sense it will become an instrument of policy rather than its guiding influence — a situation already realized in the Soviet Union.' Bonavia 1978, p. 192. In this process, the Chinese leadership appears to have largely overcome the constraints identified by some commentators in the earlier period after Mao's death. E.g. Chang 1977, pp. 313-316, Harding 1978, pp. 83-8.
26. Nathan argues that the area of Party organisation has been the one of most substantial change since the death of Mao, with the attempt to remedy the damage done to the Party since the Cultural Revolution. See Nathan 1978, pp. 112-13. On some of the revelations of 'crimes' of Party officials and damage suffered by the Party organisation, see *China News Analysis* 1121.
27. Teiwes 1979.
28. *RMRB* 17 December 1976, pp. 1-2; *RMRB* 24 January 1977, p. 2.
29. *RMRB* 14 February 1977, p. 3; *RMRB* 16 May 1977, p. 3; Beijing Radio, 22 October 1977, *SWB* FE/5659/B11/4-5.
30. *PR* 36, 2 September 1977, p. 31.
31. Ibid., p. 29.
32. *PR* 35, 26 August 1977, pp. 47-8.
33. *PR* 22, 27 May 1977, pp. 18-19.
34. *PR* 25, 23 June 1978, p. 20.
35. *RMRB* 10 January 1978, p. 1; *RMRB* 7 October 1977, p. 3.
36. *RMRB* 22 February 1978, p. 1.
37. *RMRB* 2 February 1978, p. 2.
38. The following discussion relies largely upon Cocks 1969.
39. *PR* 36, 2 September 1977, p. 21.
40. Ibid., p. 32.
41. *PR* 52, 29 December 1978, pp. 7 and 16.
42. *RMRB* 25 January 1979, pp. 1, 3 and 4; *RMRB* 25 March 1979, pp. 1 and 3.
43. *RMRB* 25 March 1979, p. 3.
44. E.g. *RMRB* 16 May 1977, p. 3; *RMRB* 22 December 1976, p. 1.
45. *RMRB* 14 December 1978, p. 3.
46. *RMRB* 16 February 1979, p. 3. See also Whiting 1977, pp. 1029-30.
47. *RMRB* 31 January 1978, p. 2.
48. *RMRB* 27 May 1978, pp. 1-2.
49. *PR* 36, 2 September 1977, pp. 30-2.
50. *Hongqi* 9, 1977, pp. 73-4.
51. *PR* 25, 23 June 1978, pp. 16-17.
52. *PR* 52, 29 December 1978, p. 14.

53. *RMRB* 11 January 1979, p. 1. See also *RMRB* 29 December 1978, p. 1.
54. *RMRB* 1 February 1979, pp. 1-2.
55. *PR* 52, 29 December 1978, p. 16.
56. *BR* 6, 9 February 1979, p. 6.
57. *RMRB* 1 February 1979, pp. 1-2.
58. E.g. the *Jiefangjunbao* articles, translated in *PR* 45, 5 November 1976, pp. 5-6; *PR* 47, 19 November 1976, pp. 7-8; *PR* 49, 3 December 1976, pp. 8-10.
59. *RMRB* 24 January 1977, p. 2; Beijing Radio, 22 October 1977, *SWB* FE/5659/B11/4; *PR* 15, 14 April 1978, p. 8.
60. *RMRB* 14 February 1977, p. 3. This article also makes clear that the major antagonism was between the revolutionary committee, or rather the mass representatives on the revolutionary committee, and the Party organisation.
61. *RMRB* 28 November 1976, p. 1.
62. *Hongqi* 5, 1978, pp. 39-40.
63. *Hongqi* 9, 1977, pp. 71-2.
64. Fuzhou, Fujian Radio, 11 June 1978, *SWB* FE/5843/B11/18; *RMRB* 8 November 1978, p. 1; *PR* 44, 3 November 1978, pp. 17-22.
65. On trade unions, see the report by Ni Zhifu, *PR* 44, 3 November 1978, p. 11.
66. See Ye's report on the revision of the State Constitution, *PR* 11, 17 March 1978, pp. 18-20; also *RMRB* 25 December 1978, p. 4.
67. *RMRB* 13 November 1978, p. 3.
68. *RMRB* 26 December 1978, p. 2; *RMRB* 3 January 1979, p. 1.
69. Reprinted in *RMRB* 13 November 1978, p. 3.
70. *PR* 52, 29 December 1978, p. 14.
71. *RMRB* 21 February 1979, pp. 1 and 4.
72. *RMRB* 28 September 1978, pp. 1 and 4.
73. *RMRB* 21 December 1978, pp. 1-3.
74. *RMRB* 5 April 1979, p. 1.
75. *BR* 27, 6 July 1979, pp. 10-11.
76. Teiwes 1979.
77. Goodman (1977, p. 136) suggests a more complex division among cadres as a result of the Cultural Revolution. See also Lee 1978, pp. 938-51; Liao 1977.
78. E.g. *RMRB* 24 January 1977, p. 3; *RMRB* 17 December 1976, p. 2; *RMRB* 7 January 1977, p. 2. Many articles linked the 'Gang's' treatment of the relationship between old and new cadres to Trotsky's activities in attempting to create divisions within the CPSU: e.g. *GMRB* 30 January 1977, p. 3; *RMRB* 19 March 1977, pp. 1 and 4.
79. *RMRB* 5 January 1977, p. 3.
80. E.g. *GMRB* 31 January 1977, p. 4; *RMRB* 24 January 1977, p. 3.
81. E.g. Hua in *PR* 1, 1 January 1977, p. 39; *Hongqi* 2, 1977, p. 8.
82. Some commentators have used rather tenuous evidence to assert Hua's opposition to Deng's rehabilitation: e.g. Domes 1978, p. 6. See also Wayne (1978, pp. 131-3) on the 'crisis' over Deng from December 1976 to January 1977.
83. *RMRB* 15 November 1978, p. 1.
84. *Hongqi* 6, 1978, p. 2.
85. Ibid., pp. 2-4.
86. NCNA 9 February 1978, *SWB* FE/5738/B11/4.
87. *RMRB* 15 November 1978, p. 1.
88. *RMRB* 19 January 1978, p. 1; *RMRB* 2 February 1978, p. 2.
89. As pointed out by Lee (1978, pp. 935-6), there is a difference between 'liberation' and 'rehabilitation'. The former implies that cadres can resume positions because they have corrected the mistakes for which they were properly accused. The latter implies that the original accusations were not proper, and that the cadres should be exonerated from blame. Thus, while the post-Cultural Revolution return of cadres involved 'liberation', the post-1976 return involves 'rehabilitation'. An interesting

case is the removal of the label from those classified as 'rightists' in 1957, at the end of 1978. As an *RMRB* editorial explained, this did not necessarily involve a re-examination of the cases. Nor did it suggest that the original classification had been improperly given. Thus, this was neither a 'rehabilitation' nor a 'liberation'. It was recognised that, in some cases, people had been wrongly designated — and would have to be rehabilitated — showing that rehabilitation did not apply to the rest. Hence, this was simply a case of expediency, departing from the Party's usual concern with handling political designations: *RMRB* 17 November 1978, pp. 1 and 4.

90. *PR* 36, 2 September 1977, p. 36.

91. *Hongqi* 2, 1977, pp. 9-10; *RMRB* 30 May 1977, p. 3.

92. See the documents in Guangzhou Gongren Daibiao Dahui Zhengzhibu 1968.

93. *RMRB* 24 January 1977, p. 2; *GMRB* 21 January 1977, p. 3; *GMRB* 30 January 1977, p. 1.

94. *RMRB* 20 April 1977, p. 3.

95. *RMRB* 30 May 1977, p. 3.

96. *RMRB* 7 October 1977, p. 3.

97. E.g. Ma Tianshui in Shanghai, *RMRB* 3 January 1978, p. 3.

98. *PR* 1, 1 January 1977, p. 38.

99. *PR* 2, 7 January 1977, pp. 12-13.

100. *PR* 19, 6 May 1977, p. 23.

101. *PR* 35, 26 August 1977, p. 33.

102. Ibid., pp. 44-5.

103. *PR* 36, 2 September 1977, p. 36.

104. *RMRB* 6 August 1977, p. 1.

105. *Hongqi* 10, 1977, p. 21.

106. *RMRB* 7 October 1977, p.3; *RMRB* 29 October 1977, p. 1.

107. *Jiefangjunbao* articles, reprinted in *RMRB* 10 January 1978, p. 2; *RMRB* 28 January 1978, p. 2; *RMRB* 31 January 1978, p. 2.

108. *RMRB* 6 August 1977, p. 1.

109. *RMRB* 23 March 1978, p. 1.

110. Nanchang, Jiangxi Radio, 20 March 1978, *SWB* FE/5775/B11/3.

111. *Jilin Ribao* 17 May 1978, *SWB* FE/5824/B11/2.

112. *PR* 25, 23 June 1978, p. 20.

113. *PR* 10, 10 March 1978, pp. 16-18. See also *Hongqi* 4, 1978, pp. 45-6; Zweig 1978 (b), pp. 85-6.

114. E.g. in the New Year's Day editorial, *RMRB* 1 January 1978, p. 1; Hua at the National Finance and Trade Conference, *PR* 30, 28 July 1978, p. 7.

115. *RMRB* 22 February 1978, p. 3; ibid. p. 1; *Heilongjiang Ribao*, Harbin, Heilongjiang Radio, 13 April 1978 and 20 April 1978, *SWB* FE/5806/B11/14-17.

116. *RMRB* 2 February 1978, p. 2.

117. E.g. *RMRB* 29 August 1978, pp. 1 and 4; *RMRB* 3 July 1978, p. 4. See also Deng's speech at the opening of the National Science Conference, *PR* 12, 24 March 1978, p. 18. Also the tendency to criticise responsible members of Party organisations in terms of their incompetence in handling production tasks rather than their political faults, as in *PR* 45, 10 November 1978, p. 31.

118. *RMRB* 18 January 1979, p. 1.

119. *RMRB* 19 February 1978, p. 1.

120. *RMRB* 4 October 1978, p. 1.

3 Industrial Development and the Four Modernisations

ANDREW WATSON

The demise of the 'Gang of Four' and subsequent developments in China have placed questions of economic theory and economic policy in the forefront of almost all activities. Indeed, even before October 1976, during the long period of factional struggle between the supporters of the 'Gang' and its opponents which dominated Chinese politics after the attempted coup by Lin Biao, efforts to undermine the 'Gang's' position were by and large initiated through debate over economic issues. Then, as now, the basic criticism of the 'Gang' was that it denied that development in China was, at heart, a problem of increasing gross output, raising the productivity of labour and speeding up the rate of growth of output. Although the 'Gang' and its supporters countered by underlining the economic results of their policies as exemplified by model enterprises in Shanghai and elsewhere,[1] much of their response was at first expressed at a theoretical level or in relation to cultural issues. It was not until the debate on questions of 'bourgeois right' and proletarian dictatorship got under way in March 1975 that they attempted to present a more careful analysis of economic questions.[2] Essentially, the 'Gang' stressed that economic development was not simply a question of gross output and productivity but also of the distribution of wealth and political power.

During 1975, the 'Gang's' efforts led to considerable discussion in the Chinese media of such things as the eight-grade wage system, the role of economic incentives, the nature of commodity production and distribution in socialist society, and questions of enterprise management. The immediate effect of this debate, however, was to provoke renewed factionalism within factories which caused serious disruption to industrial production and transport.[3] It was subsequently reported, for example, that during the period 1974 to 1976 there was a loss in production of more than 20 million tons of steel and that in 1976 steel output fell below the level of 1971.[4] Hua Guofeng, in his speech to the First Session of the Fifth National People's Congress in 1978, stated that more than ¥100,000 million in the gross value of industrial output had been lost over the same period.[5] Not surprisingly, the most fundamental line of attack on the 'Gang' and its supporters since October 1976 has concentrated on economic issues. It is alleged that they disregarded practical economic policy and pursued their own ends by concentrating on theoretical analysis. Considerable evidence has been presented to suggest that both in motives and in practice the 'Gang' had many failings, but, whatever the merits of such criticisms, the nature of this debate has once again highlighted one of the major issues which has confronted China since 1949. How can China build socialism in conditions of extreme scarcity? The policies of the First Five-Year Plan and the consolidation period of the early 1960s produced good rates of growth in output. They also raised questions about the nature of the society which was being created. The Great Leap Forward and the Cultural Revolution attempted to find alternative paths for socialist development but each, in turn, created many practical problems and led to a slowing-down in the rate of economic growth. During the period 1974-6, the calls for mass debate on political and economic issues were made in a context of political factionalism and inevitably implied losses in current production. The experience of the past 30 years has, therefore, underlined that the relationship between social revolution and planned economic development is complex and not easily handled. The compelling problems of immediate material scarcity place urgent practical restraints and demands on those who conceive of development as a combined political and economic process. 'Correct theory' cannot, for long, compensate for any lack of practical success.

In putting forward the call for the four modernisations (of industry, agriculture, national defence, science and technology), the current leadership has explicitly declared that, at the present stage, the key to development in China is the growth of output. The crucial argument made is that the changes in the system of ownership of the 1950s guarantee the building of socialism and, therefore, the true test of current policy is whether it increases production and productivity. This point is central to the changes in policy which have taken place since, if the system of ownership is seen as the key feature of socialist transition, most other policy questions come to be regarded as secondary and technical. Although it is recognised that problems of inequality and distribution may arise, it is believed that these can be remedied by government action and by increased output. They are not felt to be threats to the building of socialism. As a result, the articulation and extension of the economic policies associated with the four modernisations now dominate all aspects of political life. Work in education, the arts and the sciences has been reshaped to concentrate on training the specialists needed for technological modernisation. The reorganisation of the Party, the 'hundred flowers' policy in the arts and the concern for the democratic rights of the individual are seen as providing the necessary social and political background for rapid economic growth. There is an overall concern to develop the incentives to persuade people to devote themselves to the economic development of the country. In effect, the current leadership has responded to the problems of relating social revolution to economic growth by arguing that the latter now encompasses the former. The argument advanced during the Cultural Revolution that socialist revolution in the relations of production is necessary to ensure the consolidation and development of the economic base has been reversed by the argument that the relations of production must correspond to and be defined by the development of an economic base which is already, in essence, oriented towards socialism. The fall of the 'Gang of Four' has thus marked a decisive shift away from the concept of development that has characterised Party policy at least since the Cultural Revolution.

In what follows, I shall first examine some of the theoretical aspects of the debate between the 'Gang of Four' and the new leadership over economic issues. I shall then look at developments in industrial policy over the period 1969 to 1979 and at the major changes in planning, economic management, centralisation and decentralisation, the role of the banks, investment policy, forms of industrial specialisation, types of co-operatives and enterprise management. Throughout, it will be made clear that the call for increased output and productivity now dominates both theoretical economic discussion and the framing of practical policies.

The Theoretical Debate[6]

At the most fundamental level, the theoretical differences between the 'Gang of Four' and its opponents, as represented by Deng Xiaoping, have been expressed in terms of the relationship between the superstructure and the economic base and between the relations of production and the productive forces. The fact that the relations of production form part of both the superstructure and the base has added to the difficulty of evaluating the respective positions. A Chinese textbook published in early 1976 argues that, in general historical development, the system of ownership of the means of production determines the other aspects of the relations of production, that the productive forces (defined as consisting of the labour force and the means of production) determine the relations of production, and that the economic base determines the superstructure.

In the case of each of these relationships, however, the book goes on to argue that under certain conditions this relationship of determination may be reversed and it quotes historical examples to prove the point.[7] The argument developed by the 'Gang of Four' during 1975 was that, during the period of socialist construction, progressive revolution in the relations of production and in the superstructure formed an essential basis for economic policy.[8] By contrast, Deng Xiaoping took the position that change in the system of ownership of the means of production was the key to revolution in the relations of production. Once a change in ownership had been achieved, further change in the relations of production should be guided by the demands of the development of the productive forces. Such development should now become the focus of economic policy.[9] As its starting point, the 'Gang' took the position that:

> In human society, people always form certain relations of production and engage in productive activities to solve problems of their material well-being. The relations of production consist of three aspects, the system of ownership of the means of production, the relations between men and the methods of distribution. Of these, the system of ownership of the means of production is basic and determines the other two aspects of the relations of production. The two other aspects, however, also react on the system of ownership and, under certain conditions, play a determining role.[10]

Proceeding from this, the 'Gang' went on to argue that the continued existence of 'bourgeois right' in China in the form of the eight-grade wage system, payment according to labour, exchange by means of money, a commodity system, and different status between people in production was a threat to the continuation of the socialist revolution. Thus, first priority should be given to controlling and reforming the relations of production and to extending the scope of the revolution in the superstructure:

> It is necessary to adhere to the Party's basic line, *bring into full play the dynamic role of the socialist superstructure in consolidating and developing the socialist economic base*, restrict bourgeois right under the dictatorship of the proletariat, do away with the idea of bourgeois right, and warm-heartedly support the new things which are conducive to gradually narrowing the three major differences and which contain the sprouts of communism.[11]

As the 'Gang' saw it, the Cultural Revolution had marked a decisive step forward in this process and the changes it had made in the superstructure had inevitably entailed great advances in production.[12]

In contrast to this position, Deng placed overwhelming emphasis on the 'major determining role of the productive forces, practice, and the economic base in general historical development'.[13] While conceding that, under certain conditions, the relations of production and the superstructure could play a determining role, he argued that politics and economics existed as a unity of opposites and that, while politics should be in command, the aim of political work was 'to guarantee the completion of economic work and serve the economic base'. He alleged that, in contrast to himself, 'political swindlers like Lin Biao' (i.e. the 'Gang of Four') had set politics and economics in opposition to each other. The true test of a political line, therefore, was whether or not it promoted the development of the productive forces.[14]

Deng developed his case further by arguing that the more industry, science and technology developed, the more strict and complex become their demands on the social system. Forms of enterprise management, which did not conform to the demands of such developments, had to be abandoned since they would not be able to resist the pressures created by modern industrial techniques. This was true of capitalist, socialist and communist societies. He backed up this reference to technological imperatives by quoting Engels' 'On Authority' to the effect that:

> If man, by dint of his knowledge and inventive genius, has subdued the forces of nature, the latter avenge themselves upon

him by subjecting him, in so far as he employs them, to a veritable despotism independent of all social organisation. Wanting to abolish authority in large-scale industry is tantamount to wanting to abolish industry itself, to destroy the power loom in order to return to the spinning wheel.[15]

Although this position is not one that is completely accepted by all Marxists,[16] it was arguments of this kind which lay behind the revival of interest in Lenin's view of the positive aspects of the Taylor system (i.e. scientifically determined technical management[17]), and in the import of foreign technology and foreign managerial methods.[18] By asserting the neutrality of science and technology, Deng was able to put forward an 'objective' yardstick against which to measure the correctness of political and economic policy. Furthermore, he pointed to the factionalism, industrial disruption and lost production in the Cultural Revolution and in the period 1974 to 1976 as examples of how incorrect policy hindered production.[19]

In the years since the fall of the 'Gang of Four', this analysis by Deng has been extended and generalised, particularly with regard to the determining role of the system of ownership and the political neutrality of science and technology. As for the former, the position has been taken that, once the system of ownership of the means of production has been transformed, objective economic laws which had a capitalist content in the old society become socialist in content and must still be observed. With respect to such things as the law of value, the role of profit, capital, credit, interest rates, payment according to work done, material incentives, and the division of labour, the case is made that it is a distortion of Marxism to confuse their functioning under socialist ownership with their functioning under capitalist ownership. They should all be fully employed to promote the growth of the socialist economy.

A typical example of this kind of argument can be found in the article, 'The Category of Profit and Socialist Enterprise Management', by Wu Jinglian, Zhou Shulian and Wang Haibo.[20] This article establishes the position of the 'Gang of Four' by quoting from its Shanghai textbook on political economy to the effect that socialist economic accounting requires the economic category of profit 'but, although the system of ownership is different, this category is ultimately the legacy of the private economy'.[21] In contrast to this position, the articles goes on to argue that economic categories are the theoretical expression of the relations of production and, Marx had said in 1846, both the categories and the relationships they express are temporary historical phenomena. Thus, the economic category of capitalist profit created alongside capitalist relations of production will, of necessity, disappear with the destruction of capitalism. The capitalist category of profit reflects the exploitative relationship between the capitalist class and the proletariat. But, the authors argued:

> Under the socialist system, this kind of relationship no longer exists. Therefore, the category of profit derived from surplus value also no longer exists. *Socialist profit is an entirely new category.* It is the value expression of the surplus product created by labourers for society — part of the net income of an enterprise.[22]

The article concludes, therefore, that the 'Gang of Four' was guilty of confusing Marxist categories. Socialist profit is not a suspect remnant of the old society but a necessary goal even of socialist enterprises. Similar arguments abound in respect of a wide range of economic questions.

The second area in which Deng's arguments have been extended is with regard to the political neutrality of science and technology. This question has received considerable emphasis in discussions of the role of foreign trade and foreign imports. Management techniques under capitalism, it is argued, have two aspects.[23] One is to exploit surplus value and thus reflects capitalist relations of production. The other is to organise large-scale, socialised production and thus reflects the productive forces.

> From the point of view of the productive forces, production in capitalist enterprises and socialist enterprises is large-scale, socialised production based on modern technology. In this respect, there are no basic differences in the nature of the two and the two types of enterprise management must have points in common.[24]

The implied position, that both technology and the relations of production it embodies have no class nature, was made explicit in the foundation editorial of the journal *Jingji Guanli* (*Economic Management*). This states that modernised production technology requires modernised management. 'Science and technology have no class nature in themselves' and, unlike those aspects of management techniques which are determined by the relations of production, 'those aspects of management techniques determined by the productive forces also have no class nature'.[25]

It is not my purpose here to assess the theoretical validity of the arguments presented. Clearly, many schools of Marxism would dispute the analysis which is being made in China and whether the relationship between the superstructure and the base is adequate as a framework to deal with the problems being tackled. The important point is that, although the theoretical arguments used against the 'Gang of Four' have been elaborated at great length over the period since 1976 and practical economic policies have also been transformed, in essence the roots of the arguments made to support new initiatives were already clearly stated in Deng Xiaoping's speeches of 1975. Furthermore, these arguments have served to place at the heart of all policy the narrowly-defined concept of development as the development of the productive forces.

The Evolution of Industrial Policy 1969-1979

The period between the Ninth Party Congress in April 1969 and the removal of the 'Gang and Four' in October 1976 was characterised by an uneven but consistent trend of withdrawal from the innovations of the Cultural Revolution.[26] At the enterprise level, the period 1969 to 1971 was dominated by pressure to restore order and production, and to put an end to factionalism. This was accompanied by the gradual reconstruction of Party organisation, the decline in authority of the mass organisations, and the initial moves to phase the army out of its role in revolutionary committees. After the fall of Lin Biao, attention shifted to the problems of strengthening discipline, of raising product quality, and of improving technical management by fully employing the skills of veteran technical cadres. Waste, losses in production and organisational problems which had originally been blamed on the lingering influence of Liu Shaoqi were now attributed to the anarchy created by the 'ultra-left' during the Cultural Revolution. Thereafter, models for good management stressed such things as strengthening rules and regulations, using experienced managers, reducing costs, good economic accounting, the introduction of systems of responsibility at one's work post, and efficient attainment of production targets.[27] In contrast to the all-round reliance on mass activism which had characterised the period 1966 to 1971, the workers were now called upon to distinguish between 'grasping production for the sake of revolution' and the reactionary theory of 'production first', between economic accounting for the sake of the revolution and 'profits in command', between observing labour discipline for the sake of the revolution and the old system of 'controlling, restricting and suppressing the masses', and between reasonable rewards and the reactionary theory of 'material incentives'.[28] At the same time, there was a significant reconstruction of revolutionary committees in enterprises. The military was finally phased out, veteran cadres returned and, in many cases, the numbers of mass representatives declined. The most obvious symbol of these developments was the rehabilitation of Deng Xiaoping in April 1973. As a result of all this, by the middle of 1973 enterprise management in China was beginning to resemble the pre-Cultural Revolution situation more closely than one would have thought possible after the events of 1966 to 1969.

It was at this point that the 'Gang of Four' and its supporters stepped up their efforts to prevent the restoration of the old system. The criticism of Lin Biao was transformed from criticism of the 'ultra-left' into criticism of the 'ultra-right' and the symbolic campaign to criticise Lin Biao and Confucius was launched.[29] The immediate result was to cast doubts on the trends in industrial management which had appeared after the fall of Lin Biao.

> Because, for a period of time in 1972, after the factory Party committee strayed from the Party's basic line over certain questions and mistakenly criticised Lin Biao's ultra-right revisionist line as ultra-left, criticism increasingly changed direction so that even things denounced during the great Cultural Revolution were brought back again.[30]

During the first half of 1974, discussion of backsliding in enterprise management revealed that the return of pre-Cultural Revolution practices had been fairly widespread.[31] In contrast, the innovations of the Cultural Revolution, typified by reliance on the creative role of the workers which derived from a self-conscious sense of revolutionary discipline, were reaffirmed, and models were publicised claiming to show the advantages of this approach.[32] Since the fall of the 'Gang of Four', these models have been denounced as falsifications aimed at creating anarchy and furthering the 'Gang's' own ends.[33]

Inevitably, proponents of the restoration of order and discipline attempted to defend themselves and concentrated on appeals for stability and unity, stressing that the basic interests of all workers were the same and that there was no need to divide into factional groups.[34] While they had to make concessions to the need to defend the great achievements of the Cultural Revolution, such concessions were accompanied by insistence that the development of production was both the goal of the revolution and necessary to consolidate the socialist system; 'in the last analysis, labour productivity is the most important thing for ensuring the victorious development of the new socialist system'.[35] The bulk of reports on managerial problems and on provincial conferences on industry during 1975 took this approach.[36] Perhaps this was inevitable, given the concern expressed for discipline in production in a July 1974 circular from the Central Committee[37] and the emphasis placed on the four modernisations by Zhou Enlai at the Fourth National People's Congress. Nevertheless, the very existence of these calls for order is indicative of the fact that the campaign against restoration was having an effect in many enterprises throughout China. The period 1974 to 1976 was, therefore, one of persistent local disruptions, losses in production and considerable variation in management practices.

Despite these important developments at the enterprise level, the overall strategy of industrial development was not significantly altered during this period.[38] The policies of 'agriculture as the foundation and industry as the leading factor', of regional decentralisation of industrial ownership and planning, and of regional balance in investment, with a strong emphasis on strategic dispersal as a military necessity, remained. There was also a continued reliance on a mixture of technologies, on a wide range of size of industrial enterprises (typified by the slogan 'walking on two legs') and on balanced investment between producer and consumer goods. All these items retained the importance they had gained in the late 1950s and early 1960s. Even the policy of 'self-reliance' was not significantly dented by the imports of large plants and foreign technology which took place in the years 1972 to 1975. These imports were widely interpreted as contributing to China's capacity to become industrially independent and to the development of urgently needed goods to support agriculture. Such purchases were not supported by foreign aid or loans and the Chinese retained full control over all new investment. Internally, 'self-reliance' as a policy for stimulating local capital accumulation and local initiative was still dominant. The alternative approaches, as represented by Soviet-style planning and by the 'Libermanist' experiments of the years before the Cultural Revolution, remained unacceptable. It was not until 1975, when Deng Xiaoping put forward a new formulation to speed up the rate of industrial development, that change began to occur in this general strategy.[39]

Although Deng still employed much of the vocabulary of the Cultural Revolution, the reforms he advocated represented a clear shift of emphasis both in terms of enterprise operation and in terms of general industrial policy. At the enterprise level, he argued that a key problem was to restore sound leadership. Calls for 'rebellion' and 'going against the tide' had to be balanced by emphasis on stability, unity, and the prevention of factionalism. In fact, he argued, it was time for the status of the bulk of managers, engineers and technicians to be restored. Many enterprises were dogged by 'weak and sloppy political and ideological work, chaotic administration, low productivity, poor product quality, excessive consumption of raw materials, high costs and numerous accidents, all of which cause great losses'.[40] The solution was to strengthen management and establish effective functional organs which would be responsible for meeting the eight prescribed economic and technical targets (output volume, product type, quality, consumption of materials and fuel, labour productivity, costs, profit and use of liquid capital). While active worker participation in management would help assure these goals, it was also necessary to establish clear rules for responsibility at work posts, attendance, technical operations, quality control, the management and maintenance of equipment, safety and economic accounting. Most of Deng's arguments amounted to a reversal of the changes in management brought about by the Cultural Revolution.[41]

Dealing with overall strategy, Deng argued that the policy of downward transfer of enterprise control to provincial and municipal level which had taken place since 1970 was sound and should continue. In fact, with the exception of transport and communications which crossed provincial boundaries, large oil fields, and other key enterprises and key investments, this policy should be extended. He did not envisage any recentralisation of control but he did argue for more effective co-ordination and guidance at a regional level. He criticised any tendency for provinces to attempt to develop their own complete industrial systems. Furthermore, the central authorities had to retain control over the appointment of key personnel, general strategy, major production targets, major investment, distribution of important materials, distribution of key commodities, the budget, the currency, employment, wages and prices. In particular, it was necessary to strengthen unified central planning so that the relationships between the different economic sectors and activities could be made to conform to overall policy. While planning still had to allow some leeway, enterprises were required to carry out their assignments quite strictly. In context, Deng's comments implied a greater degree of central control over industry than had been the case in the previous period but this was still seen within the framework of a decentralisation of ownership to the lower administrative levels with dual control (central and local) mediated through the leadership of the Party committee at the level concerned. He was, therefore, not advocating any fundamental changes in this area of policy.

Turning to sectoral relations, Deng reaffirmed the long-standing emphasis on agricultural development and said that priority in planning should go to agriculture, light industry and heavy industry, in that order.[42] Industry should strive to supply goods for agricultural modernisation. Cities should form close links with suburban *xian*, stimulating the growth of agricultural subsidiaries to supply urban needs and helping with the development of commune industries. Where suitable, industrial enterprises could either develop their own agricultural subsidiaries, in the same way as the Daqing Oilfield, or they could form links with particular communes. A new note sounded by Deng, however, was a call for large-scale development of the raw materials, fuel, and motive power industries. In particular, he stressed mining and steel production. He also argued that, within the existing industrial base, the key problem was to make full use of capacity, to carry out technical reform and innovation, and to rationalise organisation with a clear-cut division of labour and better co-operation between trades, between regions and between enterprises.

Considering new investment, Deng argued for much stricter control of basic construction. All projects should be controlled by central or provincial-level authorities. Non-urgent construction should be stopped and only projects with a guaranteed supply of materials, labour and equipment should be undertaken. Furthermore, Deng criticised attempts to get round central investment guidelines. He criticised enterprises which used earmarked maintenance funds, liquid capital, depreciation funds, and profit and tax accounts for unauthorised investment in new machinery or other fixed capital. He suggested that the banking system might be used to enforce stricter investment discipline. His most radical major initiative in this area, however, was his call for the import of modern technology from abroad. 'Self-reliance', he argued, was not an excuse for self-conceit or for ignoring advanced technology because it was foreign. Payment for such imports should come from increased exports, particularly of coal and oil. Deng even envisaged the possibility of seeking credit. Purchases could be made against the future sales of raw materials and foreign suppliers could be paid either by delayed payment or by periodic payments. As is explored elsewhere in this book, this proposal was fraught with implications for China's relationship to the world economy and it provoked a sharp, critical response from Deng's opponents.

Finally, Deng argued that greater attention should be given to the use of economic incentives to increase productivity. The principle of payment according to work done should be supplemented by bonus systems and by greater concern for welfare, housing, safety arrangements and so forth. While echoing calls for ideological education and for selflessness, he believed that it was too egalitarian to ignore current material conditions if distribution of income took no account of variations in the amount and quality of work performed.

In sum, although Deng's proposals did not entirely negate the general framework of industrial policy, they did call for changes in the areas of 'self-reliance', enterprise management and economic incentives. These, in fact, negated some of the key reforms of the Cultural Revolution. They also implied that economic growth rather than class struggle should be the goal of Party policy. As a result they were roundly denounced by the 'Gang of Four'.[43] From late 1975 until the end of 1976, Deng's policies were typified as promoting the 'theory of productive forces'. Since Deng had explicitly acknowledged an emphasis on production, this accusation was easily justified. Nevertheless, in the context of the disruption of production brought about by the factional struggle of the period[44] and the losses caused by the Tangshan earthquake of July 1976, Deng's proposals must have appeared attractive to large numbers of those involved in the planning and execution of industrial policy, if not to many of the workers to whom he had promised wage increases, bonuses and improved welfare. Certainly, most observers noted that the campaign to criticise Deng during 1976 after his second dismissal was marked by a considerable lack of general enthusiasm.[45]

After the removal of the 'Gang of Four', Deng's policies were rapidly restored. At first, this was done in the context of Mao's speech 'On the Ten Major Relationships', officially published in December 1976 some twenty years after it was originally delivered. It was set against the background of a renewed emphasis on building up the economy and realising the four modernisations, the new tasks put forward by *Renmin Ribao's* New Year's Day editorial of January 1977.[46] The Anshan Charter, published in March 1977,[47] and the Daqing model were invoked to support reforms in enterprise management advocated by Deng. Detailed new management rules, adopted by Daqing in January 1977, defined the ways to strengthen leadership and discipline, and provided rules for responsibility at one's work post, shift management, inspection, repair and maintenance, quality control, economic accounting and so forth.[48] These trends came together at the National Conference on Learning from Daqing (20 April to 13 May 1977) where Yu Qiuli reiterated most of Deng's proposals.[49] Finally, a conference on foreign trade (14-28 July), held at about the same time that Deng was officially rehabilitated at the Third Plenum of the Tenth Central Committee, endorsed Deng's position on the need to import foreign technology and to export raw materials in payment.[50]

With Deng's position now vindicated and his policies restored both in name and in fact, a large number of conferences on economic questions were held throughout the year to discuss the campaign against the 'Gang of Four', to establish or re-establish policies and procedures and to examine the practical implications of Deng's proposals for each sector and trade.[51] Although much of the discussion was still couched in terms which suggested a need to defend the direction policy was taking against the kind of charges the 'Gang of Four' had previously raised, there was little doubt about the ultimate intentions. A major article by the State Planning Commission in September 1977 commemorating the first anniversary of Mao's death, for example, devoted a long introductory section to the need to 'grasp revolution and promote production', to 'take class struggle as the key link', to ensure true Marxist leadership, to guard against a capitalist restoration and to develop the relations of production.[52] Nevertheless, it also insisted that 'increasing or decreasing production is an important criterion in judging whether a revolution is successful or not' and proceeded to restate many of Deng's points. The article also referred to the need to increase accumulation of capital.

This theme had been the subject of a *Renmin Ribao* editorial in

August.[53] Enterprises were called upon to make more profits to contribute to socialist accumulation and to help raise living standards. Huge losses due to poor management were to be eliminated by greater economic democracy, stricter economic accounting, tightening up on the payment of profits and taxes to the state, and preventing upper levels from exacting funds and man-power from enterprises. An article on the same theme by the theory group of the Ministry of Finance stressed that socialist profit was the 'monetary expression of part of the surplus product created by the working class for society' and should not be confused with 'surplus value which the bourgeoisie exploited from the working class'.[54] The article established a direct link between current policy, Deng's call for economic accounting in 1975 and a national conference on economic accounting held in 1972 during the period of criticism of Lin Biao. It alleged that all the previous efforts had been quashed by the 'Gang of Four', resulting in losses, misappropriation of funds and corruption. While the profit target was not explicitly established as the key target for enterprises, fulfilment of that target was henceforth to be given considerable emphasis.

Given that the above calls and conferences were taking place during a period when considerable energy was also being devoted to the criticism and removal of the 'Gang's' supporters and to reforms and reorganisation in many areas of policy, implementation of the new industrial policies was still uneven and uncertain. Yu Qiuli admitted this in a speech to the Standing Committee of the Fourth National People's Congress in October 1977 when he stated that 'the readjustment of economic management and management of enter-prises has just begun and no marked improvement has yet been made'.[55] He did, however, announce that a wage reform affecting over half of all industrial employees had begun and that this was in line with the policy of improving the people's living standards, a point that was shortly afterwards further elaborated by renewed interest in bonus incentives. Nevertheless, Yu also stressed that many shortages and other problems remained. He laid down six tasks for the acceleration of economic growth over the period 1976 to 1985, covering some of the areas which would later be elaborated by Hua Guofeng in his speech to the Fifth National People's Congress in February 1978.

The first task was to continue criticism of the economic theory and practice of the 'Gang of Four'. The second was the need to continue efforts to build up Daqing and Dazhai-style enterprises according to criteria such as better management, better quality and cost control and better maintenance systems. Next came a call for improved planning, based on establishing a balance between central and local authority. Fourthly, Yu called for greater emphasis on agricultural growth, on the development of the power, fuel and raw material industries and on communications and transport. Fifthly, Yu argued that problems related to prices, employment, wages, incentives and technological modernisation had to be solved. Finally, Yu called for more effort in dealing with problems of welfare, housing, urban food supplies and public utilities.

As had been the case with economic policy throughout the year, Yu was still working within the framework of the balanced model for development put forward in Mao's 'On the Ten Major Relationships' and the practical adjustments to policy advocated by Deng Xiaoping. While some aspects, such as the growing attention being paid to profits and economic incentives, were reminiscent of the period before the Cultural Revolution, there was, as yet, no indication of any tendencies to modify the existing planning and distribution procedures. The eight major targets for enterprise performance and state control of the distribution of raw materials, intermediate products, capital goods and major commodities, remained unaltered.

Building on the calls for accelerated economic growth made during 1977, the Fifth National People's Congress adopted a draft Ten-Year Plan for economic development which embodied the aspirations of the four modernisations more clearly than any other document. Based on a revision of a plan originally put forward by the State Council in 1975, the draft set ambitious targets for agricultural and industrial growth rates over the period 1976 to 1985, including an annual rate of growth of the value of industrial output of ten per cent.[56] State investment, over the eight years, 1978-1985, was to equal the entire amount invested during the previous 28 years. Agriculture was to remain the foundation with emphasis given to its development. With regard to industry, the key stress remained upon steel and the familiar areas of power, fuel, raw materials, transport and communications. Technological modernisation was to be led by the completion of some 120 large-scale projects. Though Hua's report to the Congress repeated the long-standing commitment to the simultaneous development of large, medium and small-scale plants, he made it clear that the needs of the large enterprises should be guaranteed. Yet again, the importance of foreign trade was raised as was the need for more carefully co-ordinated planning, stricter economic accounting, and the linking of wages and bonuses to productivity. In addition, Hua also drew attention to a theme which was to gain increasing importance throughout 1978; that was the call for greater reliance on financial and monetary methods of managing the economy.

> The law of value must be consciously applied under the guidance of the unified state plan. . . . We must fully utilise finance, banking and credit in promoting and supervising economic undertakings so as to spur all enterprises to improve management, pay due attention to economic results and accumulate more capital for the state.[57]

While these points did not form a major part of Hua's introduction to the draft plan, they became the centre of intense interest in theoretical discussions of economic policy during 1978 and eventually contributed significantly to the reassessment of economic policy at the end of the year. Ultimately, it was concern with these issues which laid the basis for the complete restoration of the economic policies of the early 1960s which had been denounced during the Cultural Revolution. Such a concern also brought about a shift from material balance planning to the form of 'market socialism' which was endorsed by the Third Plenum of the Eleventh Central Committee in December 1978. Although the end result went beyond Deng's original proposals, it can be seen as the logical outcome of placing economic growth at the core of all policies.

Inevitably this process was not a smooth one. It took place within the context of a drive to articulate the draft plan put forward by Hua and, as Sullivan has discussed above, amid considerable disagreement over the political implications of the new direction which policy was taking. At the heart of the matter was the problem of evaluating Mao's role. So long as economic policy was still loosely cast in the framework of 'On the Ten Major Relationships', the innovations of the Cultural Revolution could be undone without explicitly negating Mao's role. The restoration of the early 1960s' framework, however, entailed criticising Mao's economic policies as far back as the Great Leap Forward. In retrospect, one of the most significant moves in this direction was the publication in *Guangming Ribao*, on 11 May 1978, of an article entitled 'Practice is the Sole Criterion for Verifying Truth.' This article denounced the 'Gang of

Four' for relying on dogma rather than testing theory against practice. Though it was not explicitly stated, the succession of articles and speeches on the theme which followed all implied that Mao's Thought was not absolute and could be modified by practice. If the argument were accepted, the way would be clear to dispense with many of the economic ideas most closely associated with the late Chairman.

Although, as Sullivan describes, this fundamental issue remained the centre of political dispute throughout 1978, *three key developments* in economic policy took place in July. The *first* was the publication of the Central Committee draft 'Decision on Several Questions Concerning the Acceleration of Industrial Development', known as the 'thirty points'.[58] In essence, these points reiterated and expanded on Deng's 1975 document, with amendments and additions to reflect the changed economic situation and the goals of the Fifth National People's Congress. The various systems for responsibility at one's work post and rules and regulations for enterprise management were spelt out in more detail, with considerable emphasis laid on the professional independence of the factory general manager and engineers under the unified leadership of the factory Party committee. Success in fulfilling the state plan was made the major criterion with which to judge enterprises and political work had to 'reflect the requirements of economics'.[59] Against that background, enterprises were now required to implement the 'five fixes': (1) fixed nature and scale of production; (2) fixed personnel and organisation; (3) fixed consumption and supply quotas for raw materials, semi-finished products, fuel, power and tools; (4) fixed liquid capital and fixed assets; and (5) fixed relations of co-operation with other enterprises. Once these were determined on a stable basis, each enterprise was expected to meet the eight standard targets. If it did so, it could retain a proportion of its profits in an enterprise fund to be used for bonuses, collective welfare and new investment. In addition, the 'thirty points' called for a reorganisation of industry along lines of specialisation and co-operation between enterprises, paving the way for the reintroduction of trusts and other forms of interlinked industrial systems (see below).

The relationship between central and local authorities was also spelt out more clearly. The economic aspects of key enterprises were placed under central control, with such things as political work and services handled by the locality. Where possible, such enterprises could also use surplus capacity to meet local demands. All remaining enterprises would be controlled at local levels in accordance with the demands of the plan, with considerable care given to guaranteeing material balances. Co-ordination had to be ensured by much more careful planning and by the establishment of a command system of economic committees at all levels. Furthermore, special attention had to be given to product quality and type with consumers having the right to refuse to accept substandard goods. Although in some respects these proposals transferred important economic powers to individual production units, they did not imply any fundamental changes to the long-standing policy of decentralisation to geographic units of administration.

In addition, the 'thirty points' covered the familiar ground of the need for industry to support agriculture, the need to develop the fuel, raw material and power industries and the importance of transport and communications. They stressed, once again, the requirement to relate productivity to material income, to produce stricter economic accounting and to foster greater accumulation. When promulgated, the document was seen as an experimental outline to be modified by the end of the year. Although many of the organisational points it made were subsequently implemented in Chinese enterprises, in many other respects its proposals have been superseded by the two other initiatives which were launched in July and a revised version had not yet surfaced by the time of the Second Session of the Fifth National People's Congress in June 1979. In retrospect, it would appear that the 'thirty points' were drawn up within the conceptual framework provided by Deng's 1975 speeches and, to some extent, Mao's 'On the Ten Major Relationships'. When this framework was replaced by the 'market socialism' approach of the early 1960s, many, though not all, of its proposals needed modification.

The *second important development* of July 1978 was a National Finance and Trade Conference on Learning from Daqing and Dazhai (20 June-9 July). Speeches were given by Hua Guofeng, Li Xiannian and Yu Qiuli.[60] By its very nature, this conference dealt with those financial and monetary issues which Hua had only touched briefly upon at the Fifth National People's Congress. In doing so, it spelt out their implications much more explicitly. The central theme was the need to work according to 'objective economic laws'. Such things as finance and trade, commodity circulation, distribution of capital, foreign trade, prices, taxes and credit policy should be actively used to stimulate development. Quoting Mao in support, Hua underlined the importance he attached to the functioning of the law of value which was interpreted to mean that the value of commodities was determined according to the socially necessary labour time required to produce them.

> In a planned socialist economy, the correct use of the law of value is of great importance for promoting socialist production. In this respect, our financial and trade work can play a major role through buying and selling commodities, through the allocation of funds, and through such economic levers as pricing, taxing and providing loans. If we do not turn the law of value to good account, or if we violate it, our economic work will not be able to proceed correctly or effectively or achieve full results with minimum expenditure, and we will be punished by this objective law in terms of the inevitable serious waste and losses and disruption of socialist production.[61]

Apart from the fact that reliance on these economic levers to plan the economy means reliance on market forces and reliance on profit as a measure of performance, a further important aspect of this line of reasoning is the implication that material balance planning and administratively determined prices may lead to waste and losses. A report on the problems of price-fixing released during the conference stressed this very problem.[62] Thus, the point at issue was not only a rejection of the 'Gang of Four's' economic philosophy but also the nature of the planning system itself.

Li Xiannian, in his speech to the conference, located the root of this failure to appreciate the law of value in the habits and methods of small producers as typified in the rural economy before collectivisation. As a result of these habits all economic units attempted to be self-sufficient and many of the people who managed the economy did not know how to 'make full and correct use of the law of socialist commodity production and the law of value'. Li urged those working in financial and trade areas to develop their professional knowledge, learn from abroad so that their enterprises 'get maximum results at minimum costs and meet the needs of consumers while ensuring a reasonable profit'.[63]

Both Hua and Li referred to waste, embezzlement and malpractices, such as 'going through the back door', as serious problems which resulted from the 'Gang of Four's' neglect of the correct economic levers. Subsequent elaborations of these problems listed a number of examples. Enterprise supply agents were criticised for using 'research expenses (such as cigarettes and wine)' to bribe suppliers of needed materials.[64] Cases were cited of enterprises building excessive stockpiles of raw materials or of capital equipment to be cannibalised or used for unofficial inter-enterprise deals in times of need.[65] Many enterprises also indulged in unnecessary investment in little used resources so as to avoid putting themselves at the mercy of unpredictable outside suppliers.[66] Many of these problems are, of course, familiar in the Soviet Union where the malpractices they represent are collectively known as *blat*.[67] Clearly they were not so much caused by the 'Gang of Four' as by the functioning of the planning system itself. In sum, the conference was pointing towards the resurrection of the 'Libermanist' or 'market socialism' methods of the early 1960s.

The *third important event* of July 1978 was the speech by Hu Qiaomu, at a meeting of the State Council, entitled 'Observe Economic Laws, Speed up the Four Modernisations'. This speech was not published until October, the long delay reflecting perhaps the controversial nature of the content.[68] Hu argued that economic laws were like objective natural laws which apply independently of human will. Social changes might change the form in which the laws operate but they did not change the laws themselves. The superiority of the socialist system, therefore, could only be realised if arbitrary administrative methods of economic management were abandoned in favour of observance of these objective laws. In order to understand the laws properly, it was necessary to learn from 'the modernised, highly efficient planning and other managerial functions carried out in today's big (capitalist) corporations'. This was particularly the case with respect to economic results, productivity, quality control, and economic accounting. Unified planning had to be based on the law of value so that

... all enterprises make strict economical use of time, constantly strive for the best possible ratio between the expenditure of labour and material (materialised labour) and economic results, practise strict business accounting, strive to lower the unit-cost of production, and raise labour productivity and the rate of profit on the funds invested.[69]

Price policy had to play a greater role in the planning process and prices had to be set so as to allow enterprises to achieve a reasonable profit. Moreover, in order to improve the use of capital, profit had to be calculated in relation to fixed assets (defined as materialised labour) rather than in relation to costs. As an added incentive, the material interests of workers and staff had to be linked directly to the success of their enterprise as expressed in this new profit target. Significantly, Hu pointed out that this vital target was not included in the recently published 'thirty points'.

The issue was more than one of minor adjustment. As subsequent discussions illustrated, it was one of basic approach. Administrative methods of running the economy were attributed first to the pre-1949 experience of running the self-sufficient economy in Yan'an which had generated the mentality of the small producer. They were said to be due also to the experience of the Soviet model in the 1950s. Copying this model was necessary in the situation at the time but Mao, as early as 1954, had criticised it as 'metaphysical and troublesome'. Nevertheless, 'for a variety of reasons, no great improvements have been made and, right up to the present, we have basically still worked according to these methods'.[70] The implication was that the 'thirty points', in part at least, also fell within the category of administrative methods of managing the economy.

Hu's argument was that, if the economic laws governing such things as profit, prices and incentives were employed, economic administration could be considerably simplified. Errors in the system, which he saw as originating in a decision-making process not based on economic criteria, could thereby be eliminated. Hu proposed a number of organisational changes to overcome these problems. He called for the use of legally enforceable contracts between producers and consumers as a means of implementing the plan. The state should only be concerned with overall targets. He proposed the development of specialised companies (such as trusts) or integrated groups of specialised producers. He advocated a greater role for the banking system in supervising investment through the administration of interest-bearing loans. Finally he called for a stronger system of economic legislation.

The points, raised by Hu, have since dominated all theoretical discussion of economic problems. Most issues of the journal *Jingji Yanjiu* (*Economic Research*), published since July 1978, have devoted several articles to these points as have the economic and business management pages of the *Guangming Ribao*. In many respects, the discussion has retraced much of the ground covered by the arguments over the law of value and the role of profit voiced in the early 1960s.[71] Indeed, many of the protagonists have been the same people who were involved at that time. Nevertheless, as indicated above, it was not until the question of the evaluation of Mao's role was decided, at the Third Plenum in December 1978, that these theoretical discussions could have an impact on policy and the full restoration of the early 1960s' policies could take place. Thus, by March 1979, *Renmin Ribao* could state that the only two good periods of economic development in China were the First Five-Year Plan and the period 1962 to 1965.[72] The reversal of the pre-October 1976 official position was now complete.

After the Third Plenum, the goals of the draft economic plan put forward at the Fifth National People's Congress were revised and scaled down. At the same time, the process of adjusting agricultural and industrial policy to correspond to the use of the new economic levers was begun. In January, the press called for a liberation of economic policy.[73] In early February, Deng's famous saying that it did not matter whether a cat is black or white so long as it caught mice (i.e. that it is economic results that count) was revived.[74] Subsequently, the virtues of a mixed economy, where the plan and market competition are used to complement each other, were extolled. It was said that a mixed economy helped to overcome bureaucratism, co-ordinate the interests of the state, the collective and the individual and ease the problems of attempting to plan everything for the nation's 380,000 industrial enterprises as well as other economic units.[75] It was, however, noted that the use of the market mechanism could intensify competition between administrative levels. This could lead to the collapse of the economically weak and the growth of disparities in income, but this was seen as a reason for care rather than for not proceeding.[76]

In February, a banking conference was held to discuss how best to use the banking system to regulate the economy through the use of credit and interest rates to direct investment.[77] At the same time, greater independence in the operation of enterprises was encouraged. Thus, enterprises could have some freedom in negotiating contracts with other units. They might be given rewards for contract fulfilment and be allowed to market their extra-contractual production themselves at government controlled prices.[78] Those enterprises currently not making a profit had to find ways to do so as soon as possible or face the prospect of closure.[79] Ultimately, the ambitious targets of the draft Ten-Year Plan were adjusted not only because of such things as foreign exchange problems and the excessive weight given to heavy industry but also because of lack of profitability of many projects. They were also adjusted because of waste created by investment in underused capacity while shortages occurred in other areas, and because they were based on the use of state-allocated unpaid-for capital investment rather than interest-bearing loans and negotiated contracts.[80]

Thus, the 1979 economic plan, announced at the Second Session of the Fifth National People's Congress in June 1979, laid greater stress on agriculture and light industry and on profitability as a guide to investment.[81] Particular emphasis was laid on resolving shortages in energy supplies and on the production of goods for export. This underlined the fact that the reassessment of economic policy derived essentially from the concern with profitability and the expanded role of the market, rather than from any reconsideration of the role of foreign trade and the import of modern technology.

The above chronological account of the evolution of economic policy in recent years has demonstrated three main things. First, the roots of economic policy in the immediate post-Mao period had been clearly enunciated by Deng Xiaoping in 1975 and can be traced back to the efforts of the opponents of the 'Gang of Four' over the entire period since 1969. Until early 1978, economic policy was essentially an elaboration and development of those 1975 policies. Secondly, the evolution of economic policy since 1976 has passed through three stages: (1) October 1976 to January 1978, which was dominated by the idea of the four modernisations within the framework of the 'Ten Major Relationships' and the policies advocated by Deng; (2) January 1978 to December 1978, when the case was mounted for the use of economic levers rather than administrative planning, and when Mao's approach to economic questions was re-evaluated; and (3) December 1978 onwards, when the process of building a form of 'market socialism' was begun. Finally, this account has shown that the current leadership in China is now so centrally concerned with growth in output and productivity that all other aspects of organisation and policy are subordinated to it. The result has been a reversal of most, if not all, of the economic policies associated with Mao Zedong.

Perhaps the impression has been given here that this process of development was a relatively smooth one with the turning point coming somewhere in the first half of 1978. But, as the other contributors to this volume have made clear, it was, in fact, a process involving considerable political dispute, and disagreements over industrial policies related to debates in most other social areas. Inevitably, the evolution of economic policy was a central feature of all those other disputes. It must also be emphasised that the whole period has, to an extent, been one of exploration and experiment. While various economic models have been put forward (as discussed below), there is still a considerable amount of variation in actual practice.

In what follows, I shall examine the impact of the changes outlined above on the key areas of planning and economic administration, centralisation and decentralisation, the role of banks, the forms of industrial specialisation and co-operation and enterprise management.

Planning and Economic Administration

During late 1978 and early 1979, a spate of articles appeared in economic journals discussing the nature of economic planning in China and ways in which it should be reformed.[82] In reviewing past experience, these articles agreed that during the 1950s China lacked economic skills and resources and had to undertake highly centralised planning through a state command system. This played a role in concentrating capital, manpower and materials, ensured the completion of key investment projects and, at the same time, provided support for backward areas. Chinese planners, however, were unable to distinguish between the basic principles of a socialist economy and the particular methods of Soviet practice. The articles suggested that many Chinese had confused a command economy and a planned economy. As a result, command planning was seen as the only alternative to bourgeois competition and any attempt to change this was denounced as 'revisionist' or leading to capitalist restoration.

Nevertheless, long years of experience had shown that many problems were created by a command economy. Consumption was determined by production. Production and consumption were not directly linked. There was no incentive to seek good economic results. Production units were only concerned with value and volume of output. There was a large number of projects which required long periods of gestation and little effort was made to seek quick returns or produce new commodities. Drawing up the plan became a process of haggling and involved struggles for investment and materials. What is more, since everything culminated at the end of the year, there was a lot of expensive 'storming' to meet requirements.

It was argued that piecemeal solutions could not solve these problems. For example, if the new enterprise contract system was based on plan requirements, then one was still essentially operating within a command economy. If the eight economic and technical targets were maintained, there would still be no enterprise independence and consumer demands would still have no effect on production. Thus, it was necessary to realise that the command economy and the planned economy were not the same. Plans were necessary but they could not be comprehensive. The Chinese economy was too complex to allow them to be. The alternative was to replace the stultifying system of production and construction targets with a system whereby the state set the major goals of the plan period and the key proportional relationships, and then proceeded to direct economic policy by economic means. In this way, the state would determine the general speed of development, the level to be reached and the relationships between economic sectors over the long term. It would also determine such things as the proportion of the national income devoted to accumulation and the proportion devoted to consumption. With regard to the relationship between enterprises and localities, however, plans should be flexible, providing guidance but not having binding force. In practice, enterprises should be free to plan production according to their sales contracts, orders, and market conditions, without needing approval from higher levels of administration. This would produce a system of indirect planning similar to that currently used to direct agricultural production in the communes.

The state should use a variety of economic levers to direct the plan. Prices and relative prices would become important and, while producers would be free to establish prices according to contract, the state should be able to intervene and establish an upper limit. Tax policy should be used to prevent enterprises from making windfall profits due to externalities. Credit should be used to direct enterprise investment and interest levels should control the use of capital. Enterprise profit should, to a significant extent, remain within enterprises. Unlike the present situation, however, that profit should come directly from the market and reflect consumer preferences rather than take the form of a payment from marketing organisations. Indeed, some theorists argued that 'consumer power' should become an important stimulus to producers.[83] Other levers which the state could use include levying duties, the control of foreign trade, adjusting the currency, depreciation rates, altering wages and incentives, and granting financial subsidies. Administrative measures, such as licensing, prohibitions and personnel appointments, should only be used when absolutely necessary.

Needless to say, proposals on this scale, if adopted, would entail the wholesale abandonment of all planning practices used since 1949. The advocates of such proposals were, at least, cautious enough to suggest a gradual process of trial, with experiments first being carried out in less vital areas.[84] By June 1979, many of these proposals had not yet been taken up, but, as the above discussion of policy since late 1978 has shown, they were actively under consideration. What is important to note is that the discussion no longer centred on overthrowing the policies of the 'Gang of Four'. The 'Gang' was seen as an obstacle which had prevented a serious analysis of the issues involved but the aim was to reappraise economic policy over the entire period since 1949.

Centralisation and Decentralisation

Until 1978, the division of authority in the Chinese industrial system was still that prescribed in the late 1950s. As outlined by Deng above, it involved central control over key commodities, targets and the planning process, with ownership and operation decentralised to regional units of administration (Schurmann's Decentralisation II).[85] In calling for a greater degree of centralised co-ordination and more careful planning, Deng had reaffirmed this principle. He had insisted that control of the bulk of industrial enterprises should be transferred downwards to provincial or municipal level 'but no further'.[86] This call was repeated in the 'thirty points' of July 1978.[87] By late 1978, amid calls for enterprise independence and the re-establishment of specialised companies or trusts, the emphasis had shifted to decentralisation of operation to the units of production (Schurmann's Decentralisation I).

In the discussion, most authors typified centralisation as 'administration by lines' (*tiaotiao guan*) and decentralisation to regional units as 'administration by lumps' (*kuaikuai guan*).[88] Both were seen to be administrative rather than economic ways of managing the economy and both were felt to hinder the formation of economic links between enterprises and between regions. In past experience, 'administration by lines' involved completely separate planning within ministries, each with independent lines of control and operation. Co-ordination, at the regional level, was impossible and competition between ministries was strong. As a result, many things, such as the comprehensive utilisation of resources, could not be achieved. 'Administration by lumps', on the other hand, broke the links between regions and established boundaries for economic operations which could not be crossed. Each time there was a tendency towards centralisation, the ministries 'stretched out their hands' to control their subordinate enterprises, and the localities could do nothing. When this policy was changed into one of decentralisation, the localities went their own way and the ministries did nothing; the result was chaos and lack of co-ordination. It was argued that Chinese industry had passed through several cycles of centralised stultification and decentralised anarchy. Both involved large bureaucracies, hierarchical chains of command, mounds of paperwork, and a plethora of meetings. Not unexpectedly, the authors of this analysis advocated complete decentralisation of operation and control to the enterprise level, with the state maintaining simply the role of guidance and overall planning through economic methods. Discussions in the media during 1979 of the methods of inter-enterprise contracting and of the operation of specialised companies indicated that the process of implementing this form of decentralisation had begun.[89] Once again, this was an area of policy where the thrust of Deng Xiaoping's attack on the 'Gang of Four' was superseded by the goal of introducing 'market socialism'.

The Role of the Banking System

Consideration of the role of the banking system intensified after Hu Qiaomu's speech on economic laws. In August 1978, an article in *Guangming Ribao* suggested that banks should supervise the use of capital within enterprises and help them with economic accounting. They should also act as an economic 'thermometer', which could give the leadership some indication of economic trends.[90] By early 1979, these basic ideas had been elaborated considerably.

Many of the points raised at the banking conference in March 1979 had been the subject of articles published in the previous months.[91] Looking back at the development of banking, it was noted that Lenin had seen capitalist banks as the nervous system of capitalism and as laying the foundations for socialist banks. He had wanted them to play a central role in social regulation, measuring and supervising production and distribution, and in economic accounting. In the 1930s, Stalin had made the banks the controllers of the money supply and credit, and instruments with which to settle accounts. But, investment capital for fixed assets was supplied by the state and liquid capital was supplied in part in this way and in part by temporary interest-bearing loans from the banks. After 1949, the Chinese banking system had played an important role in stabilising the currency and transforming the economy but, essentially, it had been modelled on the Stalin pattern. This system fully accorded with the administrative way of operating the economy and suggestions that it should be reformed had been firmly resisted by the 'Gang of Four'. The 'Gang' saw relationships based on currency exchanges as the 'soil from which capitalism grew' and denounced savings, interest and bank involvement in economic accounting as 'bourgeois' and 'a form of oppression'.[92]

If banks were to play a positive role in the four modernisations, these old methods had to change. Six proposals were put forward.[93] First, all liquid capital had to be provided through banks in the form of credit. This system currently operated in commercial units and should be extended to all production units. Such a system would do much more than simply force enterprises to be more responsible in their use of cash. It would prevent enterprises with a large state allocation of liquid capital from ignoring the banking system and those with too little from continuously attempting to balance one source of income off against another.

Second, this system should be extended to all capital used for fixed investment. Currently, enterprises received these funds from state allocation. Thus, they competed actively to obtain investment funds but, once they were obtained, they were not obliged to show that funds were being used to the best advantage. They did not have to meet any target which reflected the productivity of the fixed assets employed. If this capital were issued in the form of bank loans, the banks could influence the efficiency of the investment. By charging interest, they could force enterprises to be economical in their use of capital and make them carry out strict economic accounting. Since cash credit was a form of distribution of materials, the key task for the banks was to plan credit in such a way that cash supply corresponded with the supply of materials and the currency remained stable. If this reform were carried out, it would imply decentralising practical control of capital investment from the central financial authorities to the banks at local levels. These local banks, in turn, would be required to administer loans according to the general guidelines set by the centre. Enterprises would repay their interest from the proportion of profits which they would be allowed to retain.

Third, interest rates should be adjusted, as required, in order to influence the circulation of capital and affect the level of savings. Since the 1950s, interest rates in China had generally declined which was, by and large, a good thing. They could, however, be adjusted as needed. Currently, they were too low and didn't encourage savings or strict accounting. Fourth, the banks should play an important role in the drawing up and settling of contracts between enterprises. They could supervise all parties and ensure that the best results were realised. Fifth, banks should help supervise foreign trade and act as a channel for attracting foreign investment. Finally, the banks should be placed in a position to maintain general supervision of the economy as a whole. After all, they have knowledge of the movement of cash and capital and the reasons for it, of potential problem areas, and of any emerging irregularities. This and much other information could be supplied to the leadership as required.

An interesting sidelight on the problems was provided by a disagreement between some economists on whether depreciation funds could be used for basic investment.[94] It was noted that, before 1967, all depreciation funds were handed to the state and issued to enterprises, as requested, under four categories. After 1967, the funds were decentralised to enterprises or to localities, with the result that a large amount of capital remained outside the planning system and its use could conflict with planning and material allocation. This capital was also a potential source of corruption. In 1975, a reform had been put forward so that 30 per cent should go to centre, 30 per cent to the locality, and 40 per cent to the enterprise. This had been implemented after the fall of the 'Gang of Four' and was working more satisfactorily than other systems.[95] It was a good example of the way in which economic problems were seen as the creation of the planning system itself. The 'Gang of Four' was again essentially seen as an obstacle to a change which placed maximising return on investment at the heart of policy.

Despite disagreements, the consensus was that the banking system should move in the direction outlined above through the establishment of a number of specialised banks under the general control of the People's Bank of China. Such a move follows, of course, from the shift from administrative regulation to economic control through financial means.

Specialisation and Co-operation

The reorganisation of industrial enterprises into specialised integrated companies or into clusters of closely linked undertakings has received a great deal of attention throughout the period since October 1976.[96] This has long been a major organisational issue in China[97] and, as we have seen, is one on which Deng Xiaoping placed considerable emphasis.

Specialisation is now defined as a necessary adjunct of technological development. Its advantages include improvements in productivity and less capital investment as enterprises cease to strive to be 'large and comprehensive' and do not waste resources on underused capacity. It leads, moreover, to lower costs and greater efficiency because of the large volume production of articles which can be used by a variety of consumers. There is, consequently, a reduction in the amount of capital tied up in stocks and improved management through its concentration on a small number of products. Specialist enterprises may produce either as independent units, supplying a large number of consumers with standard products (e.g. electrical parts), or as subunits within a trust.

Co-operation may work either on the basis of contractual relations between enterprises, or by enterprises combining to form a large joint company which acts as a single accounting unit. A large variety of combinations are possible according to product or technology. Companies may be organised on a provincial or urban basis or on an inter-provincial basis. They may develop vertically to include everything from raw materials to the finished product, or horizontally to produce a range of technologically related products. Many authors have stressed that these companies should be free from outside interference if they are to succeed. Ultimately this stress has led to the complete rehabilitation of the trust system denounced during the Cultural Revolution.[98]

Joint companies are seen to have a number of advantages. They generate increased production, lower costs and higher profits. They reduce the need for enterprises to participate in planning conferences since material supplies between subordinate factories become a matter of internal movement rather than part of state planned distribution. They also lead to the disappearance of considerable paperwork and of the now notorious 'supply agents'. A further saving is that intra-company costs are reduced. Materials, parts or subassemblies, which would have borne a production tax and a profit levy had they been transferred between independent enterprises, may be considered as internal transfers and hence bear neither. It is, nevertheless, still necessary to ensure that accounting procedures recognise the productivity of subfactories so that their employees may receive suitable rewards to stimulate their enthusiasm. Furthermore, the formation of companies has to have a strong economic rationale. If not, there is a danger of simply inserting another administrative level between enterprises and governmental agencies. Many of these points have been illustrated by examples of earlier joint companies of the period 1962 to 1966.[99]

Two models of specialisation and co-operation have been put forward. These are the Shanghai Electrical Machinery Company, as an example of an integrated company,[100] and the Changzhou 'dragon' system, as an example of urban integration and co-operation.[101] Both were cited as models in the 'thirty points'.[102] Particularly interesting is the claim that both experiments evolved continuously throughout the 1960s, despite the alleged opposition of the 'Gang of Four'. If this was so, it is an example of how grass roots implementation can vary, to some extent, from the dominant official policy.

The Shanghai Electrical Machinery Company was organised from a number of independent enterprises in 1964. It consists of some 42 factories producing a variety of interrelated products including electrical machinery, wiring and cables, and materials and equipment for electrical engineering. The entire company employs some 32,000 people. Its total output value, in 1977, was 1.37 times greater than in 1965, and the profit made had increased by 85 per cent. The first stage of development, from 1964 to 1973, had concentrated on the standardisation of products and the division of labour between subordinate plants. The second stage, after 1973, had centred on technological development and specialisation. Details have been given of how this system has raised productivity (for some products, to three or four times the national average), improved quality, reduced costs, uncovered latent resources, improved technology and increased the number of products.

The Changzhou 'dragon' has been popularised as an example of high-speed industrial development in a small-to-medium sized city. The term, 'dragon', is intended to imply a cluster of enterprises, some subordinate to others and some independent but all contractually linked; these work together to produce a range of related end products. Changzhou initially developed some industry during the

Great Leap Forward but most of the factories were small and not interrelated. Their technological sophistication and levels of productivity varied considerably. As a result, it was very difficult to expand production. In 1959, the city's industrial bureau decided to initiate a process of specialisation and co-operation. This involved choosing a few major products, based on some key enterprises, and then carrying out co-ordinated production by building links between a large number of factories with different degrees of subordination and different levels of ownership.

Changzhou's first 'dragon' system was based on cotton cloth production. In 1963, it developed one based on hand tractors. By 1978, some sixteen 'dragons' were in operation producing such things as transistor radios, plastics, glass, bicycles, cameras, electric motors and industrial sewing machines. Each system was distinguished according to the product, the production process, or the raw materials used. As a result, the city's gross value of industrial output had increased at an annual rate of 13 per cent over the period 1965 to 1977.

The operation of this model required strong leadership from the municipal industrial bureau. The independence of factories, particularly those which were not part of the state-owned system, had to be respected but they had to be encouraged to see the value of close co-operation. Problems of technological disparities, product specification, quality control and inter-factory prices had to be solved. For example, if prices for a particular part were set too high, there would be no stimulus for a consumer factory to use that part instead of producing it itself. On the other hand, if prices were too low, the subordinate factory would not get a sufficient return. The solution, found in Changzhou, was to fix prices within the 'dragon' according to the needs of the system and not at the levels prescribed by the state. The supply of raw materials was handled through a number of municipal agencies and allocated according to the needs of each 'dragon' rather than balancing the independent demands of each enterprise. This not only assured production but meant that stocks could be reduced. Similarly, capital investment could be directed according to the overall needs of the production process. Thus, there was both the incentive and the means to raise the technological level of the small, collective handicraft factories which were incorporated into the system.

The attractions of this model are in many ways self-evident and include many of those listed for joint companies above. In addition, it is stressed that managerial skills have developed quickly together with the sense of working together for the sake of the collective. Perhaps most important of all is the impact on the small handicraft-style factories. These are owned at residential and district level or within communes and brigades. Since they have been established in clusters around key factories and production processes, it is argued that their economic security is assured and conditions are right for the rapid improvement of their technological level. This may be brought about either through help from related factories or by investment from the city authorities.

In 1977, there were 243 such factories (61 per cent of all factories).[103] Of these, 65 were owned at residential, commune or brigade level and were known as 'small collectives' and 178 were owned at municipal, ward or bureau level and were known as 'large collectives'. The latter were a particularly important group. They had originated in four ways. Some had been 'small collectives', set up in the 1950s and subsequently purchased by the municipal authorities. Some had been hived off from the state-owned structure during the period of readjustment from 1961 to 1963, but, since there had been no payment to the state for capital equipment, they still essentially belonged to the state. Some had been formed when workshops split away from established factories to form independent accounting units according to the needs of specialisation; (14 of these had been set up since 1976). Finally, some had been established by direct investment by the municipality or ward. Their rate of growth had exceeded the city average. This was because they were able to employ local labour and capital very flexibly without any reference to central authorities and could, therefore, easily respond to the needs of the 'dragon' system.

Unlike the 'small collective' which is owned by its employees, controls its own profit and depends on output for its income, the 'large collective' is still owned by the state (in the form of the municipality or ward). Its profit is handed in to the authorities and its employees are paid according to the eight-grade wage system, regardless of enterprise income. Most important, however, is that, unlike local state-owned enterprises, the 'large collectives' do not depend upon the central authorities for planning and development, finance and labour administration. Although owned at the municipal level, they operate outside the central plan and have considerable freedom to respond to the local economic situation. Among the many interesting implications of this situation is that the urban authorities are not just the local representatives of the central government but operate as independent entrepreneurs in the manner of rural communes and brigades. Furthermore, the success of the 'dragon' system has depended very heavily on the flexibility of these 'large collectives' in supplementing the state-owned sector proper and on the ability to operate outside planning norms and procedures. Thus, the key plan is that drawn up by the city industrial bureau. In some ways, this model is, therefore, an urban equivalent of the rural industrialisation programme. It also appears to combine the means to encourage local initiative and to raise technical levels in the established way of 'walking on two legs'.

Although the process will take considerable time and will be modified by practice, Chinese industry is now being encouraged to reorganise along the lines of these two models. This will require considerable economic independence for companies to develop along lines dictated by economic and technological rationale. It will also necessitate the decentralisation of economic power to units of production. Such a reorganisation can only take place in the context of the changes in the planning structure and economic management outlined in the previous two sections.

Enterprise Management

As I have shown elsewhere, the entire period since 1969 has seen a gradual erosion of the management reforms introduced by the Cultural Revolution.[104] Gone is the emphasis on worker participation in management, on mass mobilisation and political education, and on simplification of management procedures. In its place is the argument that managerial forms should be shaped by the needs of developing the productive forces and the demands of technological processes.

As described above, it is now argued that individual enterprises should be given considerable economic independence.[105] The state should establish the general limits within which enterprises operate. It should also require these enterprises to meet their various targets or contracts, although some economists are even saying that the target system should be abandoned and enterprises should be allowed to make contracts according to their individual economic situation.[106] Enterprises must also hand over designated profits and taxes. All other matters such as production, supplies, sales, labour and finances should remain within their own control. They should be free to retain a proportion of profits for their own use, either for bonuses or investment, and they should be free to borrow funds and develop production on their own initiative. State planning should be realised largely through legally enforceable contracts between the state and the enterprise and between enterprises.[107] Surplus capacity should be used at the factories' own discretion to achieve the best economic results.

The concern with economic levers to manage the economy described above has meant that the profit target is now defined as the key measure of enterprise performance, efficiency and survival.[108] Furthermore, profit should be calculated in terms of return per unit of fixed capital rather than in any other way. Profit itself is defined as 'the surplus product of the workers to be used for socialist accumulation in order to develop expanded reproduction'. Capital is seen as 'materialised labour' and considerable effort has been devoted to arguing that this does not mean that capital creates value but that 'materialised labour' provides the conditions for the best employment of 'living labour'.[109] Thus, using this profit target will ensure the most economical use of capital and labour, and the strictest economic accounting. An important concomitant of this is that prices should be set on the basis of production prices, that is they should be set according to average production costs plus a rate of profit determined by the average rate of profit per unit of fixed assets for the industry multiplied by the amount of fixed assets employed.

Whether or not the full extent of these proposals for enterprise independence and the use of the profit target will be realised is not yet clear. It has been reported that at the beginning of 1978 the central authorities called for a complete examination of all fixed assets.[110] This suggests that serious consideration was being given to changing the method of distribution of fixed capital and its employment. Other economists, however, have argued for a full reintroduction of both the 'five fixes' of the 'thirty points' (fixed products, employment, material supplies, capital and co-operation relations) and the 'five guarantees' (guaranteed product specifications, fulfilment of the wages bill, meeting of the costs plan, handing over of profit and use of capital equipment), which were first put forward together in the 'seventy points' of 1961, as the basis for state-enterprise relations.[111] Any enterprise which meets its 'five guarantees' in return for the 'five fixes' supplied by the state would be allowed to keep some of its profits. Although still cast within the 'market socialism' framework, this latter proposal would put more limitations on enterprise operation than the wider freedoms outlined above.

Management practices themselves have returned to the system of 'divided responsibility between the enterprise Party secretary and the factory general manager'.[112] The Party secretary is responsible for major decisions, general strategy, and political and ideological work. The factory general manager has authority over production and the use of enterprise assets. He takes the day-to-day decisions and is responsible for technical operations, discipline, welfare and so forth. In addition, he represents the enterprise to outside bodies, to upper levels and to the employees' committees. Various rules and regulations define the relationships between employees and set out their work responsibilities. Although this has led to a proposal for the rehabilitation of the much-reviled concept of 'one-man management' in order to underline the importance now placed on establishing a clear system of command and defining responsibilities,[113] it has not meant a complete disappearance of the idea of worker participation in management. The trade unions have been strengthened in their role as representatives of the workers' interests. Factory general managers are expected to report to and listen to the opinions of workers' congresses. What is more, a new system of election by secret ballot is being used for the appointment of heads of workshops, shifts and work groups.[114] Unlike the innovations of the Cultural Revolution, however, these forms of participation are based on a representative rather than a participatory principle. They depend also on a system of material rewards and punishments for fulfilment of work tasks alongside appeals to political ideals and moral incentives.

The need to link productivity with material return, as an incentive to increase production, has now become a guiding principle not only of enterprise performance as a whole but also of individual income.[115] As has been noted, at the enterprise level this is reflected in such methods as allowing factories to keep a proportion of profits and permitting efficient producers to use surplus capacity for their own benefit. For the work-force, the principle of 'payment according to work done' is firmly established and has been interpreted not only as payment according to time at work but also as various forms of piece-work wages. Enterprises have also been encouraged to experiment with a wide range of bonus systems in order to find the one which best suits their methods of production. Some of the discussion has revealed that the pre-1966 bonus payments did not entirely disappear during the Cultural Revolution but were renamed 'supplementary wages'. These were paid to all workers, as a standard part of the wages bill, though technically they were not included in the rates defined by the eight-grade wage system.[116] Thus, workers employed before the Cultural Revolution have continued to receive an extra payment above standard wages even though this is made regardless of actual work performance. Discussion of implementing the new bonus systems has insisted that these supplementary wages should not be taken away and replaced by the new bonuses since such a move could entail a drop in living standards for many veteran workers.

A further problem, encountered in the new system, has been a tendency to give excessive incentives or award them equally to everyone regardless of work done.[117] The ideal is to design rewards which provide sufficient incentives for workers but which do not create too great a disparity between levels of income. Furthermore, it is argued that bonuses should be directly linked to enterprise profits.[118] During the First Five-Year Plan, bonuses were based on a profit target which was not defined in terms of fixed assets. It was set at a minimum of four per cent and a maximum of ten per cent of the total wages bill. As a result, bonuses reflected performance in terms of administratively established targets rather than in terms of productivity measured against use of capital. At that time, enterprises tried to get a low profit target in order to earn higher bonuses. The Second Five-Year Plan followed a similar pattern though it tried to set an average rate for payment based on performance during the First Five-Year Plan. In the early 1960s, the 'seventy points' related bonuses more directly to productivity. This experiment, however, was stopped and the system of tying bonuses to target fulfilment was reintroduced. The maximum rate of bonuses was set at 3.5 per cent of wages bill, provided six key enterprise targets were met. One-sixth of this percentage was deducted for each unfulfilled target. In addition, ten per cent of surplus profits could be retained for enterprise incentives. Once again, no relationship was established between productivity and rewards, and enterprises tried to increase their labour force in order to expand their wages bill and hence the amount available for bonus payment. Replacing these methods by systems directly relating profits and incentives will inevitably lead to inequalities between enterprises and between individuals. Profit will also become the major factor influencing employment policy and management methods. Currently, it is suggested that piece-work wages relate productivity and income most directly.[119] What is more, examples of incentives employed in various enterprises have not indicated any outside limit for bonus payments but suggest that each bonus can be tailored according to the work done and the profit generated.[120]

Doubtless, the above changes in management practices will produce a wide range of variation in the actual running of factories throughout China. Initially, at least, this will lead to a return to the situation observed during the early 1960s when the extent of enterprise independence was determined by its level of importance in the economy as a whole. As Richman noted, sensitive military production was more likely to be controlled from the centre than shoe production in each major city.[121] Within enterprises, the division of authority between people will to a large degree come to be based on economic and technical performance. The managerial methods, first outlined in the 'seventy points' of 1961 and reintroduced in the 'thirty points' of 1978, are thus likely to be further developed. As I have noted many times, this amounts to a complete rejection of the innovations of the Cultural Revolution which are now officially discredited as ineffective and counter-productive. Moreover, as Japanese and American managerial models are increasingly adopted, many management systems from even earlier periods will also disappear or be modified.[122]

Conclusion

This chapter has demonstrated that, over the entire period since 1969, there has been a persistent trend within China to modify most, if not all, of the innovations in the industrial economy attempted during the Cultural Revolution. After the fall of the 'Gang of Four', this trend immediately became dominant. Until 1978, the framework within which this discussion took place was that put forward by Deng Xiaoping in his speeches of 1975. This framework negated the argument, at the heart of the Cultural Revolution, that development in a society attempting to build socialism was as much political as it was economic. In its place, the argument was made that, after the crucial changes in the system of ownership which took place in the 1950s, the key to development was the growth of the productive forces as represented by the increase of gross output, productivity, and the rate of growth. Nevertheless, this framework did not entail the abandonment of all the experience of economic management built up in China since 1949 and it encouraged people to look towards the period before the Great Leap Forward of 1958 for inspiration.

Since the middle of 1978, this approach has been replaced by a model of development which has grown from the 'market socialism' ideas of the early 1960s. While, in some respects, this appears to be a logical outcome of some of the initiatives originally put forward by Deng, the result goes far beyond his initial perspective. In effect, the negation of the economic ideas represented by the 'Gang of Four' is no longer the centre of the debate but has become one aspect of a complete reappraisal of economic policy. By making material economic growth the focus of all efforts, the result has been not only to change the nature of the ideology, which the Chinese Communist Party has always insisted should be at the heart of economic theory, but also many of the practical policies as well. The contrast with the Cultural Revolution could scarcely be more marked. What, then, has caused these changes?

Central to any answer to this question is an evaluation of the role of the 'Gang of Four'. There can be no doubt that the lines of argument advanced by Yao Wenyuan and Zhang Chunqiao in their articles of early 1975[123] were based on economic ideas advocated by Mao Zedong and reflected the consistent trend of his thinking on problems of development since the Great Leap Forward. Yao and Zhang also attempted to place these ideas within the scope of an analysis of the problems of class struggle during the period of socialist development.[124] This attempt was made, however, at a time when the advocates of the approach represented by the 'Gang' were already on the defensive, if not in full retreat. In addition, the many political and social failings of the Cultural Revolution, exacerbated by the factionalism and violence which it had engendered, had to a large extent rendered any delayed theoretical refinement redundant. Since Yao and Zhang were in the position of defending a movement which was already in the process of rejection and with which they were closely associated as members of the Central Committee's Cultural Revolution Group, the basis for defending their theoretical position was already extremely weak. As much evidence suggests, the fact that the personal motives and methods of leadership of the members of the 'Gang' bore little resemblance to the Mass Line, which they advocated, did little to help them defend their position. As events have shown, their control over much of the press and their ability to have Deng Xiaoping dismissed for a second time in 1976 masked a fundamental weakness. There were no safeguards sufficient for them to maintain their influence.

Leaving aside the question of the relative strength of the different groups within the Chinese leadership, a question of even greater significance is the relationship between the theory and the practice of the ideas the 'Gang' put forward. As I have detailed above, there is considerable evidence to show that the innovations of the Cultural Revolution were either circumvented in practice or did not work to provide greater social equality. Despite the continuous debates provoked by the 'Gang', social inequality remained unaffected. Indeed, the essence of the 'Gang's' argument on bourgeois right was that much remained to be done in these respects. Thus, the theoretical perspectives of the Cultural Revolution did not provide any workable solutions to China's problems either in terms of equality or in terms of greater output. This chapter has stressed that it is in this area of material failure that the strongest attack has been mounted on the 'Gang of Four'. It is the area where the problems of material scarcity exert their strongest influence on the options open to those who attempt to weigh economic policies against longer-term political goals.

Analysis of the past 30 years of economic development now divides the period into two phases of fast and effective growth and two periods of losses and deceleration.[125] The two phases of effective growth are listed as the First Five-Year Plan and the period 1962 to 1965. It is pointed out that the annual rate of growth of the gross value of industrial output, during 1953 to 1957, was 18 per cent, and that, in most industries, 1965 was the year of best-ever performance. By contrast, it is stated that the Great Leap Forward and the Cultural Revolution were characterised by decline and disruption. In response to those within China who point out that the annual rate of industrial growth over the period 1949 to 1977 was 13.5 per cent and that even during the Third Five-Year Plan (1966 to 1970) and the Fourth Five-Year Plan (1970 to 1975), when the influence of Lin Biao and the 'Gang of Four' was strongest, the growth rate was still 11.7 per cent and 9.1 per cent respectively, it is argued that per capita productivity remained low, product specifications were slipshod, quality was poor, costs were high and there was serious waste. Although the annual growth rate of the gross value of industrial output appeared high, many products were not satisfactory or were consumed within the production process. Socially useful products were few.[126]

These growth-rate figures are very close to those calculated from provincial data by Field, Lardy and Emerson.[127] They also bear out the general conclusion of most observers that the First Five-Year Plan period was one of exceptional growth and that the 1960s saw a general decline in the overall growth rate.[128] Although they do not reflect the structural changes which took place over this period and, therefore, understate many of the important advances in agriculture, industrial-agricultural relationships and the nature of industrial output which were made,[129] the continued decline in the rate of growth into the 1970s does attest to the continuing problems in the way of accelerating industrial development. This failure to accelerate growth may have done more to undermine the policies advocated by the 'Gang' than any other factor. The failure is all the more significant given the speed with which growth accelerated after 1976. If the potential existed, why could it not be mobilised by the policies of the 'Gang'? Certainly, the figures quoted at the Second Session of the Fifth National People's Congress in June 1979 do show a sharp upsurge in the growth rate for 1977 to 1978, with the latter year recording a 13.5 per cent increase, equal to the long-term trend rate.[130] This sharp rate of increase is borne out by the figures for individual industrial commodities, illustrated in Table 3.1.

Table 3.1: China's Economic Performance, 1969-1978: Selected Commodities (million tonnes)

Commodity	1969	1970	1971	1972	1973	1974	1975	1976	1977	1978
Steel[a]	16.0	17.8	21.0	23.0	25.5	23.8	25.0[b]	21.0[b]	23.7[c]	31.8[c]
Coal[a]	258	310	335	356	377	389	430[b]	483[g]	550[c]	618[c]
Crude Oil[a]	20.3	28.5	36.7	43.0	54.5	65.3	75/80[b]	87[g]	93.6[c]	104[c]
Chemical Fertiliser[d]		14.0	16.8	19.9	25.0	25.4[e]			38.0[f]	48.0[f]
Cement[a]	19.6	19.8	23.0	27.5	29.9	31.6			55.7[c]	65.2[c]

Sources:
a. 1969 to 1974: Field 1975, pp. 165-7.
b. MacDougall 1977.
c. *BR* 27, 6 July 1979, p. 37.
d. 1970 to 1973: Chao 1975.
e. Eckstein 1977, p. 217.
f. *BR* 2, 12 January 1979, p. 8. Note: *BR* 26, 29 June 1979, p. 10 gives 1978 production as 42.1 million tonnes.
g. *BR* 25, 22 June 1979, p. 10.

If this potential existed, why was it that the calls for mass mobilisation and the restrictions on the emergence of a technocratic élite, which had characterised the Cultural Revolution, could not realise it? The evidence strongly suggests that the concern with revolutionary theory had left revolutionary practice behind.

In sum, the need to promote material growth in the economy was urgent, yet the initiatives taken by the 'Gang of Four' and its supporters inevitably inhibited the full use of existing resources and entailed losses in current production. By contrast, the policies of the current leadership promote growth at the expense of the Communist Party's previous political goals. The problem of being both 'red' and 'expert' is still unresolved. Although the new policies may generate a period of rapid industrial growth, they will also lead to growing inequalities between regions and between individuals — a fact which the current leadership is aware of, as discussion in the Chinese media shows. Thus, political problems will be created which can be expected to become pronounced should the rate of economic growth falter. Furthermore, many of the changes in economic policy stress greater economic freedom and independence at the expense of the central government and the authoritative role of the Communist Party. The dilemma facing the Chinese leadership is, therefore, one of where and how to draw the line between using 'objective economic laws' to stimulate activism at lower levels and ensuring that Party authority is not completely set aside.

Notes

1. See the arguments in Beijing Renmin Chubanshe 1974; Zhongguo Caizheng Jingji Chubanshe 1976.

2. Yao Wenyuan, *Hongqi* 3, 1975, *PR* 10, 7 March 1975, pp. 5-10; Zhang Chunqiao, *Hongqi* 4, 1975, *PR* 14, 4 April 1975, pp. 5-11.

3. Contemporary accounts of these problems can be found in *SWB* FE/4967/B11/1-7; *SWB* FE/4969/B11/1; *SWB* FE/4981/B11/1-4; *SWB* FE/4982/B11/4-7; *SWB* FE/4988/B11/1-5; *SWB* FE/4993/B11/1; *SWB* FE/4994/B11/16-20.

4. CCP.CC *Zhongfa* 37 (1977) *Issues and Studies*, Vol. XIV, No. 11, November 1978, p. 103.

5. Hua Guofeng, 26 February 1978, *PR* 10, 10 March 1978, p. 12.

6. Some of the argument in this section is drawn from Watson 1979.

7. Beijing Renmin Chubanshe 1976, pp. 1-16.

8. In particular, see *PR* 10, 7 March 1975, pp. 5-10; *PR* 14, 4 April 1975, pp. 5-11; *Hongqi* 5, 1975, pp. 8-13; *RMRB* 5 March 1976, p. 1; *Hongqi* 5, 1976, pp. 45-52; *Xuexi yu Pipan* 4, 1976, pp. 28-35.

9. Deng Xiaoping, 7 October 1975; Deng Xiaoping, 2 September 1975, in *Zhonggong Nianbao* 1977, Section 5, pp. 58-67; ibid., Section 5, pp. 67-76 (reference to these). Also in Chi Hsin 1978, pp. 203-38, 239-76 and in *Issues and Studies*, Vol. XIII, No. 8, August 1977, pp. 77-99; ibid., Vol. XIII, No. 7, July 1977, pp. 90-113.

10. *Hongqi* 5, 1975, p. 8.

11. Ibid., p. 11, my emphasis.

12. *Hongqi* 6, 1976, pp. 52-5.

13. Deng Xiaoping, 7 October 1975, *Zhonggong Nianbao* 1977, Section 5, p. 62.

14. Ibid., pp. 62-4.

15. Engels 1892, p. 377. Quoted in Deng Xiaoping, 7 October 1975, *Zhonggong Nianbao* 1977, Section 5, p. 65. Excerpts from Engels were subsequently published in *RMRB* 17 February 1977, p. 1.

16. See Brugger 1979.

17. *PR* 14, 1 April 1977, pp. 23-6.

18. See, e.g., the articles on foreign technology and methods published on the enterprise management page of *GMRB* 11 July 1978, p. 4; *GMRB* 12 August 1978, p. 4; *GMRB* 26 August 1978, p. 4; *GMRB* 23 September 1978, p. 4; *GMRB* 21 October 1978, p. 4; *GMRB* 2 December 1978, p. 4; *GMRB* 10 February 1979, p. 4.

19. Deng Xiaoping, 7 October 1975, *Zhonggong Nianbao* 1977, Section 5, pp. 68-70.

20. Wu Jinglian, Zhou Shulian and Wang Haibo, *Jingji Yanjiu* 9, 1978, pp. 15-25.

21. Quoted in ibid., p. 15.

22. Ibid., my emphasis.

23. Jiang Xuemu, *GMRB* 23 September 1978, p. 4.

24. Ibid.

25. *Jingji Guanli* 1, 1979, p. 3.

26. For a discussion of this trend, see Watson 1978, pp. 176-182.

27. See, e.g., *Hongqi* 7, 1972, pp. 63-7; *SWB* FE/3930/B11/11; *SWB* FE/3962/B11/7.

28. *RMRB* 2 March 1972.

29. A useful collection of documents from this campaign is Price 1977.

30. *Hongqi* 5, 1974, pp. 57-8.

31. *SWB* FE/4530/B11/14-15; *SWB* FE/4538/B11/1-2; *SWB* FE/4545/B11/2-14; *SWB* FE/4554/B11/5-13; *SWB* FE/4556/B11/13-16; *SWB* FE/4566/B11/13-17.

32. This discussion was launched in *RMRB* 1 February 1974, p. 3. A useful collection of related articles is Beijing Renmin Chubanshe 1974.

33. *RMRB* 29 June 1978, p. 1.

34. *Hongqi* 11, 1973, pp. 3-7; *Hongqi* 4, 1974, pp. 68-72; *Hongqi* 5, 1975, pp. 39-42.

35. Anhui Radio (quoting Lenin), 28 April 1975, *SWB* FE/4893/B11/12.

36. *SWB* FE/4869/B11/1-3; *SWB* FE/4872/B11/14 ff; *SWB* FE/4874/B11/6 ff; *SWB* FE/4876/B11/3 ff; *SWB* FE/4882/B11/3 ff; *SWB* FE/4896/B11/3-6; *SWB* FE/4933/B11/5-6; *SWB* FE/5017/B11/25-26; *SWB* FE/5090/B11/7.

37. *Issues and Studies*, Vol. XI, No. 1, January 1975, pp. 101-4.

38. Cheng 1978, pp. 126-133.

39. Deng Xiaoping, 2 September 1975, *Zhonggong Nianbao* 1977, Section 5, pp. 67-76.

40. Ibid., p. 69.

41. See the discussion in Watson 1979.

42. Deng Xiaoping, 2 September 1975, *Zhonggong Nianbao* 1977, Section 5, p. 71.

43. *Xuexi yu Pipan* 4, 1976, pp. 28-35.

44. See, e.g., *SWB* FE/5405/B11/6-8; *SWB* FE/5407/B11/6-12; NCNA 13 January 1977, *SWB* FE/5414/B11/1-6.

45. Brugger 1978, pp. 266-8.

46. The text of both is in *Hongqi* 1, 1977, pp. 3-24 and 70-3.

47. *Hongqi* 4, 1977, pp. 3-4. See also *Hongqi* 3, 1977, 66-70.

48. *Lianhuan Huabao* 4, 1977, pp. 12-14; *RMRB* 16 February 1977, p. 1; NCNA 16 February 1979, *SWB* FE/5445/B11/1-5.

49. *PR* 22, 27 May 1977, pp. 5-23.

50. NCNA 28 July 1977, *SWB* FE/5580/B11/12-15.

51. References to many of these conferences can be found in 'Quarterly Chronicle', *CQ*, 70-3, 1977-8.

52. *PR* 39, 23 September 1977, pp. 7-14.

53. *RMRB* 27 August 1977, p. 1.

54. *Hongqi* 8, 1977, pp. 70-3. See also ibid., pp. 74-6.

55. *PR* 45, 4 November 1977, pp. 6-9; *RMRB* 25 October 1977, p. 2.

56. *PR* 10, 10 March 1978, pp. 7-40.

57. Ibid., p. 25.

58. *RMRB* 4 July 1978, p. 1. Full text is in *Zhonggong Yanjiu*, Vol. XII, No. 10, October 1978, pp. 122-134.

59. Ibid., p. 125.

60. *Hongqi* 8, 1978, pp. 24-41. See also *PR* 30, 28 July 1978, pp. 6-17.

61. *PR* 30, 28 July 1978, p. 11.

62. NCNA 5 July 1978, *SWB* FE/5863/B11/11-13.

63. *Hongqi* 8, 1978, pp. 33-41.

64. *GMRB* 13 January 1979, p. 4. See also *GMRB* 18 November 1978, p. 3; *Jingji Yanjiu* 1, 1979, p. 76, for references to 'supply agents flocking everywhere'.

65. Liang Wensen and Tian Jinghai, *Jingji Yanjiu* 4, 1979, pp. 16-24.

66. Qiao Rongzhang, *Jingji Yanjiu* 7, 1978, pp. 20-4.

67. For a discussion of *blat* in the Soviet Union, see Berliner 1957, pp. 182-199.

68. *RMRB* 6 October 1978, p. 1ff. Translated in *PR* 45, 10 November 1978, pp. 7-11; *PR* 46, 17 November 1978, pp. 15-23; *PR* 47, 24 November 1978, pp. 13-21.

69. *PR* 46, 17 November 1978, p. 18.

70. Liao Jili, *Jingji Yanjiu* 12, 1978, pp. 26-31.

71. Lee 1965, pp. 72-8.

72. *RMRB* 16 March 1979, p. 3. See also Li Chengrui and Zhang Zhuoyuan, *Jingji Yanjiu* 2, 1979, pp. 2-11.

73. *RMRB* 12 January 1979, p. 1. See NCNA 12 January 1979, *SWB* FE/6018/B11/6.

74. Mo Fei, *Gongren Ribao* 3 February 1979, *SWB* FE/6041/B11/9-11.

75. See, Chengdu, Sichuan Radio, 4 February 1979, *SWB* FE/6038/B11/1-2; NCNA 13 February 1979, *SWB* FE/6067/B11/6-7; *GMRB* 17 March 1979, p. 4, *SWB* FE/6081/B11/6-7. The figure for the number of enterprises was given in *Jingji Yanjiu* 1, 1979, p. 54.

76. *GMRB* 17 March 1979, p. 4.

77. NCNA 8 March 1979, *SWB* FE/6065/B11/8; NCNA 13 March 1979, *SWB* FE/6068/B11/11.

78. Chengdu, Sichuan Radio, 11 March 1979, *SWB* FE/6068/B11/14.

79. NCNA 16 March 1979, *SWB* FE/6071/B11/10.

80. See NCNA 22 March 1979, *SWB* FE/6077/B11/17-19; *RMRB* 24 March 1979, *SWB* FE/6080/B11/1-4; NCNA 28 March 1979, *SWB* FE/6082/B11/1.

81. *BR* 29, 20 July 1979, pp. 7-24.

82. See, e.g., Liao Jili, *Jingji Yanjiu* 12, 1978, pp. 26-31; Li Chengrui and Zhang Zhuoyuan, *Jingji Yanjiu* 2, 1979, pp. 2-11; Liao Jili, *Jingji Guanli* 2, 1979, pp. 9-11; Luo Jingfen, *Jingji Guanli* 2, 1979, pp. 12-14.

83. Huang Fanzhang, *Jingji Guanli* 2, 1979, pp. 25-7.

84. *Jingji Guanli* 2, 1979, p. 14.
85. Schurmann 1966, pp. 175-8, 196-9.
86. Deng Xiaoping, 2 September 1975, *Zhonggong Nianbao* 1977, Section 5, p. 70.
87. *Zhonggong Yanjiu*, Vol. XII, No. 10, October 1978, p. 127.
88. E.g. Liao Jili, *Jingji Yanjiu* 12, 1978, pp. 26-7.
89. E.g. Beijing Radio, 2 January 1979, *SWB* FE/6013/B11/1-2; *Beijing Ribao* 19 February 1979, *SWB* FE/6053/B11/6-8.
90. *GMRB* 26 August 1978, p. 4.
91. Liu Guangdi, *Jingji Yanjiu* 1, 1979, pp. 29-35; Ye Xiangzhi, *Jingji Guanli* 2, 1979, pp. 17-18; Tian Chunsheng, *Jingji Guanli* 2, 1979, pp. 48-51.
92. Quoted in *Jingji Yanjiu* 1, 1979, p. 31.
93. Ibid., pp. 31-5.
94. Tian Chunsheng, *Jingji Guanli* 2, 1979, pp. 48-51; Tian Jianghai and Liang Wensen, *Jingji Guanli* 2, 1979, pp. 52-4.
95. *Jingji Guanli* 2, 1979, p. 50.
96. See *GMRB* 29 July 1978, p. 4; *GMRB* 18 November 1978, p. 3; *GMRB* 30 December 1978, p. 4; *GMRB* 24 March 1979, p. 4. See also Qiao Rongzhang, *Jingji Yanjiu* 7, 1978, pp. 20-4; Wu Jiapei, *et al.*, *Jingji Yanjiu* 7, 1978, pp. 25-31; Research Section of the Number One Ministry of Machine-Building, *Jingji Yanjiu* 7, 1978, pp. 32-6; Wu Jiapei, *et al.*, *Jingji Yanjiu* 11, 1978, pp. 55-60; Ye Ji, *Jingji Yanjiu* 1, 1979, pp. 75-6; Zhou Muchang, *Jingji Guanli* 2, 1979, pp. 14-16; Shao Liang, *Jingji Guanli* 2, 1979, pp. 22-4.
97. Schurmann 1966, p. 300.
98. *Jingji Guanli* 2, 1979, p. 16.
99. *Jingji Yanjiu* 1, 1979, pp. 75-8; *Jingji Guanli* 2, 1979, pp. 22-4.
100. *Jingji Yanjiu* 7, 1978, pp. 32-6.
101. *Jingji Yanjiu* 7, 1978, pp. 25-31; *Hongqi* 11, 1978, pp. 47-53; *Jingji Yanjiu* 11, 1978, pp. 55-60.
102. *Zhonggong Yanjiu*, Vol. XII, No. 10. October 1978, p. 126.
103. *Jingji Yanjiu* 11, 1978, pp. 55-60.
104. Watson 1978; Watson 1979.
105. *GMRB* 9 September 1979, p. 4; *GMRB* 13 January 1979, p. 4; *Jingji Yanjiu* 12, 1978, pp. 26-31; *Jingji Yanjiu* 2, 1979, pp. 2-11.
106. *Jingji Yanjiu* 12, 1978, p. 31.
107. *GMRB* 7 October 1978, p. 4; *GMRB* 13 January 1979, p. 4; *Jingji Guanli* 2, 1979, pp. 9-11 and pp. 19-21.
108. *GMRB* 11 July 1978, p. 4; *GMRB* 26 August 1978, p. 4; *Jingji Yanjiu* 4, 1978, pp. 8-16 and pp. 17-20; *Jingji Yanjiu* 9, 1978, pp. 2-14, pp. 15-25 and pp. 26-31; *Jingji Yangjiu* 1, 1979, pp. 47-59; *Jingji Yanjiu* 4, 1979, pp. 16-24.
109. These were the arguments of 1963-4, summarised in Lee 1965, pp. 72-8.
110. *Jingji Yanjiu* 9, 1978, p. 27.
111. Ibid., p. 24.
112. *GMRB* 23 September 1978, p. 4; *Jingji Yanjiu* 6, 1978, pp. 17-22.
113. *Jingji Guanli* 2, 1979, p. 46.
114. *RMRB* 1 May 1978, pp. 1-2; *PR* 42, 20 October 1978, pp. 6-7; *GMRB* 16 December 1978, p. 4; *BR* 23, 8 June 1979, pp. 9-23.
115. *GMRB* 21 October 1978, p. 4; *Jingji Yanjiu* 9, 1978, pp. 47-50; *Jingji Yanjiu* 12, 1978, pp. 37-43; *Jingji Yanjiu* 1, 1979, pp. 6-13; *Jingji Yanjiu* 2, 1979, pp. 49-53; *Jingji Guanli* 2, 1979, pp. 40-3.
116. *Jingji Yanjiu* 9, 1978, p. 50.
117. *RMRB* 25 January 1979, *SWB* FE/6033/B11/1-2; *RMRB* 14 March 1979, *SWB* FE/6069/B11/5; Beijing Radio, *SWB* FE/6071/B11/9-10; Beijing Radio 31 March 1979, *SWB* FE/6086/B11/5-6; Beijing Radio, 3 April 1979, *SWB* FE/6089/B11/12-13.

118. *Jingji Yanjiu* 12, 1978, pp. 39-41.
119. *Jingji Yanjiu* 2, 1979, pp. 49-53.
120. *Jingji Guanli* 2, 1979, pp. 40-3.
121. Richman 1967, Chapter III.
122. *GMRB* 11 July 1978, p. 4; *GMRB* 12 August 1978, p. 4; *GMRB* 26 August 1978, p. 4; *GMRB* 23 September 1978, p. 4; *GMRB* 21 October 1978, p. 4; *GMRB* 2 December 1978, p. 4; *GMRB* 27 January 1979, p 4; *GMRB* 10 February 1979, p. 4; *Jingji Guanli* 1, 1979, pp. 55-9; *Jingji Guanli* 2, 1979, pp. 58-64.
123. *PR* 10, 7 March 1975, pp. 5-10; *PR* 14, 4 April 1975, pp. 5-11.
124. Brugger 1978, pp. 261-3.
125. *Jingji Yanjiu* 2, 1979, pp. 2-11. See also Hu Qiaomu, *PR* 46, 17 November 1978, p. 22.
126. *Jingji Yanjiu* 2, 1979, pp. 3-4.
127. Field, Lardy and Emerson 1975, p. 433.
128. Eckstein 1977, pp. 218-19.
129. Rawski 1973, pp. 1-33.
130. *BR* 27, 6 July 1979, pp. 37-41.

4 *Rural Policy*[1]

BILL BRUGGER

In the previous chapter, which discussed industrial policy, Watson presented a periodisation somewhat different from that which Sullivan outlined in Chapter 1. This chapter, which will discuss rural policy, will follow Sullivan's periodisation. It will focus, in particular, on the second and third periods since the downfall of the 'Gang of Four' (mid-1977 to late-1978 and late-1978 to the present). In the first period (October 1976 to mid-1977), there were few major discussions of rural policy, despite the exhortations of people such as Chen Yun to reopen the debate about the Great Leap Forward. Thus, if one compares the speech made by Hua Guofeng to the 1975 Conference on Learning from Dazhai in Agriculture[2] and official statements of late-1976[3], one is not aware of any significant change in policy towards the countryside.

At the core of the 1975 strategy, which was reiterated in early 1977, was the policy of making one-third of the country's approximately 2,100 *xian* (counties) into Dazhai-type *xian* by the year 1980.[4] The criteria for establishing these *xian* were much the same as those which applied to advanced areas in the 1960s and the quantitative targets for output and yields were based upon the National Programme for Agricultural Development (NPAD) of the 1950s.[5] There were six main criteria.[6]

1. In providing core leadership, the *xian* Party committee should adhere to the Party line and be 'united in struggle'.
2. In order to wage struggles against capitalist activities and to supervise and remould 'class enemies', the *xian* Party committee should establish the dominance of the 'poor and lower middle peasants'.
3. Cadres at *xian*, commune and brigade level should participate regularly in collective productive labour, like those of the model

135

Xiyang *xian* (in which Dazhai is located).
4. Rapid progess should be achieved in farmland construction, agricultural mechanisation and scientific farming.
5. The collective economy should steadily be expanded so that the production and income of the poorer communes and brigades should reach or surpass the present level of the average communes and brigades in the same locality.
6. There should be an all-round development in agriculture, forestry, animal husbandry and fish farming. There should be large increases in output, large contributions to the state and a steady improvement in peasants' living standards.

The above six criteria were quite vague. Without any clear discussions of policy one is not sure what was meant by 'united in struggle' and who exactly 'class enemies' were. Nor was it at all clear what 'leadership by the poor and middle peasants' might imply. Back in the Socialist Education Movement of 1963-6, the institutional means chosen to limit the activities of 'class enemies' and to revitalise local Communist Party branches took the form of 'poor and lower middle peasant associations'. It was, at that time, rather difficult to form these associations and initial measures to launch the struggle against 'class enemies' were promoted by work teams and sometimes by the people's militia. Prior to the demise of the 'Gang of Four', it appears that the same means were used to foster class struggle in the countryside, only by then poor and lower middle peasant associations were part of the establishment.[7] Being unable to form indigenous peasant bodies which might restrict capitalist activity, those who sought to promote changes in the countryside soon resorted to 'commandism'. Ever since the demise of the 'Gang', therefore, there has been criticism of the excessive use of the militia to promote class struggle[8] and of rusticated youth being used by the 'Gang' to place its agents in positions of authority.[9]

It was only after the rehabilitation of Deng Xiaoping, in mid-1977, that there was any really serious discussion of theory and policy and an attempt was made to define 'class enemies'. In this, the second period since 1976, it became clear that 'class enemies' were no longer to be defined according to the generative view of class developed by Zhang Chunqiao and Yao Wenyuan in 1975.[10] This view, discussed in Chapter 1, held that society undergoing socialist transition was characterised by 'bourgeois right' whereby equal rights were given to people made unequal by their economic location. Unless restricted, this 'bourgeois right' would entrench inequalities so that differences in status and power would grow into class differences (defined in Marxian terms according to the means of production). Thus, a new class could develop. Class struggle, therefore, had to be the motive force of all social and economic policies if the process of socialist transition were not to go into reverse in the same manner as the Soviet Union. In repudiating the 'Gang's' views of 'bourgeois right'[11] the Party designated as 'enemies' those sworn followers of the 'Gang' who held precisely that view. There was inaugurated a massive campaign to root out followers of the 'Gang' and many cadres, who had risen to power during the Cultural Revolution, were removed from their posts and replaced by people who had once been criticised for 'revisionism'.[12] It is not at all clear, however, just how deep this movement went. It was probably the case that commune level cadres remained in office and it was mainly cadres at *xian* level and higher who suffered. In any case, the removal of these higher level cadres was to have an impact on rural policy as the Party embarked on its general reassessment of economic strategy.

As Sullivan has noted, much of the economic thinking of late-1977 and 1978 was reminiscent of the Great Leap of 1958-9. Ambitious targets were put forward and moves were made to decentralise decision-making authority to local areas (Schurmann's Decentralisation II). The Great Leap scenario, however, did not fit in with the new stress on 'great order across the land' nor with policies of export-led growth. These latter policies had implications not just for national self-reliance but also *regional* self-reliance. Though the new strategy centred on the export of large amounts of oil and coal, there was also scope for the export of agricultural products. This implied a greater concentration on cash crops, regional specialisation and a modification of the policy of 'taking grain as the key link'. It was such considerations, together with others outlined by Watson in the previous chapter, which led, in late-1978, to a repudiation of the Great Leap and an affirmation of Libermanist 'socialist market relations'[13] — the position for which Liu Shaoqi had been lambasted in the Cultural Revolution.

As we have seen, the dominance of the Libermanist position was to be confirmed at the Third Plenum of the Party Central Committee in December 1978 and there was ushered in a new period in contemporary Chinese history. The Plenum announced the basic completion of large-scale class struggle and, at about the same time, full political rights were restored not only to 'rightists' capped since 1957 but also to former landlords who were deemed to have reformed.[14] The position, criticised in 1975 as the 'theory of the productive forces', was affirmed and much was made of the independent operation of economic laws.[15] More important still, in the context of this chapter, the Plenum approved a general programme for accelerating agricultural development and a new sixty article draft document for work in the communes based upon that sixty article document of the early 1960s which had been denounced in the Cultural Revolution.[16]

The new policy for agriculture was set within the framework of 'centralised policy and dispersed operations'. This, however, was not the same framework which had informed the Yan'an model and the Great Leap Forward where operational authority had been decentralised to local areas. Rather, as Sullivan notes, it was that odd amalgam of centralisation and decentralisation to economic units (Schurmann's Decentralisation I)[17] which had long been associated with Chen Yun. Thus, planning, financial control, irrigation and other capital construction, provisions for mechanisation and the conduct of agricultural research were to be increasingly centralised. Individual rural economic units, on the other hand, were, like their industrial counterparts, to enjoy much greater autonomy and were to be integrated by the operation of market forces. The following examination of rural policy in the two periods since mid-1977 will focus on this issue of centralisation and decentralisation. The first part, which deals with general strategy, will note the trend towards centralisation, whilst the second part, which discusses the rural administrative system, will focus on the decentralised operation of communal sub-units.

General Strategy

The confusion which attended the second period (mid-1977 to December 1978) was such that one was presented with Great Leap-type targets without much else of the Great Leap strategy. The first set of targets concerns yields per hectare. Over the past 20 years, land reclamation in China has enjoyed considerable priority and a certain amount of new land has been brought under cultivation.[18] This, however, has not kept pace with the loss of land to urban development and China's cultivated area has declined from 107 to about 100 million hectares.[19] Though, in 1978, it was planned to extend the cultivated area to 108 million hectares by 1985,[20] the key to meeting the target of 400 million tonnes of food-grains which Hua Guofeng set for 1985 (and consequently increasing the agricultural growth rate from between two and three per cent to between four and five per cent)[21] was to raise crop yields. Research into high yielding seed strains was to be the major concern of twelve key agricultural areas which were to provide models for the rest of the country.

With regard to raising yields, rice cultivation had enjoyed the most success. In 1977, output of this grain was about 126 million tonnes[22] (44 per cent of the total food-grain output of 283 million tonnes).[23] China's version of the 'green revolution' had extended the area given over to this crop to 36 million hectares[24] and rice was grown in 28 out of the 29 provincial level units (the one exception being Qinghai).[25] The main area of rice cultivation, however, was still south of the Huai River and it was doubtless the anticipation of future success in rice cultivation which caused China's planners to stipulate that the old NPAD target of six tonnes per hectare for all grains in the region should be met by 1980.[26] The average national yield for rice in 1977 was some 3.5 tonnes per hectare[27] and, since some 70 per cent of the rice lands in the South were double cropped,[28] this did not seem an impossible target. What was, however, quite ambitious was Mao's 1957 target for the end of the century; that is, that yields in this region might reach 15 tonnes per hectare.[29]

Wheat, on the other hand, had not profited so much from the development of new seed strains and, in 1978, constituted only some 43-50 million tonnes[30] (15-18 per cent of the total). The national average yield for wheat was only some 1.6 tonnes per hectare[31] and consequently the yields anticipated north of the Huai River were much lower than those in the South. In the region north of the Huai River and south of the Yellow River, the reiterated NPAD target for all grains was 3.75 tonnes per hectare[32] and this would seem to imply the rapid extension of rice cultivation. Around the turn of the century it was hoped that this figure might reach 7.5 tonnes per hectare.[33] Though rice had been introduced into the region north of the Yellow River, its development was still only rudimentary and consequently the planned target yield for all grains in that area was only 1.5 tonnes per hectare,[34] with the hope of six tonnes at the turn of the century.[35]

The third major crop to have profited by hybridisation was maize. By 1978, some 30 million tonnes were produced and this figure might be expected to rise as maize replaces *gaoliang* (sorghum).[36] After a slight decline, the production of soy beans

(10-17 million tonnes)[37] was also increasing. These are customarily included in the figure for food-grains (*liangshi*), as are peas and beans (10 million tonnes),[38] potatoes and sweet potatoes (calculated in the overall figure as one-fifth of output).[39]

The 1978 targets were put forward at a time of quite serious drought and it was reasonable to doubt whether, under such circumstances, they could be realised. As the modified Great Leap scenario of 1978 gave way, in 1979, to the reiteration of the early-1960s position, it was felt that agricultural plans would be modified in the same manner as certain industrial plans.[40] Furthermore, although it was claimed that grain production in 1978 (305 million tonnes)[41] showed a spectacular increase over 1977, the achievement of grain targets over the whole country has been played down in favour of agricultural specialisation.

The 1979 stress on specialisation and rationalisation has led to a concentration on agricultural zoning[42] and a reinterpretation of the policy of 'taking grain as the key link'. Though that slogan is still used, great pains are taken to argue that areas which are more suited to pasture, forestry and the growing of industrial crops should concentrate on those specialities even if it means that they cease to be self-sufficient in grain. The idea that 'only growing grain constituted socialism' is seen as an 'ultra-leftist' error of Lin Biao and the 'Gang of Four'. It has been pointed out that, in the past, some areas were content if they fulfilled the NPAD targets in grain production even though the development of industrial crops was retarded. Excessive concentration on grain caused soil erosion, the reclamation of land at the expense of waters rich in fish, the retardation of light industry due to insufficient production of industrial crops (especially cotton) and the destruction of forests.[43] This last item received considerable attention following the promulgation of a draft Forestry Law in early-1979.[44] Plans were put forward to increase the forest area from the current 12.7 per cent of the total land area to 30 per cent (averaging 40 per cent for *xian* in mountainous areas, 20 per cent for those in hilly areas and 10 per cent for those on the plains).[45] To this end, 27 million hectares of trees were to be planted by 1985[46] to augment the current 122 million hectares, though no date is given as to when the target of 253-288 million[47] will be reached. In the same way, plans have been formulated to expand the pastoral area to some 287 million hectares.[48]

Though there is undoubtedly much truth in the descriptions of the deleterious consequences of a policy of regional self-reliance which stressed grain production, it is difficult to see how the present policy will prevent wide disparities in wealth between different areas. A policy of specialisation, according to economic zones and between production units, will require a far greater degree of central control than has existed hitherto. This will probably lead to a far greater amount of direct state investment in agriculture. There has always been some degree of direct state investment in agriculture, particularly in the state farm sector and the collective sector during times of natural calamities (though the normal form of state aid in this case is a reduction or waiving of agricultural tax).[49] There has even been some direct state aid given to the collective sector under normal circumstances as is clear from articles warning against the misuse of such aid[50], but this was probably quite small. The major form of state aid in the collective sector was always indirect and effected through pricing policy. For two decades, efforts have been made to close the 'price scissors' (between agricultural and industrial goods) and the price of goods sold to the peasants has declined considerably in relation to the price of agricultural products. By the end of 1978, the state purchase price of grain had been raised eight times since liberation and was double the figure for 1949.[51] The Third Plenum, in December 1978, decided to accelerate this closure of the 'price scissors' by planning to raise the price by a further 20 per cent in 1979 (with a 50 per cent rise in the price of grain sold above quota)[52], and the effect of this will be enhanced by earlier plans to pass on to the peasants a major part of an anticipated 20 per cent reduction of the production cost of farm machinery.[53]

The above moves will significantly boost peasant incomes and increase the sums agricultural units have for investment. But they will do so differentially — in short, the richer units will get richer and the gap between them and the poorer units will grow. It is significant, therefore, that most of the Dazhai-type *xian* appear to have been traditionally well-off *xian*[54] (with notable exceptions such as Xiyang where Dazhai itself is located). The twelve key grain producing areas, moreover, will profit most from indirect state investment precisely because they are already relatively well-off.

It must be stressed that the above features of indirect investment, which have been reiterated after the Third Plenum, are not new. Despite its commitment to 'egalitarianism' in other areas, the 'Gang of Four' does not appear to have advocated any measures to rectify the inegalitarian consequences of indirect investment. This may have been because it felt that this negative aspect of self-reliance was more than offset by the positive virtue of generating local commitment. What does appear to be new, however, follows from the logic of specialisation. It is likely that the above pattern of indirect investment will be coupled with a new policy of direct investment in agriculture through the banking system.

In March 1979, the State Council announced the restoration of the Chinese Agricultural Bank which had been dissolved in October 1965. The bank has been reconstituted as an organ directly under the jurisdiction of the State Council and charged with the management of funds to support agriculture. Specifically, its functions are to supervise the payment of agricultural tax and the deposits paid by commercial departments upon the conclusion of contracts for the supply of agricultural produce, to handle the normal banking operations of peasants, rural production units and supply and marketing co-operatives, to make appropriate loans and to assist rural units in accounting.[55] If, as I suspect, the bank becomes the major organ of state in the rural areas, we might expect bankers' logic to apply to rural finance and investment and loans to be channelled into fields which will guarantee the greatest financial return. This will probably produce a degree of inequality greater than the old system of self-reliance and will be much less amenable to local democratic control. Banks are not noted for being particularly responsive to popular democracy.

The new stress on rationalisation implies much more than the centralisation of the rural financial network. It might be anticipated that agricultural research activity will also be increasingly centralised. In the aftermath of the Cultural Revolution, a major part of research activity was carried out in the production units themselves, on the grounds that peasant creativity was just as important in developing new seeds as agricultural scientists working in isolated laboratories. The result, many Western agronomists noted, was the development of an excellent agricultural extension system but a very slow pace of basic research.[56] Despite the slowness, however, by conducting research in basic level production units and involving the peasants in experimentation, China has, in the recent past, avoided one of the major problems faced by many Third World countries — that of persuading the peasants to try out new seeds. Now, with the emphasis on speed, an attempt is being made to correct what is seen to be an imbalance in research activity[57] and experiments concerning the adaptation to Chinese conditions of seed strains imported from the Philippines (rice) and Mexico (wheat) are carried on by central institutions. Such a change could give rise to acute problems when it comes to changing patterns of inter-cropping to accommodate quick-ripening varieties. Labour habits will have to be altered and new planting techniques developed. All this will involve considerable risk[58] which is not likely to be minimised if the peasants feel cut off from the initial process of experimentation.

Because rationalisation, since the Third Plenum, has been often interpreted in much the same way as in the early-1960s, it is likely that it will involve the closure of a number of industrial or quasi-industrial plants located in the countryside in the same manner as at that time. Indeed, demands were made in the press in early-1979 for the closure of backward enterprises which lose money or which do not have easy access to transport.[59] Though considerable efforts continue to be made to assist local enterprises,[60] less attention, it seems, is now being paid to their educative effect or the extent to which they mobilise funds which might otherwise never become productive capital. As yet, it is too early to make any generalisations about the fate of rural industries, but something must be said about the most important of these — the fertiliser industry — because it provides the key to the whole programme of boosting yields.

Commenting on the 1985 targets for economic development, the 'Decisions of the Central Committee of the Chinese Communist Party on Some Questions Concerning the Acceleration of Agricultural Development', submitted to the Third Plenum in December 1978, demanded that chemical fertiliser production be increased to 80 million tonnes.[61] In 1978, the bulk of nutrients in agriculture came from organic fertiliser (172 kg per hectare)[62] though chemical fertiliser production had increased rapidly and stood at some 42-8 million tonnes.[63] Such a dramatic increase in chemical fertiliser output had been due, in large part, to the development of small-scale fertiliser plants in the countryside after the Cultural Revolution (though these, like so much else, owe their origin to policies introduced in the late-1950s). The motivation behind the development of these plants was both political (they played a part in closing the urban-rural gap) and economic (they made use of local resources and, unlike plants now scheduled for closure, their *raison d'être* was poor transportation facilities). One suspects, however, that short-term economic considerations were the most important. The initial expansion in the early-1970s, it is said, was in no small measure prompted by the escalating cost of imported fertiliser during the oil crisis.[64] Since China, at that time, was developing an indigenous petroleum industry, policy shifted to importing large fertiliser plants from overseas. It was anticipated, therefore, that as these large plants came into operation, there would be a decline in local fertiliser production from the peak (over 60 per cent of total production) of the early-1970s.[65] Economic logic, therefore, would deal a heavy blow to the political logic of rural industrialisation. This, then, was one of the reasons why the 'Gang of Four' was said to have opposed the importation of complete fertiliser plants from overseas.[66]

I am not at all sure, however, that, from the 'Gang of Four's' perspective, the situation is all that bleak. There is little evidence that transport problems have been overcome and there will still be a need for small-scale nitrogenous plants. As far as phosphates are concerned, severe problems were encountered in converting ores in local plants but, in recent years, there has been a veritable explosion in the production of humic acid fertiliser in plants at *xian*, commune and brigade levels.[67] In 1977, it was estimated that humic acid production was being carried on in 1,500 *xian*. At *xian* level and above, there were some 400 plants, at commune level there were 9,000 plants and at brigade level some 100,000 plants.[68] Some of these plants must be extremely primitive, but these figures suggest that the importation of large complete plants from overseas will not alter drastically the contribution which local fertiliser production has made to introducing rudimentary industrial techniques into the rural areas.

Though one might have some qualms about the new stress on rationalisation and centralisation, there is one field in which only a centralised policy may dramatically change the present situation and that is irrigation. Currently, some 50 per cent of China's cultivated area is irrigated[69] but the situation north and south of the Changjiang (Yangtze) is quite different. In the south, the cultivated land has long been adequately irrigated and very little improvement is immediately necessary. In the dry north, however, considerable efforts were made in recent years to dig tube wells and harness the Huai and Huang (Yellow) Rivers. In the last few years, some two million tube wells have been sunk in the North China Plain[70] though these have at times run dry.[71] Attempts to control the major rivers have met with some temporary success, though north China constantly faces problems of silting. Much more needs to be done and can only be done by huge programmes of capital investment undertaken by the central government. First, the Huang River is to be brought under full control and this task will probably take another forty years.[72] Secondly, it is planned to divert waters from the Changjiang to the north.[73] These two schemes are seen as the key to a comprehensive water control programme for north China and the sums of money required for them will be colossal. Even though the central government has, in early-1979, attempted to rectify an overcommitment on capital construction plans,[74] these long-term projects are still the subject of much discussion and forward planning. In the meantime, much of the irrigation work is handled locally and is highly labour intensive. The increase in the horsepower capacity of irrigation works from 60 million (1977) to 66 million (1978)[75] is only the first step on a very long march which must lead to greater central control.

Arguments in China about centralisation and decentralisation have, in the past, always accompanied arguments about the relationship between mechanisation and social change. In the mid-1950s, advocates of mechanisation first were also advocates of central control whilst Mao, in stressing social reorganisation first, also advocated regional decentralisation. Mao's position, however, has to be seen in the context of a labour surplus which was to be rectified in the Great Leap Forward. In 1979, on the other hand, there appears to be a labour shortage.

To understand the structure of rural employment, we need to be able to relate the figure of 285 million for the rural labour force[76] to an estimate of the maximum potential labour force. This is extremely difficult to do in the absence of reliable demographic data. If, however we take the official figure of 958 million[77] and subtract the 21 per cent who are urban dwellers, we get a rural population of 757 million. This rural population has been growing at an estimated two per cent per annum, though the rate has slowed to under two per cent and may be approaching the official national figure of 1.2 per cent.[78] It has been estimated that some 25 per cent of the population is under nine years of age and six per cent is between nine and fifteen. If we discount this 31 per cent plus the four per cent who are over sixty,[79] we get a figure of 492 million, which is 1.7 times the official labour force. Allowing for pregnancy, sickness, etc., we may deduce from this figure that about half the adult female population forms part of the rural labour force, which is quite remarkable in the light of the Chinese tradition.

There is, therefore, room for some expansion of the rural labour force but not very much. The recruitment of more women will undoubtedly require two things which were fundamental concerns of the discredited 'Gang of Four'. The first of these is equal pay for equal work. The evidence would seem to show that China still has some way to go before this is universally achieved though there is no evidence that the present leadership is any less committed to the goal than that which it replaced.[80] The second requirement for recruiting more women into the work force is an education campaign aimed at eradicating old ideas which keep women confined to the home. A considerably under-researched aspect of the now discredited campaign to 'Criticise Lin Biao and Confucius' of 1974-5 (which was launched by the 'Gang of Four') aimed precisely at emancipating women and recruiting them into the work force.[81] In the last three years, less seems to have been done in this regard than in the preceding two.

Unemployment in the Chinese countryside is not, therefore, a major problem. But is underemployment? There are few statistics which may help us answer this question. The figure for the labour force cited above refers to people who fulfil half of the assigned work quota (*ban laodongli*) (about 150 labour days per annum) as well as those who fulfil the total quota (*zheng laodongli*)[82] (about 300 labour days) and we have no information as to the relative size of these two categories. Doubtless, in any society which depends upon the annual cycle of sowing and harvesting, there must be periods of relative underemployment but the indication is that, in China, these are few and far between. In recent years, (and especially in the periods of serious drought), between one-third and one-half of the total rural work force has been engaged in farmland construction and irrigation work[83] and, in some areas, between 40 and 50 per cent of the year's labour days for the entire labour force is spent levelling and enlarging fields[84] (a prerequisite for the future use of farm machinery). But perhaps the most convincing evidence that labour shortages exist at most times of the year are the numerous accounts which appear in the press complaining that farming tasks, in the teams, are being harmed by too much labour being taken away for industry run at higher levels or for capital construction work.[85] Efforts have been made at harvest time, in the past year, to retain some 80 per cent of the labour force in the teams[86] but sometimes the authorities have found it difficult to retain any more than 30 per cent.[87] Thus, the situation in 1978-9 seems to be the reverse of that of the mid-1950s when it was felt that social reorganisation should precede farm mechanisation. No one in China nowadays, be they the 'Gang of Four' or Deng Xiaoping, would disagree that the prime task for agriculture is mechanisation, for only in that way can the labour shortage be solved.

Alongside the rural labour shortage, there has continued to exist, in recent years, an urban labour surplus and it was partly in response to this that some 17 million educated youth have been sent down to the countryside.[88] In the early-1970s, however, ideological concerns were probably just as important as purely economic concerns (hence the stress on *educated* youth). Educated youth could overcome what was felt to be the corruption of an urban life-style; they could pass on skills to the peasants and could take part in the political movements of that time. Some of them were certainly involved in promoting class struggle and many were more sympathetic to the goals of the Cultural Revolution than local cadres. In general, however, one gets the impression that only occasionally did educated youth attain positions of authority in the communes.[89] The more usual pattern was for youth to live in segregated quarters, engaging in their own sideline activities[90] and, in 1977-8, this became the specific general policy.[91] Doubtless, many youth did achieve some degree of integration with the local peasants though one is struck by constant accounts of problems. Youth were often denied the opportunity to earn work points equivalent to those earned by indigenous peasants.[92] They were frequently welcomed by commune authorities so long as the initial resettlement subsidy from the *xian* lasted and, after that, regarded as somewhat of a nuisance.[93] In general, they rarely took a full part in team discussions and the struggle sessions associated with political campaigns.[94] As a result of this (and a general distaste for rural life), many went back to the cities without ration tickets and became a burden on their relatives or friends. Aware of these problems, Mao (and the 'Gang of Four') were very concerned about the future of the movement and, from 1973 on, a number of remedial measures were taken.[95] After all, what was at stake was a great social experiment and a major attempt to contribute towards closing the urban-rural gap.

At first, the new leadership did not seem particularly concerned to alter the present arrangements for sending youth to the countryside. Youth were enjoined to stay where they were[96] and plans were made to improve their training.[97] Such a policy appealed not only to those who were ideologically committed to closing, in the short run, the urban-rural gap but also to those who were concerned about the urban employment situation. At a conference on rusticated youth towards the end of 1978, however, it became clear that the new leadership was motivated mainly by economic concerns. A very influential article in *Zhongguo Qingnianbao* (*China Youth News*)[98] noted that, in the 1950s, the policy of *xiaxiang* was justified because urban industry and commerce could not absorb all the middle school graduates but, by the 1960s, the situation had changed. In the Cultural Revolution, too many young people had been sent to the countryside. Now, in the 1970s, as the 'four modernisations' took place, the demand for educated labour in the cities would cause the number of youth sent to the countryside to diminish. The article went on to pour scorn on the comments of the 'Gang of Four' to the effect that the *xiaxiang* movement was a 'socialist new thing', 'a great revolutionary movement' and an 'orientation that must forever be kept to'. It was pointed out that integrating with the workers and peasants did not necessarily mean physical integration. Integrating with the workers and peasants could simply mean 'emulating the fine qualities of the workers and peasants, studying assiduously and working actively for the four modernisations'. When it came down to it, the main way of closing the gap between town and country was to develop the productive forces. Because of the 'interference of Lin Biao and the ''Gang of Four''', the *xiaxiang* movement had done nothing in this respect.

One would anticipate, therefore, a winding-down of the programme to send educated youth to the countryside, but the conference documents make it clear that, because of employment problems in the cities, this is not likely to occur very quickly.[99] Indeed, in 1979, some educated youth who had read the signs and had returned to the cities were persuaded to return to the countryside once again.[100] There is no doubt, however, that the long-term consequences of winding down the rustication programme will be very significant. The informal back-up which some rusticated youth gave to the rural education system will be weakened and there will be more reliance on the (often inadequate) formal education structure. The decentralisation of services, in which educated youth played a major part, will slow down and there will be a greater tendency for bright, ambitious, young people to want to migrate from the communes to the cities.

As significant as the above changes in the programme of rusticating educated youth are those concerning the rustication of qualified technical personnel. The principle of cadre participation in manual labour is still stressed. *Xian* level cadres were still being sent down to the countryside in 1977 and plans were made to ensure that they worked at least 100 days per year in the fields. Similarly, commune level cadres were expected to work 200 days and brigade level cadres 300 days.[101] The new administration, however, is less willing to countenance the large-scale downward transfer of technicians and doctors. These technical personnel have, in the past, played a major part in training skilled workers and para-medical personnel.[102] In 1977, for example, it was reported that there were some 1.5 million 'bare-foot doctors' in China[103] (averaging two per brigade). This development has only been made possible by the despatch of fully qualified doctors from the cities to train them. Though the technical proficiency of these 'bare-foot doctors' may not have been very high, few can deny that they have achieved much in extending the medical network and in providing technology for reducing the birth-rate; (though one would be rash to claim that birth control technology can ever be a major cause of population reduction, it is clearly an important factor).[104] It is with some degree of apprehension that one contemplates the future of such a programme, but it is unlikely that this shift in emphasis will be achieved too sharply. The present leadership's desire to lower the birth-rate to under one per cent by 1980[105] and to double the number of technicians servicing agricultural machinery would indicate some caution.

Though the despatch of educated people from the towns may have done something to ease the urban labour surplus and has probably done much to spread skills and services among the peasants, it can have had little effect on the general rural labour shortage. As I have suggested, this can only be tackled by mechanisation. At the First Conference on Learning from Dazhai in Agriculture in 1975, it was announced that 'basic mechanisation' would be achieved by 1980[106] and this was subsequently spelt out as the mechanisation of 70 per cent of the main jobs in farming, forestry, animal husbandry, sideline occupations and fish breeding. It was felt that this would contribute significantly to solving the labour shortage, since the mechanisation of ploughing, drainage, irrigation and transport alone would be the equivalent of more than doubling the rural labour force.[107] In 1978, this target was restated as the basic mechanisation of 80-85 per cent of all important tasks by 1985.[108]

Commenting on the target for 1980, the Shanghai political economy textbook indicated that this would mean increasing the 100,000 approx. standard (15 hp) tractors and the 100,000 'hand' (7 hp) tractors, which China had in 1970, to 800,000 standard and 1.5

million hand tractors by 1980.[109] This figure is consistent with a 1963 estimate that China needed one standard tractor for every 100 hectares.[110]

One is tempted to extrapolate the 1975 textbook target to 1985. This would suggest that China anticipates having 970,000 standard tractors and 1.8 million hand tractors by that date. Such an extrapolation would, however, be somewhat misleading since there was a change in policy in 1978 in favour of standard models. According to Vice-Premier Li Xiannian, China had enough small tractors and efforts should be directed to producing the larger type.[111] Thus, there was to be a 70 per cent increase in standard tractors by 1980 but only a 36 per cent increase in hand tractors.[112] This decision, impeccably rational in economic terms, will facilitate the process of centralisation. It will tend to take tractors away from the production teams and weaken the identification which ordinary peasants have with the programme of mechanisation. It will also strengthen the position of the machine tractor stations, which remained in existence throughout the 1970s, and might occasion some of the same type of criticism which was directed against them during the Cultural Revolution.

How do these targets for 1985 compare with current holdings? According to recent (June 1979) State Statistical Bureau figures, China had, in 1978, 557,000 large and medium-sized tractors and 1.37 million hand tractors.[113] Even though it is claimed that 26 out of the 29 provincial units are capable of producing the larger tractors,[114] it is clear that China intends to import a significant proportion of the half million needed to meet the target. It may well be, therefore, that the drain of foreign currency reserves in 1978 explains why the programme of mechanisation is proceeding more slowly than expected. Imports of foreign tractors, however, are probably seen as particularly necessary since the general quality of domestically produced tractors is not high and many complaints have been voiced in the press to that effect.[115] In the near future, one might anticipate that imported modern tractors will rapidly be copied by Chinese factories.

Because tractors are still used for purposes of transportation as well as farming (a major factor in over-use), China will need to increase greatly its supply of farm trucks in the next few years. Since transportation is a year-round activity, it is likely that control over these trucks will remain in the hands of basic level production units. It might also be anticipated that provision for the production and repair of farm implements, which has been built up steadily over the past decade at *xian*, commune and brigade levels, will not be subject to any increase in central control. Doubtless some central planners, appalled at the lack of standardisation in farm equipment[116] resulting from previous programmes of self-reliance, would like to impose greater control, but I fail to see how such control might be achieved. In the meantime, major efforts are being undertaken to boost the supply of farm equipment. In the period 1978-1980, it is planned to increase by 110 per cent the number of machines hauled by large and medium-sized tractors, and the state supply of rolled steel for farm equipment is to be increased by 50 per cent (compared with 1975-7). The state supply of fuel and lubricants for farm machinery is to be 120 per cent more than 1977 and, as has been noted, a major reduction in the purchase price to rural units is envisaged. It is, moreover, planned to double the number of technicians trained to operate and service the machinery.[117] Finally, provision has been made for an adequate supply of electric power for agricultural tasks. In 1963, it was estimated that the mechanisation of agriculture would require some 8 billion kwh.[118] When one considers that some six per cent[119] of China's total electric energy consumption of 257 billion kwh[120] is consumed by agriculture, one may see that this target has been surpassed.

The above strategy for modernisation implies a far greater degree of centralisation in Chinese agriculture than hitherto. This was implicit in what I have referred to as the second period since 1976 and much more explicit after the promulgation of the new 'sixty articles' in the third period after December 1978. The new stress on specialisation, new provisions for rural finance, considerations of the profitability of rural industries and the logic of mechanisation might be expected to exacerbate inequalities between regions. But this might be a price the Chinese are willing to pay in order to develop the productive forces to a degree sufficient to advance to a more socialist form of society. It was Mao's view, however, that one could not separate means and ends in such a way since they interacted dialectically and it is significant that Mao's post-1957 economic policies are under implicit attack following the reinterpretation of Peng Dehuai's criticism of the Great Leap Forward.[121] To understand fully, however, the local structure of inequalities which the new strategy might produce, we must now turn to an examination of the rural administrative system.

The Rural Administrative System

China's present leadership claims that the 'Gang of Four' favoured a policy of centralising administration within the communes. By prematurely upgrading the unit of account, imbalance was created between the various components of the 'three level system of ownership' and production suffered.[122] Since the demise of the 'Gang', therefore, efforts have been directed toward restoring this balance and guaranteeing the integrity of the teams. Before evaluating this, it is necessary to describe the current rural organisational structure. This is set out in Tables 4.1 and 4.2.

Table 4.1: The Three Sectors of Agriculture

	Area Farmed	No. of Persons	Labour Force	Land /Pop.	Land/Labour Force
State	4mha[a]	13m[b]	5m[c]	0.3ha	0.8ha
Collective	91mha	744m	280m	0.1ha	0.32ha
Private	5mha[d]				
	100mha[e]	757m[f]	285m[g]	0.13ha	0.35ha

Sources:

a. *RMRB* 26 January 1978, p. 2.

b. Five million workers multiplied by the ratio of the total rural population to the rural workforce (i.e. 757 ÷ 285).

c. *RMRB* 26 January 1978, p. 2.

d. In 1966, five per cent of arable land in most teams was given over to private plots, NCNA 19 February 1966, *SCMP* 3644, p. 26. There is no evidence that this proportion has changed significantly. See NCNA 10 November 1978, *SWB* FE/5971/B11/17.

e. CCP. CC *Zhongfa* 4 (1979), *Issues and Studies*, Vol. XV, No. 7, July 1979, p. 109.

f. State Statistical Bureau 27 June 1979, p. 9. Figure multiplied by 79 per cent to exclude urban dwellers.

g. Deng Xiaoping (18 March 1978, *PR* 12, 24 March 1978, p. 12) stated that the average output per farm worker was one tonne. Since grain output was about 285 million tonnes in 1977, one may deduce that the rural labour force was 285 million. A similar figure (286 million) is reached by multiplying the number of communes (54,000) by the labour force per commune (5,300), *Shehuizhuyi Zhengzhi Jingji xue* 1975, p. 76. Li Xiannian (22 July 1978, NCNA 15 August 1978; *SWB* FE/5897/B11/14) spoke of over 300 million and this was echoed by Yu Qiuli in June 1979, *SWB* FE/6155/C1/4.

Table 4.2: The Collective and Private Sectors of Agriculture

	Av. Area Farmed, Collective	Av. Area Farmed, Private[a]					
China	91mha	5mha	No. in China				
Commune	1,700ha[b]	85ha	54,000[c]	Av. No. in Commune			
Brigade	147ha	7ha	680,000[d]	13	Av. No. in Brigade		
Team	21ha	1ha	4.8m[e]	90	7	Av. No. in Team	
Household	6,000 sq. metres	300 sq. metres	169m[f]	2,900[g]	250	35[h]	Av. No. in Household
Labour Force Units	3,500 sq. metres	175 sq. metres	280m	5,300[i]	410	58	1.7
Individuals	1,300 sq. metres	65 sq. metres	744m	14,000[j]	1,100	154	4.4[k]

Sources:

a. This column is five per cent of the total area for each collective unit.

b. 91 million hectares ÷ 54,000.

c. 1973 figure. *Shehuizhuyi Zhengzhi Jingji xue* 1975, p. 76.

d. *RMRB* 26 February 1979, p. 1.

e. Ibid.

f. 744 million ÷ 4.4.

g. *Shehuizhuyi Zhengzhi Jingji xue* 1975, p. 76.

h. Ibid., p. 89, gives a figure of 'over 30'. 35 is derived from 169 million ÷ 4.8 million.

i. Ibid., p. 76.

j. 744 million ÷ 54,000

k. US Congress, Joint Economic Committee 1975, p. 409. For some other figures, see Croll 1977(b), pp. 790-1.

It will immediately be apparent, from Tables 4.1 and 4.2, that the average size and population per unit is much smaller than most of the units visited by foreigners on short trips to China. This would indicate that suburban communes (the most accessible) are significantly larger than those far from the cities. Indeed, there seems to be considerable variation in the size of communes. It is, moreover, extremely difficult to work out any precise relationship between communes and traditional marketing areas, since the size of the communes appears to have been increased significantly in the late-1960s (the number being reduced from some 75,000 to 54,000). Similarly, it is very difficult to discover any clear relationship between brigades, teams and natural villages. Sometimes a natural village is organised as a brigade and sometimes as a team.[123] Considerable research needs to be done on this question if we are to be able to make any meaningful generalisations about future changes in the unit of account.

Judging from the political economy textbook produced in Shanghai under its aegis, the attitude of the 'Gang of Four' towards the system of commune ownership was most cautious:

> The three level system of ownership within rural people's communes, which takes the team as the basic accounting unit, is able to integrate the different levels of development and different requirements of the productive forces in the countryside ... (It has), therefore, very great flexibility and superiority and must be maintained stable and unchanged for a quite long period of time.[124]

Such a position, which would be endorsed heartily by Deng Xiaoping, held that any future changes would be dependent upon the development of the productive forces; these were described as 'the most active element in social production'. What was on the current agenda was not the large-scale transfer of the unit of account from team to brigade level but the appropriate management of quantitative changes consequent upon the development of these productive forces.[125] Quantitative changes here refer to changes in the relative income generated at different levels. Table 4.3 shows these changes in income in Shanghai suburban communes for the period 1970-4 and they are contrasted with 1977 national figures and those for a less affluent provincial unit (Jilin, 1978).

Table 4.3 shows that communes in Shanghai municipality were quite atypical. In that region, in 1975, 34.2 per cent of the total collective assets were held at commune level and 15.1 per cent at brigade level.[126] This, however, was well below the minimum set

*Table 4.3: Percentage of Income Generated in the 'Three Level'
System of Ownership in Rural Communes*

	Shanghai 1970[a]	Shanghai 1974[b]	National 1977[c]	Jilin 1978[d]
	%	%	%	%
Commune	10+	30.5		14.6
			23	
Brigade	5	17.2		
Team	80+	52.3	77	85.4

Sources:
a. *Shehuizhuyi Zhengzhi Jingji xue* 1975, p. 90.
b. Ibid. These figures are also in Zhang Chunqiao, *PR* 14, 4 April 1975, p. 8.
c. *PR* 4, 27 January 1978, p. 30. Note: this figure refers to income from industries. This is the main form of brigade and commune income but not the only form. Sometimes brigades and communes take responsibility for a limited amount of grain production (which, in this case, is referred to as a sideline activity).
d. Changchun, Jilin Radio, 16 February 1978, *SWB* FE/5749/B11/5.

down by Mao for transferring the unit of account (i.e. when the bulk of assets were held at the higher level). The 'Gang', therefore, (or Zhang Chunqiao, at least) did not advocate the blanket transfer of the unit of account in that region. Despite the charges, I doubt whether the 'Gang' advocated it in other areas and whether much premature upgrading had occurred since the 'flying leap' of 1969-70. In China as a whole, there are few brigades which constitute basic accounting units. In Jilin, for example, only 698 brigades (5.7 per cent) were so designated in early-1978.[127]

In the period up to the Third Plenum, in December 1978, one gets the impression that few changes occurred concerning the unit of account. The integrity of the production team was stressed, as before, though some moves continued to be made to upgrade units. Indeed, such a policy would fit in well with the new stress on mechanisation. In Jilin, for example, plans were under way, in early-1978, to engage in selective upgrading.[128] In Heilongjiang too, each *xian* was asked to designate two or three places where brigades might become basic accounting units and small groups of people were organised to investigate the task.[129] It was stressed, however, that upgrading might only be undertaken when the productive forces were sufficiently developed. I doubt very much whether, in 1978, the policy-makers in Beijing would have disagreed with the long-term goal articulated in the 1975 Shanghai textbook:

In the future, along with the development of the productive forces and raising the consciousness of commune members, the brigade can become the basic unit of account in the rural people's communes. This will be when the team is unsuitable to act as the basic unit to organise agricultural production ..., when the collective economy of the brigade is strong enough to help and support the lagging teams to develop swiftly and thus to bring about a general evening out of the economic levels among the teams. Then, after a long period of development, one will be able to move from the brigade to the commune as the basic accounting unit.[130]

Eventually, the Shanghai textbook believed, the collective system, with the commune as the basic accounting unit, would be replaced by a system of ownership by the whole people which, presumably, meant the reorganisation of agriculture in the form of state farms.

It is when one looks at state farms that one begins to appreciate the importance of the size of the accounting unit. State farms currently only number some 2,000 (about the same average size as a commune) and farm only 4 out of the 100 million hectares of arable land.[131] They are, however, highly productive and the recent stress on specialisation means that they will enjoy an increasingly disproportionate degree of state investment. In contrast to the collective sector, where the basic unit of account is the team of some thirty-five households, these state farms are themselves basic accounting units defined according to the same economic accounting system (*jingji hesuanzhi*) as industrial enterprises.[132] In line with the new policies introduced after the Third Plenum, which Watson has noted, a system has been promoted in Heilongjiang whereby state farms are allowed to retain 70 per cent of the profits they earn with only 30 per cent going to the state farm bureau. This is the restoration of a system in operation between 1966 and 1968.[133] It will undoubtedly lead to a much greater disparity of wealth between the state farm sector and the collective sector which does not enjoy similar economies of scale. It is significant, in this regard, to note that, following the visit of Hua Guofeng to Yugoslavia in 1978, a farm combine was set up in the Xinjiang Autonomous Region[134] modelled explicitly on agricultural organisations in a country noted for great disparities in rural income which are exacerbated by socialist market relations.

General policy, therefore, has been to stress the autonomy of the accounting unit, be it a huge state farm or a small team. In the collective sector, the integrity of the team has been stressed throughout the whole period since 1976 (and indeed since long before) but there has been a change in emphasis since the Third Plenum. In 1977-8, press comments on the integrity of the team concentrated on such matters as the upward drift of agricultural labour. This was seen as the result of laxness on the part of cadres who, having been cowed by excessive political campaigns, were too scared to adopt tough measures to rectify the situation. To remedy this, work teams were sent down from higher levels of administration.[135] Attempts were made to streamline the operation of brigade and commune level industries, to prune them of excess labour and send that labour back to the teams.[136] Since the Third Plenum, however, attempts have been made to ensure the integrity of the team by strengthening, and making legally enforceable, contractual agreements between various levels of rural organisation and between those rural units and the state.[137] This policy might ensure the optimum distribution of labour but, in the past, when applied to the industrial sector, it gave rise to a number of problems. First, local planning sometimes degenerated into being no more than the rationalisation of inter-unit contracts. Secondly, such a system was able to give a degree of permanency to different systems of payment and different pay scales. This made a uniform wages policy difficult to formulate. Currently, the wages paid by commune enterprises are lower than those paid by state enterprises[138] and brigade and team enterprises operate on a full or a partial work point system (with much lower equivalent wages). The inequalities of such a system are much easier to bear if they are not formulated in a legally enforceable contract system with precedents for institutionalising inequalities. Once the contract system acquires the force of law, 'bourgeois right' is clearly strengthened.

It is, of course, quite apparent that the advocates of 'socialist market relations', who have achieved prominence since the Third Plenum, are not worried about the strengthening of 'bourgeois right'. Indeed, inequalities between teams are actively fostered and teams are told that they should not be afraid of getting rich. Bonuses are given to units for increasing output and, in some areas, these reach ten per cent of annual income.[139] Amid criticism of the old slogan of 'grasping revolution and promoting production',[140] reference is made once again to the 'millionaire brigades' and production teams which appeared in the old days of co-operativisation.[141] Suburban production teams which approach or even surpass the average income of urban workers are praised,[142] without much consideration that the fault line between urban and rural incomes does not occur at the limits of built up areas but at the point where the municipal market garden communes cease.[143] One wonders how the 'Gang of Four' would have responded to the statement: 'the centre has proposed that some peasants should be allowed to become rich before others; this is a great policy'.[144]

In the political climate of 1979, not much of the Dazhai model is left. Over the years, the Dazhai model has been interpreted in different ways — sometimes as a model of self-reliance, sometimes as a model of egalitarianism and, at other times, as a model for mechanisation.[145] Now, it seems that the stress is on opposing the blind adherence to advanced units and opposing the absolutist nature of 'learning from Dazhai'. It is pointed out that anyone in the past who criticised Dazhai was considered a 'capitalist roader'.[146] Doubtless, some fundamentalists might have been guilty of this charge and certainly the Dazhai model was not suitable for complete implementation everywhere, but one cannot help feeling that some of the current ridicule poured on Dazhai and demands for the retirement of Chen Yonggui[147] are unjust.

I noted above that, until the end of 1978, there was little change in policy towards the unit of account. In the aftermath of the Third Plenum, however, measures were taken in some areas to deprive brigades of independent accounting status[148] and much was said about the disintegration of production teams. This latter phenomenon is largely a consequence of new patterns of remuneration within teams. Before discussing it, therefore, something must be said about the mechanics of team distribution.

Before distribution work begins in a team, state tax agencies make calculations concerning team 'needs'. Usually four calculations are made. The first of these, under the heading of 'consumption needs', consists of multiplying a stipulated per capita ration (which varies between areas) by the team's population. This is then added to calculations for seed stock and livestock fodder (worked out according to a regional norm). Finally a calculation is made for agricultural tax. This is based upon a fixed assessment for yields in a normal year and is changed relatively infrequently in order that increased production should be reflected in reduced tax burdens.

There has been no general reassessment of tax burdens since 1971[149] and not very much change since 1965 though the Second Session of the Fifth National People's Congress, in June 1979, talked about an impending reduction[150] in some areas. Currently, state agricultural tax is about 3-5 per cent of output and levies made by the brigade for management expenses constitute up to another 5 per cent.[151] If these officially determined 'needs' are lower than output, the team is considered to have a 'surplus', of which the state may purchase up to 90 per cent. It will do so according to a planned quota (adjusted usually every five years) with a fixed price and will pay substantially more for what is purchased above that quota. Available for distribution, therefore, are the proceeds of this sale, the grain already earmarked as 'consumption needs', the surplus not purchased by the state, the income from team industries and compensation paid to the team for the use of team labour by brigade and higher level industries.[152] Before this distribution takes place, however, the team makes deductions for loan repayments and (according to set formulae) administrative expenses, the capital accumulation fund, the welfare fund and sometimes a contingency fund. What remains is distributed to individual households.

In recent years, four kinds of method of team distribution have been used. The first of these is an egalitarian system of distribution based on work attendance. According to this method, the same number of work points is awarded to all those who turn up for work, regardless of output, though this work-point allocation might be varied after discussion at team meetings. Not since the Great Leap Forward has there been any general advocacy of the 'communist' policy of 'payment according to need' though this is the nearest thing to it. Here, the 'socialist' principle of 'payment according to work' is interpreted solely on the basis of attendance. This method was said to have been particularly favoured by the 'Gang of Four' since it lowered income differentials (and consequently restricted 'bourgeois right').[153] It has, of course, been rejected by the present leadership which has adopted a more rigid interpretation of the socialist principle of 'payment according to work'.[154]

The second method is one of payment according to fixed grades. Peasants are classified into grades according to skill and work capacity and work points are attached to each grade. This is much the same as the time-work method of payment for industrial workers except in two very important respects. First, it is work points which are awarded and not wages and, secondly, grading is arrived at as a result of discussion. The problem of assigning grades in the rural sector, therefore, is much more complicated than in the industrial sector where there are guidelines laid down by the state and periodic mass promotions to higher grades. As was suggested earlier, a particular problem seems to have been the grading of rusticated intellectual youth who frequently complained that they were assigned to the lowest grade.[155] Women also might find themselves assigned to grades lower than men though press articles have gone to great pains to show that women are, on the whole, much better off when assigned to fixed grades than when they were subject to assessment by (male) discussion.[156] Though moderately favoured by the present leadership, this system might provoke a degree of tension and it is for this reason that the fixed grade system has been sometimes supplemented by meetings which might alter assessment determined strictly by grades. Needless to say, such a system was unlikely to find favour with supporters of the 'Gang of Four' who saw the (industrial) eight grade system as a breeding ground for 'bourgeois right'.[157]

The third method awards work points solely on the basis of team discussions. It is, therefore, the best method for accommodating considerations of 'labour attitude'. Clearly, however, such discussions cannot take place without norms for payment and these norms will tend over time to provide the basis for a system of grading. This seems to be what happened to the original Dazhai system of remuneration. In Dazhai, norms were originally set by pace-setters (1962) and peasants discussed what they thought they were worth according to these norms. When a work team visited Dazhai in 1964, it was clear that the system had not yet developed into a formal system of grading and the method was criticised for failing to distinguish between slackers and those who worked hard.[158] Such criticisms were dismissed as 'revisionist' in the Cultural Revolution but it appears that, in the 1970s, the Dazhai system of remuneration was interpreted as a form of grading plus discussion. The original Dazhai system is said to have depended upon a high level of political consciousness and would seem to run counter to the current interpretation of 'payment according to work'. I doubt very much, therefore, whether the criticisms of the 1964 work team would still be regarded as 'revisionist'.

The fourth method of remuneration consists of varieties of piecework. Ideally, this consists in the distribution of team income according to the amount of work points amassed during the year by each person or group, when these work points are determined exclusively by the completion of quantified jobs. Since this method requires assigning a point value to every job of work and consequently very complicated methods of calculation, its use was not widespread.[159] In the past, piece-work was objected to on ideological grounds in that it encouraged the application of the 'responsibility system' in the rural sector. This system, which was first applied in industry in the early-1950s, was experimented with in agriculture in the 1960s and was vehemently denounced in the Cultural Revolution as one of the 'crimes' of Tao Zhu.[160] The main danger of such a system, it was felt, was that it militated against team solidarity and it was, of course, opposed by the 'Gang of Four'.[161] In 1977-8, however, this system was promoted once again[162] and piece-work methods were experimented with.

In 1977-8, attempts were made to combine piece-work with some of the other methods. Sometimes, it was combined with the discussion method.[163] At other times, it might apply only to part of the distribution whilst the remainder was made according to the basic ration (which figures in the initial state calculations). Sometimes, piece-work payment applied to only 20 per cent of distribution[164] though attempts were made to enlarge the proportion and 30 per cent became more common.[165]

The main problem of piece-work, in the countryside, is how to designate the piece-work unit. Individual piece-work is often just too difficult to implement and usually piece-work groups are formed. But what should the constituency of these groups be? There is a long tradition of labour contracting (*baogong*) in China and it is significant that, during the Great Leap Forward, groups were formed to undertake specific tasks for which they were rewarded collectively. In 1977-8, the same situation occurred and self-organised capital construction teams formed and entered into contracts with permanent production units. Such groups, which were independent of the teams and removed labour from them, were soon dissolved[166] and permanent groups of piece-workers were formed within the teams. These groups were often assigned a portion of land and a number of work points (labour days) for completing certain targets.[167] As one might expect, these work groups sometimes consisted of individual households or members of the same lineage[168] and constituted, in 1979, a restoration of an important element in the *sanziyibao* formula, attributed to Liu Shaoqi and denounced in the Cultural Revolution.

Ever since the adoption of these piece-work groups, the Party has gone to great pains to insist that they should not consist of households and members of the same lineage, nor should a pursuit of higher income lead to the formation of teams of able-bodied peasants which left the poorer groups consisting exclusively of old people and children.[169] Under no circumstances was it permitted to divide up the land and abolish the production team.[170] Nevertheless, numerous accounts of the impending disintegration of teams appeared from different parts of the country in early 1979 and the Party responded with a firm hand. Judging from the tone of Party criticism, I do not foresee, in the near future, any decentralisation of the unit of account lower than the team though it cannot be denied that the permanent division of the team into work groups will hinder its cohesion.

What is lost in terms of cohesion, however, will be partly offset by ease in accounting. The confused situation in the Chinese countryside in recent years has led to some very poor accounting and local Party efforts have been directed towards improving it. A major problem exists in the 'draw-as-you-earn' system whereby households are entitled to the basic ration throughout the year. This is then adjusted when final calculations are made at the end of the year. The system has worked on the assumption that only the basic ration would be drawn, though it appears that peasants often drew more than the basic ration and were in debt to the team once final calculations were made. The problem of the 'overdrawing household' sometimes became quite serious. In Yunnan province, for example, 1977 accounts showed that 30 per cent of households were overdrawn with the cumulative debt of ¥137 million.[171] In 1978, major efforts were made to ensure the repayment of overdrafts and to promote peasant solvency.[172] Many of the press articles made much of the extravagant expenditure of cadres who negotiated loans which they could not repay and sometimes took bribes;[173] doubtless the credit system has been much abused. There remains the problem, however, of how the ordinary peasant in difficulties or who seeks to raise the money to build a house (which can cost over ¥1,000)[174] will get along in the new credit squeeze and press articles have urged caution when demanding debt repayment.[175] But this is a problem familiar to people in most countries.

The problem of accounting has, of course, not been helped by what seems to be a very substantial increase in private sector activity in 1978 and 1979. The importance of the private sector in the Chinese rural economy must not be underestimated. Sideline activities supplement food and provide raw materials for local handicraft production. The private plots (though only some 300 square metres on average)[176] produce most of the rural households' vegetable supply (estimated on average at about 400 kg per annum)[177] and quite a substantial proportion of the nation's livestock. Most of the 94 million draught animals are not privately owned but some of the 170 million sheep and goats are.[178] More important still, some 73 per cent of the country's 301 million pigs are raised privately[179] (compared with 83 per cent in 1956).[180] It has been estimated that livestock production constitutes some 13.9 per cent of the gross value of agricultural production[181] and I would not be surprised if half of this were privately generated. We do not have enough information to assess, with any degree of confidence, the contribution of the private plot to peasant incomes and it is always very difficult to define income at the point where the institutional and domestic modes of production intersect. One United States estimate, however, has put forward the tentative figure of between five and ten per cent.[182]

A certain amount of evidence was published in 1977-8 which indicated that there were continued attempts by local cadres to restrict the private sector. For example, peasants were sometimes prevented from gathering wild fruit, grass for animal fodder, wood for baskets and herbs for indigenous medicine.[183] They were also criticised for keeping too many animals on their private plots.[184] Such attempts, which resemble those of the 'flying leap' of 1969-70, were vigorously condemned and, of course, such activities were blamed on the 'Gang of Four'. In so far as the 'Gang's' position might be inferred from the Shanghai textbook, it was not in fact all that radical:

> In addition to the collective economy, which occupies the dominant position in our country's rural people's communes, there also remain the commune members' private plots and their household sideline activities. Being dependent on the system of collective ownership, these supplement the socialist economy. It is necessary to permit commune members to manage small-scale private plots and household sideline activities in a situation where the productive forces of the rural collective economy are not at a high level and where there is a need to supplement certain requirements for (the people's) livelihood. It is necessary also in order to guarantee the development and absolute superiority of the

communes' collective economy. By doing this, one may make ample use of the rural labour force to increase social production, improve the commune members' livelihood and raise their income. It will also help the development of brisk rural markets.[185]

The above would suggest that the 'Gang' had no intention of severely restricting the private sector. It is clear, however, that it had no illusion about the social nature of the private sector and may have been a trifle concerned about its expansion.

> But when it comes down to considering the character of private plots and household sideline activities, they (must be seen as) a remnant of an individualised economy. This remnant of a system of small-scale private ownership provides soil for the generation of capitalism. Because of this, one must not fail to analyse the character of the private plots and household sideline activities and the necessity for their existence at this stage. One cannot abolish them prematurely but neither can one gloss over the contradictions between them and the collective economy. Nor can one adopt a *laissez faire* attitude, sit down and watch the flood of spontaneous capitalist forces attack the socialist economy. We must maintain, in combination, both socialist principles and flexibility. On the one hand, we must limit the negative function of the private plots and household sideline activities and, on the other, must foster their correct function of supplementing (the collective economy).[186]

Though I doubt whether the present leadership would disagree too strongly with the theoretical import of the above quotation, I suspect that the emphasis is far more radical than they would like.[187] This is not to say, however, that the association of cadre excesses and the 'Gang of Four' is, in any way, proven. To make that association we want to know just what the connection between the 'Gang' and its 'agents' was. We also want to know whether the alleged instances of the collapse of the collective economy in the countryside were a reaction against a 'commandist' leadership, which wanted to restrict the private sector, or whether the 'collapse' antedated the action of the 'Gang's' 'agents'. In many cases, I suspect it was the latter. How else can one make sense of articles which stated that speculation, embezzlement, dividing up the collective land and the excessive encouragement of sideline activities was not so much a reaction against the 'Gang' but carried out at its direct instigation?[188]

As I see it, the main bone of contention between the 'Gang' and the present leadership was not so much the existence of the private sector but the expansion of its activity. In 1978, efforts were made to stimulate that sector and to encourage sideline activities. Reports from Sichuan, for example, spoke of special bonuses being given for eggs and pigs sold to the state. For every kilogram of eggs sold to the state, peasants received coupons for one kilogram of rice or four ounces of sugar. For every pig they received coupons for 25 kilograms of rice and two feet of cloth.[189] The authorities have even tolerated some private trading of grain. It appears also that market prices are allowed to prevail and no attempt is made by the state to set prices for the sale of goods produced on the private plots.[190] All this has led to a rapid expansion of private trading. In 1979, it was announced that 30,000 rural trade fairs had been restored and surveys of 206 such fairs in 28 provincial level units showed that the total volume of transactions for the fourth quarter of 1978 had increased by 30 per cent over the same period the previous year.[191] In Tianjin municipality, the 18 former rural markets (which had been reduced to four under the alleged influence of Lin Biao and the 'Gang')[192] were restored and everywhere there were reports of increased private trading.

Whether it was out of fear that such an increase in private activity might reveal a tendency towards capitalism or out of concern for strict rural accounting, efforts were made in the first half of 1979 to impose some kind of control over the burgeoning local markets,[193] and it is likely that such activities might contribute to the general feeling of uncertainty which prevails in the countryside. It is probable that peasants are unsure about what prices to ask for their produce and they are not always confident that the current level of state prices will be maintained. In Zhuzhou in Hunan province, for example, the state price for pigs was raised, in the spirit of the resolutions of the Third Plenum in early-1979, and peasants crowded the procurement stations to sell their pigs just in case the price fell once again. In the panic, several pigs were said to have died.[194] One can, indeed, understand the concern of cadres who wish to see some appropriate balance reached between state and private trading and, therefore, some long-term price stability.

Conclusion

The uncertainty in the Chinese countryside extends far beyond price instability and apprehension on the part of the ten million rural cadres[195] at being urged to encourage activities which have been frowned upon in the past. At the heart of the matter is the old question of liberty and equality. As the 'Gang of Four' saw it, the liberty which exists in a socialist transitional society is much the same as in a capitalist society — equal rights are given to people made unequal by their economic location. To prevent these inequalities becoming entrenched and the basis for the formation of new classes, liberty for some had to be curtailed. But such liberty could only be curtailed with the active support of the majority of peasants and with their consultation and participation. Despite its good intentions, there is every indication that this aspect of the Mass Line was not pursued during the 'Gang's' period of dominance and peasants could welcome the greater degree of democracy which accompanied its overthrow. In the last two years, new organs of government have been elected in many rural production units without a predetermined Party ticket and apparently with much mass support.[196]

In addition to greater democracy, the new leadership has offered greater material incentive. Despite the claims that one-tenth of the Chinese population had insufficient grain in 1977,[197] it would seem that the majority of peasants are materially much better off than they were in 1976. Some indication of this is given in the claim that the average per capita income of peasants in the collective sector went up from ¥65.0 in 1977 to ¥73.9 in 1978.[198] Greater formal democracy and greater income have no doubt done much to legitimise a programme of rural economic development which can only lead to much greater inequalities. No student of development, who has studied the literature on diffusion, can doubt that the present Chinese leadership's faith in the 'trickle-down effect' from the richer areas is naïve. In this chapter, I have discussed policies which discriminate in favour of high yielding areas, the new logic of profitability, the rationalisation of local industry and the winding-down of China's unique experiment to send educated youth to the countryside. All these constitute a reversal of policy but it would be naïve to believe that the set of policies which have been superseded were without problems. 'Self-reliance', too, led to inequalities (though probably less serious ones). The former policies did not get the best out of each area, and the logic whereby every region was required to be self-sufficient in grain was sometimes economically irrational. But was it politically rational or perhaps highly rational from a defence point of view? In this chapter, I have not disguised my preference for the former policy of integrated self-reliant development nor my sympathy for the argument about 'bourgeois right'. But one could have wished that its adherents had been more practical, more democratic and more in tune with the Mass Line politics advocated by Mao since the 1940s.

A lot of the criticism of the 'Gang of Four' must be taken with a pinch of salt and no serious scholar may take at face value the portrayal of the inane clownings of Jiang Qing as she attempted to establish Xiaojinzhuang as an alternative to Dazhai.[199] To establish the 'Gang's' position, therefore, I have relied on a political economy textbook produced, it is said, under the aegis of Zhang Chunqiao in Shanghai. Despite the current distortions, I am inclined to believe some of the charges of excessive 'commandism' in the countryside in the early-1970s and, though one cannot assign all the blame to the 'Gang', it does seem to have stemmed from some of the 'ultra-leftist' behaviour manifested in the Cultural Revolution.

This chapter has argued that two sorts of policy position emerged during the second and third periods since the demise of the 'Gang'. One of these took its cue from the mid-1950s and the other from the early-1960s. At the moment, the second view is dominant and, as Sullivan argues, this is surely associated with the restoration to high office of Chen Yun. The other view, which was dominant through the second half of 1977 and much of 1978 and may more closely reflect the position of Hua Guofeng, must still be powerful and may moderate the new emphasis on 'socialist market relations'. The reiteration of the early-1960s view in 1979 cannot be unconnected with the political demise of Chen Yonggui — the architect of Dazhai, who on my visit to Dazhai in 1966 impressed upon me that there was a distinctive Chinese approach to agricultural development and that economic rationality only had meaning in terms of particular sets of values. The set of values, which was manifest in the original Dazhai model, was assailed both from the 'ultra-left' in the Cultural Revolution and from the right in 1979. It might yet survive the injunction to stop talking about 'grasping revolution and promoting production'.

Notes

1. A slightly different version of this chapter was presented at a seminar at the Australian National University, Canberra, in June 1979 and will appear in a book on peasant policies to be edited by A. Chan. My thanks to all participants in the seminar and also to D. Woodward.

2. Hua Guofeng, 15 October 1975, *PR* 44, 31 October 1975, pp. 7-10 and 18.

3. See, e.g., Hua Guofeng, 25 December 1976, *PR* 1, January 1977, pp. 31-44.

4. Hua Guofeng, 15 October 1975, *PR* 44, 31 October 1975, p. 10.

5. *RMRB* 11 December 1977, p. 1.

6. Hua Guofeng, 15 October 1975, *PR* 44, 31 October 1975, pp. 8-9.

7. These bodies still exist (see *RMRB* 15 February 1978, p. 1) but do not seem to be very active.

8. NCNA 31 January 1978, *SWB* FE/5731/B11/16; NCNA 2 August 1978, *SWB* FE/5887/B11/1; Lanzhou, Gansu Radio, 4 August 1978, *SWB* FE/5887/B11/9.

9. NCNA 24 January 1978, *SWB* FE/5723/B11/15; Beijing Radio, 23 November 1978, *SWB* FE/5980/B11/1-3.

10. Yao Wenyuan, *PR* 10, 7 March 1975, pp. 5-10; Zhang Chunqiao, *PR* 14, 4 April 1975, pp. 5-11.

11. E.g. *PR* 3, 20 January 1978, pp. 5-9 and 10-13.

12. *RMRB* 19 January 1978, p. 1; NCNA 9 February 1978, *SWB* FE/5738/B11/1-6; Changchun, Jilin Radio, 23 December 1978, *SWB* FE/6014/B11/15.

13. See *GMRB* 17 March 1979, p. 4.

14. See NCNA 2 January 1979, *SWB* FE/6008/B11/7; *BR* 7, 16 February 1979, pp. 8-10.

15. See Hu Qiaomu, July 1978, *PR* 45, 10 November 1978, pp. 7-12; *PR* 46, 17 November 1978, pp. 15-23.

16. These two documents are 'Decisions of the Central Committee of the Communist Party of China on Some Questions Concerning the Acceleration of Agricultural Development' (CCP. CC *Zhongfa* 4 (1979), *Issues and Studies,* Vol. XV, No. 7, July 1979, pp. 102-19; ibid., No. 8, August 1979, pp. 91-9) and 'Regulations on Work in the Rural People's Communes (Draft for Trial Use)' (ibid., No. 8, August 1979, pp. 100-12; No. 9, September 1979, pp. 104-15).

17. See Schurmann 1966, pp. 175-6.

18. *PR* 5, 3 February 1978, p. 31; *PR* 26, 30 June 1978, pp. 10-12.

19. CCP. CC *Zhongfa* 4 (1979), *Issues and Studies*, Vol. XV, No. 7, July 1979, pp. 105 and 109. Note: the translation is in error.

20. Ibid, p. 113.

21. Hua Guofeng, 26 February 1978, *PR* 10, 10 March 1978, p. 19.

22. NCNA (29 September 1977, *SWB* FE/W950/A/11) announced, for 1976, a 158 per cent increase in rice production since 1949. The official 1949 figure was 48.65 million tonnes (State Statistical Bureau 1960, p. 119).

23. Official figure. See State Statistical Bureau 27 June 1979, p. 4.

24. Smil 1978, p. 70.

25. NCNA 29 September 1977, *SWB* FE/W950/A/12.

26. Hua Guofeng, 15 October 1975, *PR* 44, 31 October 1975, p. 8.

27. NCNA 29 September 1977, *SWB* FE/W950/A/11.

28. NCNA 29 September 1977, *SWB* FE/W950/A/12. The total area is 13 million hectares, NCNA 18 August 1977, *SWB* FE/W944/A/4.

29. *PR* 23, 9 June 1978, p. 5; Mao Zedong, 9 October 1957, *SW*, Vol. V, p. 486.

30. Erisman 1978, p. 23; (the 1976 estimate was 50 but this fell to 43 in 1977 due to drought). Stavis (1976, p. 91) estimates 45 for 1974.

31. 1974 estimate (Stavis 1976, p. 91). The highest yield is 3.5 tonnes/hectare and the lowest 0.8.

32. Hua Guofeng, 15 October 1975, *PR* 44, 31 October 1975, p. 8.
33. *PR* 23, 9 June 1978, p. 5; Mao Zedong, 9 October 1957, *SW*, Vol. V, p. 486.
34. Hua Guofeng, 15 October 1975, *PR* 44, 31 October 1975, p. 8.
35. *PR* 23, 9 June 1978, p. 5; Mao Zedong, 9 October 1957, *SW*, Vol. V, p. 486.
36. Smil 1978, p. 70.
37. These estimates in ibid., p. 71 and in Dernberger 1978, p. 75.
38. Smil 1978, p. 70.
39. Because of the complexities of calculation, it is impossible to say with any confidence what the production of this crop might be. Stavis estimates 22 million tonnes for 1974. Erisman's (1978) estimate for 1977 is 27.8 million tonnes.
40. *RMRB* 24 March 1979, p. 1.
41. State Statistical Bureau 27 June 1979, p. 4.
42. NCNA 13 April 1979, *SWB* FE/6095/B11/16.
43. *RMRB* 28 February 1979, p. 1; Beijing Radio, 16 April 1979, *SWB* FE/6096/B11/1.
44. Text in *RMRB* 27 February 1979, p. 2.
45. Ibid., and *RMRB* 27 February 1979, p. 1, editorial.
46. NCNA 6 March 1979, *SWB* FE/6061/B11/3.
47. These two figures are derived from Beijing Radio, 16 April 1979, *SWB* FE/6096/B11/2, (3,800 million *mu*), and 30 per cent of 9.6 million sq. km.
48. Beijing Radio, 16 April 1979, *SWB* FE/6096/B11/2.
49. See *PR* 37, 2 September 1975, p. 25.
50. *RMRB* 11 December 1977, p. 2.
51. NCNA 23 November 1977, *SWB* FE/5682/B11/17.
52. CCP, 11th CC, 3rd Plenum, communiqué, 22 December 1977, *PR* 52, 29 December 1978, p. 13.
53. Yu Qiuli, 26 January 1978, *PR* 7, 17 February 1978, p. 9, and *SWB* FE/5727/B11/11. The 3rd plenum anticipated this reduction would be 10 to 15 per cent in 1979-80. CCP.CC 3rd plenum communiqué, 22 December 1978, *PR* 52, 29 December 1978, p. 13.
54. This is the tentative hypothesis reached by Dernberger (1978, pp. 93-7).
55. NCNA 2 March 1979, *SWB* FE/6061/B11/11-12.
56. See Perkins 1976, pp. 603-4.
57. See *PR* 14, 7 April 1978, p. 8.
58. See the discussion in Dernberger 1978, p. 85.
59. *RMRB* 17 April 1979, p. 3. See also Yu Qiuli, 21 June 1979, *SWB* FE/6155/C1/7.
60. Beijing Radio, 27 April 1979, *SWB* FE/6107/B11/5-8.
61. CCP. CC *Zhongfa* 4 (1979), *Issues and Studies*, Vol. XV, No. 7, July 1979, p. 114.
62. Dernberger 1978, p. 75.
63. *PR* (50, 15 December 1978, pp. 4-5) gives a figure of 48. At the Second Session of the 5th National People's Congress, Yu Qiuli announced a figure of 42, Yu Qiuli, 21 June 1979, *SWB* FE/6160/C/3. The State Statistical Bureau's figures (27 June 1979, p. 2) talk in terms of a figure of 8.7 million tonnes counted on the basis of 100 per cent effectiveness.
64. Erisman 1975, p. 334; Sigurdson 1975, p. 416.
65. Sigurdson 1975, p. 417.
66. See *PR* 49, 8 December 1978, pp. 17-18.
67. Wong 1978.
68. *RMRB* 17 October 1977, p. 4.
69. CCP. CC *Zhongfa* 4 (1979) gives a figure of 47 per cent for 1978. It was planned to increase this to 60 per cent (900 million *mu*) by 1985. *Issues and Studies*, Vol. XV, No. 7, July 1979, p. 113.

70. *PR* (1, 3 January 1975, p. 11) reported that 1.3 million wells had been dug. It is estimated that these are being added to at a rate of 200,000 per annum.

71. NCNA 19 March 1978, *SWB* FE/W977/A/5.

72. The opinion of one member of the U.S. Water Resources Delegation was that full control of the Yellow River would be achieved within 50 years (cited in Perkins 1976, p. 607).

73. Tianjin Radio, 10 April 1979, *SWB* FE/6102/B11/14.

74. Yu Qiuli, 21 June 1979, *SWB* FE/6150/C/2.

75. State Statistical Bureau 27 June 1979, p. 5.

76. See Table 4.1, note g.

77. State Statistical Bureau 27 June 1979, p. 9. The figure given is 975,230,000 and includes the population of Taiwan. The Taiwan figure (17 million) has been subtracted.

78. Ibid. The target announced by Hua Guofeng is 1 per cent. Hua Guofeng, 26 February 1978, *PR* 10, 10 March 1978, p. 29.

79. Smil 1978, p. 8.

80. See Kang Keqing, *PR* 39, 29 September 1978, pp. 5-11; Wan Li, *Hongqi* 3, 1978, p. 95; Jinan, Shandong Radio, 23 March 1978, *SWB* FE/5775/B11/9.

81. See Croll 1977(a).

82. *Shehuizhuyi Zhengzhi Jingji xue* 1975, p. 76.

83. Hua Guofeng (15 October 1975) noted that 100 million people had taken part in this work in each of the preceding four years (*PR* 44, 31 October 1975, p. 8). In the winter-spring period 1975-6, 150 million were involved, NCNA 27 December 1976, *SWB* FE/W911/A/2. In 1976-7, another 100 million took part, NCNA 4 February 1978, *SWB* FE/W916/A/1.

84. Plant Studies Delegation, cited in Dernberger 1978, p. 77.

85. E.g. *RMRB* 3 September 1977, p. 1; Wuhan, Hubei Radio, 26 January 1968, *SWB* FE/5730/B11/11.

86. Chengdu, Sichuan Radio, 30 April 1977, *SWB* FE/5504/B11/13. Ji Dengkui (1 August 1978, NCNA 17 August 1978, *SWB* FE/5899/B11/5) stipulated that, in the winter mass farmland construction campaigns, not more than 30 per cent of the available labour power should take part and that these campaigns should be limited to 50-70 days.

87. Lanzhou, Gansu Radio, 20 July 1977, *SWB* FE/5570/B11/2.

88. Chen Yonggui (NCNA 14 December 1978, *SWB* 5997/B11/5) gave a figure of 17 million. Of these, 900,000 had married and settled down permanently. NCNA (24 January 1978) gave a figure of 16 million (*SWB* FE/5723/B11/15). Of these, 10 million were said still to be in the countryside.

89. Bernstein 1977, p. 87 and pp. 100-3. Not more than 15 per cent achieved positions of authority.

90. At least half of all educated youth in 1973 were in separate youth villages, ibid., p. 79.

91. According to Chen Yonggui, NCNA 14 December 1978, *SWB* FE/5997/B11/5.

92. Bernstein 1977, pp. 89-90.

93. The settlement fee provided by the state was ¥230. It was later raised to ¥480 or ¥530. See Bernstein 1977, pp. 85-6 and 101.

94. Ibid., p. 90.

95. Ibid., pp. 91-107.

96. Beijing Radio, 25 January 1978, *SWB* FE/5725/B11/3.

97. NCNA 24 January 1978, *SWB* FE/5723/B11/15.

98. Beijing Radio, 23 November 1978, *SWB* FE/5980/B11/1-13.

99. See NCNA 14 December 1978, *SWB* FE/5997/B11/1-5.

100. Harbin, Heilongjiang Radio, 4 April 1979, *SWB* FE/6090/B11/7-8.

101. *RMRB* 11 December 1977, p. 1.

102. Some one million city doctors have gone to the countryside in the past few years, NCNA 7 March 1977, *SWB* FE/W920/A/1.

103. NCNA 7 March 1977, *SWB* FE/W920/A/1. One third of these were women. In addition there were 3.9 million paramedical workers and midwives.

104. Commoner 1975.

105. Hua Guofeng, 26 February 1978, *PR* 10, 10 March 1978, p. 29.

106. Hua Guofeng, 15 October 1975, *PR* 44, 31 October 1975, p. 10.

107. *PR* 50, 12 December 1975, p. 20.

108. Hua Guofeng, 26 February 1978, *PR* 10, 10 March 1978, p. 19. The official documents of late 1978 lowered the figure to 80 per cent. CCP. CC *Zhongfa* 4 (1979), *Issues and Studies*, Vol. XV, No. 7, July 1979, p. 114.

109. *Shehuizhuyi Zhengzhi Jingji xue* 1975, p. 200.

110. This was expressed as one standard tractor for every 1,500 *mu*. Liu Rixin, *RMRB* 20 June 1963, p. 5. Strangely, this author takes the cultivatable area to be 80 million hectares and calculates that 800,000 tractors would be needed.

111. Li Xiannian, 22 July 1978, NCNA 15 August 1978, *SWB* FE/5897/B11/9-10.

112. Yu Qiuli, cited in *PR* 7, 17 February 1978, p. 9.

113. State Statistical Bureau 27 June 1979, p. 5.

114. *PR* 8, 24 February 1978, p. 11.

115. E.g. *RMRB* 12 May 1977, p. 3; *RMRB* 6 January 1978, p. 3; *PR* 36, 8 September 1978, p. 21. According to the State Statistical Bureau (27 June 1979, p. 5), the availability of tractors in good condition was only 70 per cent on average.

116. *Hongqi* 2, 1978, pp. 54-7.

117. Yu Qiuli, 26 January 1978, *PR* 7, 17 February 1978, p. 9 and *SWB* FE/5727/B11/11.

118. Liu Rixin, *RMRB* 20 June 1963, p. 5.

119. 1974 estimate. Dernberger 1978, p. 88.

120. State Statistical Bureau 27 June 1979, p. 2.

121. See Lu Dingyi, *RMRB* 8 March 1979, p. 2.

122. See, e.g., NCNA 3 February 1978, *SWB* FE/5737/B11/15; Wuhan, Hubei Radio, 14 January 1979, *SWB* FE/6019/B11/11-12.

123. US Congress, Joint Economic Committee 1975, pp. 376-7.

124. *Shehuizhuyi Zhengzhi Jingji xue* 1975, p. 90.

125. Ibid., pp. 90-1.

126. Zhang Chunqiao, *PR* 14, 4 April 1975, p. 8.

127. Changchun, Jilin Radio, 16 February 1978, *SWB* FE/5749/B11/5. Note: reports which talk about the premature upgrading of the unit of account are not specific as to the time this occurred. See Wuhan, Hubei Radio, 14 January 1979, *SWB* FE/6019/B11/11-12. The period when this happened was probably the 'flying leap' of 1969-70.

128. Changchun, Jilin Radio, 16 February 1978, *SWB* FE/5749/B11/5.

129. Harbin, Heilongjiang Radio, 17 March 1978, *SWB* FE/5772/B11/5.

130. *Shehuizhuyi Zhengzhi Jingji xue* 1975, p. 91.

131. *RMRB* 26 January 1978, p. 2. 1,000 of these farms are run by the Army, NCNA 2 March 1977, *SWB* FE/W920/A/2.

132. *RMRB* 16 March 1979, pp. 1 and 4.

133. NCNA 11 March 1979, *SWB* FE/6069/B11/13.

134. NCNA 2 March 1979, *SWB* FE/6061/B11/15-16.

135. *PR* 10, 4 March 1977, pp. 13-14; Harbin, Heilongjiang Radio, 17 March 1978, *SWB* FE/5772/B11/5; Wan Li, *Hongqi* 3, 1978, p. 97.

136. E.g. Wan Li, *Hongqi* 3, 1978, p. 97; NCNA 13 February 1978, *SWB* FE/5743/B11/13; Haikou, Hainan Radio, 25 March 1978, *SWB* FE/5775/B11/8-9.

137. See, e.g., Jinan, Shandong Radio, 8 March 1979, *SWB* FE/6067/B11/14;

PR 16, 20 April 1979, p. 18; Shenyang, Liaoning Radio, 18 December 1978, *SWB* FE/6013/B11/7.

138. See, e.g., Morehouse 1976, p. 589.

139. NCNA 19 March 1979, *SWB* FE/6073/B11/11-12.

140. Zhang Decheng, *RMRB* 9 March 1979, p. 2.

141. Fuzhou, Fujian Radio, 13 March 1979, *SWB* FE/6073/B11/10-11.

142. Guangzhou, Guangdong Radio, 4 March 1979, *SWB* FE/6061/B11/13.

143. On this fault line, see Skinner 1978, p. 792.

144. Zhengzhou, Henan Radio, 21 April 1979, *SWB* FE/6101/B11/15.

145. See Friedman 1978.

146. NCNA 6 March 1979, *SWB* FE/6062/B11/4-5; Beijing Radio, 6 March 1979, *SWB* FE/6065/B11/17.

147. Beijing, AFP report, 12 March 1979, *SWB* FE/6067/B11/14.

148. Wuhan, Hubei Radio, 14 January 1979, *SWB* FE/6019/B11/11-12.

149. CCP, 11th CC, 3rd Plenum, communiqué, 22 December 1977, *PR* 52, 29 December 1978, p. 13.

150. Yu Qiuli, 21 June 1979, *SWB* FE/6155/C1/4.

151. *PR* 37, 12 September 1975, p. 25; *BR* 16, 20 April 1979, p. 18. In 1977, overall taxes from the rural areas accounted for only 3.35 per cent of the countryside's gross industrial and agricultural output value, *BR* 11, 16 March 1970, p. 12.

152. Note that this compensation was not always paid and failure to pay has recently occasioned stern criticism, NCNA 13 February 1978, *SWB* FE/5743/B11/13-14.

153. NCNA 31 January 1978, *SWB* FE/5731/B11/16.

154. The clearest statement of the new leadership's interpretation of 'payment according to work' may be found in *PR* 7, 17 February 1978, pp. 6-8.

155. Bernstein 1977, pp. 89-90.

156. Jinan, Shandong Radio, 23 March 1978, *SWB* FE/5775/B11/9-10.

157. Zhang Chunqiao, *PR* 14, 4 April 1975, pp. 7-8.

158. Pien Hsi 1972, pp. 191-2.

159. US Congress, Joint Economic Committee 1975, pp. 400-1.

160. *Nanfang Ribao* 26 July 1967, *SCMP* 4011, pp. 14-23.

161. Zhao Lükuan, *RMRB* 22 November 1977, p.2.

162. Wan Li, *Hongqi* 3, 1978, p. 95; Wuhan, Hubei Radio, 11 February 1978, *SWB* FE/5743/B11/15.

163. Wuhan, Hubei Radio, 11 February 1978, *SWB* FE/5743/B11/14-15.

164. Xi'an, Shaanxi Radio, 12 December 1978, *SWB* FE/6001/B11/13-14.

165. Ibid. See also, NCNA 9 November 1978, *SWB* FE/5966/B11/11.

166. Wuhan, Hubei Radio, 26 January 1978, *SWB* FE/5730/B11/11.

167. See the various reports in *SWB* FE/6071/B11/2-5. On the theoretical rationale, see Beijing Radio, 4 May 1979, *SWB* FE/6111/B11/5-7.

168. E.g. Fuzhou, Fujian Radio, 16 March 1979, *SWB* FE/6074/B11/4-5; Guangzhou, Guangdong Radio, 21 March 1979, *SWB* FE/6079/B11/13-16.

169. See, in particular, Guangzhou, Guangdong Radio, 21 March 1979, *SWB* FE/6079/B11/15.

170. See, e.g., Changsha, Hunan Radio, 10 March 1979, *SWB* FE/6067/B11/13.

171. NCNA 4 August 1978, *SWB* FE/5887/B11/11.

172. Guangzhou, Guangdong Radio, 14 January 1978, *SWB* FE/5717/B11/12-13.

173. Guangzhou, Guangdong Radio, 21 January 1978, *SWB* FE/5722/B11/3.

174. Croll 1977(b) p. 808.

175. Changchun, Jilin Radio, 12 December 1978, *SWB* FE/6001/B11/13.

176. See Table 4.2.

177. Smil 1978, p. 71.

178. Livestock numbers, from State Statistical Bureau 27 June 1979, p. 4.

179. *PR* (42, 17 October 1975, p. 23) states that every peasant household in the country raises 1.3 pigs on the average. This gives some 220 million pigs. This is 73 per cent of the official figure of 301 million.

180. Walker (1965, p. 43) notes that 70 million out of 84 million pigs were in private hands in 1956.

181. Li Xiannian, 22 July 1978, NCNA 15 August 1978, *SWB* FE/5897/B11/12.

182. US Congress, Joint Economic Committee 1975 p. 404.

183. NCNA 2 February 1978, *SWB* FE/5736/B11/15-16.

184. Hangzhou, Zhejiang Radio, 31 January 1978, *SWB* FE/5736/B11/16-17; *PR* 9, 3 March 1978, pp. 18-19.

185. *Shehuizhuyi Zhengzhi Jingji xue* 1975, pp. 81-2.

186. Ibid.

187. See NCNA 13 February 1978, *SWB* FE/5743/B11/12-13, for a criticism of the 'Gang's' view that 'legitimate' sideline production was 'the soil which generates capitalism'.

188. See, e.g., Liao Zhigao, *Hongqi* 2, 1978, pp. 45-8.

189. NCNA 10 November 1978, *SWB* FE/5971/B11/17.

190. NCNA 11 November 1978, in ibid.

191. NCNA 11 March 1979, *SWB* FE/6068/B11/9-11.

192. Tianjin Radio, 21 April 1979, *SWB* FE/6101/B11/16.

193. E.g. Harbin, Heilongjiang Radio, 2 March 1979, *SWB* FE/6061/B11/14; NCNA 11 March 1979, *SWB* FE/6068/B11/9-11; Xining, Qinghai Radio, 11 April 1979, *SWB* FE/6097/B11/9; Beijing Radio, 27 April 1979, *SWB* FE/6107/B11/4-5.

194. Changsha, Hunan Radio, 20 April 1979, *SWB* FE/6101/B11/4-5.

195. *RMRB* 26 February 1979, p. 1.

196. NCNA 6 March 1979, *SWB* FE/6061/B11/13; NCNA 15-17 March 1979, *SWB* FE/6071/B11/5-6.

197. CCP. CC *Zhongfa* 4 (1979), *Issues and Studies*, Vol. XV, No. 7, July 1979, pp. 105-6.

198. Yu Qiuli, 21 June 1979, *SWB* FE/6155/C1/2. Note: it was claimed that, in nearly one quarter of all production teams in 1977, the average per capita income was under ¥40.

199. *RMRB* 12 January 1978, p. 2.

5   The Blooming of a 'Hundred Flowers' and the Literature of the 'Wounded Generation'

SYLVIA CHAN

This chapter will examine the relationship between literature and politics in contemporary China. Following the periodisation set out in Chapter 1, it will note that, in the first period (late-1976 to mid-1977), discussion focused on the autocratic behaviour of the 'Gang of Four' concerning literary matters. As in other fields, the second period (mid-1977 to late-1978) saw a discussion of theoretical issues and a number of important contradictions were brought to light. The most important of these was the contradiction between the injunction to 'let a hundred flowers bloom' and still to adhere to the tradition of making literature serve politics. I shall explore this contradiction in the context of the history of the 'hundred flowers' policy since the mid-1950s. The third period (after December 1978) did not really resolve this contradiction though a number of other issues became clearer.

'Liu Shaoqi's sinister line on art and literature', for example, was declared non-existent. Throughout the second and third periods, large numbers of writers were rehabilitated and a number of new writers began to emerge. The chapter will conclude with a brief examination of some of the new writing. This remains quite controversial. By examining that controversy, one can understand more clearly the current relationship between literature and politics.

Literature and Politics: The Historical Context

It is generally agreed that Mao's 'Talks at the Yan'an Forum on Literature and Art' is a landmark in the development of contemporary Chinese literature. Its significance lies in the fact that it was the first and the only systematic formulation of the Chinese Commu-

174

nist Party's guidelines on art and literature since the Party became a major political force. The essay's contribution to Marxist literary theory, however, is almost negligible. It does little more than reaffirm the Leninist principle that a worker-peasant (or proletarian) literature should be created to serve proletarian politics and that this literature should be subject to Party control.[1] It sets out to answer the questions as to whom literature and art should serve and how this should be done. Both these questions, in fact, had been answered by other Party leaders before Mao. Qu Qiubai, for instance, wrote several theoretical essays urging the creation of a popular literature (*dazhong wenyi*) to further China's socialist revolution as early as 1931-2.[2] Qu's essays go further than Mao's 'Talks'. They are not confined to a discussion of general principles but also include proposals to reform the language in which literature is expressed, to educate intellectual writers and to train writers from among the workers and peasants.

Qu himself gave important theoretical and organisational leadership to the left-wing literary movement in the early-1930s.[3] Since the formation of the League of Left-wing Writers in 1930, Communist domination of Chinese literature has been complete and literature has, on the whole, served the Communist-led revolution very well.[4] To such literature, Mao himself was to pay tribute:

> 'To defeat the enemy, we must rely primarily upon the army with guns. But this army alone is not enough. We must also have a cultural army... Since the May Fourth Movement, such a cultural army has taken shape in China. It has helped the Chinese revolution. It has weakened the influence and reduced the domain both of China's feudal culture and of the comprador culture which served imperialist aggression.'[5]

Indeed, Chinese literature had already become highly political long before Mao's 'Yan'an Talks'. This was due partly to Communist influence in the 1920s and 1930s and partly to the cultural milieu out of which modern Chinese literature was born. It was a Confucian tradition that an important part of the moral education of the 'ideal man' (*junzi*) was the study of poetry and music. In traditional China, the political élite was culled from the cultural élite whose education consisted entirely in the study of Confucian classics (including the *Book of Poetry* and the *Book of Music*) together with traditional *belles lettres*. This practice further ensured the close marriage between literature and politics. In such a situation, art and literature were never pursued for their own sake but mainly for their didactic value. 'Art for art's sake' was a Western concept, imported into China towards the end of the last century. By that time, China hardly provided a congenial environment for that concept to have much effect. The stark reality of a land in the grip of poverty, ignorance, internecine war and foreign invasion demanded attention. An apolitical literature, therefore, could not but be rejected as illusory and hypocritical.

During that period of intense intellectual ferment known as the May Fourth Movement (after 1919), when the new Chinese literature began to take shape, only one of the many rival literary schools raised the banner of 'art for art's sake'. This was the Creation Society. Yet it was precisely the members of that society who, after an open recantation, were the first to put forward the slogan of 'literature for the revolution'.[6] Such a *volte face* attests eloquently to the social necessity for a politically-oriented literature. Such a literature was, indeed, not simply a creation of the Communists imposed upon an unwilling people.

What the Chinese Communist Party did was to enrol literature in the service of its own version of politics. Until the 1950s, when the Party leadership was relatively unified, literature was given a uniform set of goals. In the years after the Great Leap Forward, however, when the unity of the Party leadership began to break down, each faction was suspected of using literature to serve its own particular view of politics. Thus, the novel *Liu Zhidan* was said to be speaking for the Mao Gang faction and *Defending Yan'an* for the Peng Dehuai faction.[7] When Mao complained to the Tenth Plenum of the Eighth Central Committee in 1962 that people were using novels for anti-Party purposes, he was probably alluding to these works.[8] More famous, however, was Wu Han's play *Hai Rui Dismissed from Office* which was interpreted by Mao and his supporters as a veiled attack on the Great Leap Forward and the dismissal of Defence Minister Peng Dehuai. When Mao's interpretation was rejected by Peng Zhen and others, allegedly with the support of state Chairman Liu Shaoqi, an open confrontation occurred. This was the beginning of the Cultural Revolution.[9]

Three members of the 'Gang of Four' owed their rise to prominence to their role in this peculiar kind of literary politics. Jiang Qing, Zhang Chunqiao and Yao Wenyuan all contributed to the criticism of *Hai Rui Dismissed from Office*. Thereafter, these people were closely identified with a commitment to revolutionary culture and their political survival depended, to a large extent, on their ability to pose as its sole promoters, arbiters and vigilantes. They, therefore, felt compelled to condemn all literature and art except 'exemplary' operas, ballets and other works, created under their direct supervision. Ever since the Cultural Revolution, and particularly in the succession struggle in Mao's final years, the 'Gang' manipulated continuously the symbol of revolutionary culture to damn its opponents. Thus, as Sullivan has noted, the denunciation of Zhou Enlai was expressed in obscure and tortuous historical references to Confucianism and Legalism and in oblique criticisms of the classical novel *Water Margin*. It was, moreover, in the field of education that the 'Gang' mounted its initial attack on Deng Xiaoping.[10]

Culture, therefore, came to play a very important role in the rough-and-tumble of Communist Party politics. The authority of Mao himself had to be invoked to sanction the movie, *The Pioneers* (*Chuangye*), and a Politburo meeting had to be convened to discuss whether another movie, *Haixia*, should be released for public performance.[11] This is not to say, however, that Mao's intervention or Politburo decisions carried the day. Mao's support for *The Pioneers* was only made public after the demise of the 'Gang', and the press, under the control of the 'Gang', refused to give any publicity to *Haixia* despite Politburo approval. Such victories by the 'Gang' were, nevertheless, somewhat hollow. Of all the factions in the Communist Party, the 'Gang' was perhaps the only one to have virtually no control over any institutions of power except those in the cultural field. If one may speak of the 'Gang' having a power base, it lay only in this field and political power has never been known to grow out of the pen.

Initial Criticisms of the 'Gang of Four'

When one considers the above relationship between literature and politics, it is hardly surprising that the literary issue continued to feature prominently in Chinese politics after Mao's death. The new leadership continued to make use of this issue to articulate its own line and discredit its defeated opponents. As we have seen, the initial period after the defeat of the 'Gang' was characterised by the desire to legitimise the succession of Hua Guofeng. Several of Mao's directives, therefore, were published and these were said to demonstrate that Hua had been singled out by Mao as his successor and that the

'Gang' had been excluded. In this connection, Mao's 'directive' on *The Pioneers* was thought to be of particular value and was given much publicity.

The Pioneers tells the story of the construction of the Daqing Oilfield. This was considered to have been a monumental achievement of the Ministry of Petroleum in the 1960s under the leadership of Zhou Enlai's State Council. The oilfield, which was not particularly known for its enthusiasm for the Cultural Revolution, was portrayed as a model of the pre-Cultural Revolution interpretation of 'grasping revolution and promoting production'. It was, therefore, far from the 'exemplary' art promoted by the 'Gang'. Resisting the 'Gang's' criticisms, however, the scriptwriter appealed to Mao, and the late Chairman, it was claimed, approved of the movie. Mao apparently went on to criticise the 'Gang's' attempt to put too many restrictions on literature and art and to demand the revision of its literary policy. Mao's directive, however, was only conveyed to cultural workers in closed meetings and *The Pioneers* remained under interdict until the demise of the 'Gang'.[12] As one might expect, the new leadership took great pains to use the case of *The Pioneers* to demonstrate that, despite its protestations of loyalty, the 'Gang' had acted against Mao's instructions and that Mao had consistently opposed its line. The new leadership also used the case to show the 'Gang's' opposition to the late Premier Zhou Enlai. Clearly no one still had any doubts about the 'Gang's' enmity for the late Premier, but Zhou's popularity was so great among the Chinese people that no astute politician could fail to exploit it. In this early stage, when much of the criticism of the 'Gang' remained on an emotional and behavioural level, Zhou's personal ties with cultural circles were also freely exploited. Allegations were made that some writers and artists had been persecuted by the 'Gang' simply because of their personal friendship with the Premier.[13] It was alleged, moreover, that *Haixia* had incurred the 'Gang's' displeasure because its director had appealed to Zhou for support.[14]

The Disappearance of Liu Shaoqi's 'Sinister Line'

Earlier chapters in this book have shown that the behavioural criticisms of the 'Gang' gave way, in mid-1977, to more serious discussions of policy. In this second period, the overall concern of the leadership was to repudiate what eventually became known as the 'ultra left' cultural policy of the 'Gang'. This policy, it was felt, had created a veritable cultural desert in the previous decade. 'Ultra leftism', it seemed, had manifested itself in a nihilist attitude towards pre-Cultural Revolution art and literature. Just before the outbreak of the Cultural Revolution, in February 1966, at a forum on art and literature in the armed forces, Jiang Qing had declared that art and literature had been 'under the dictatorship of a sinister anti-Party and anti-socialist line' and that there had been 'few good or basically good works in the last decade or so'.[15] In the Cultural Revolution, the extensive persecution of writers and suppression of their works had been justified on those grounds. Thus, in 1977-8, efforts were made to refute allegations about the 'dictatorship of a sinister line'.

Yet Jiang Qing's pronouncements of early-1966 had been but a logical extension of the position adopted in the early 1960s by Mao himself. At the Tenth Plenum in 1962, it will be remembered, Mao had accused some people of writing anti-Party novels. In succeeding months, he had more than once criticised cultural circles for promoting 'feudal and capitalist art', claiming that they had slid right down to the brink of 'revisionism'.[16] Thus, Jiang Qing's statements in 1966 were considered to have been approved by Mao himself and any criticism of them might be taken as an implicit criticism of the late Chairman. In 1977-8, therefore, writers were faced with the unenviable task of having to denounce Jiang Qing's statements on art and literature whilst dutifully defending Mao's statements to the same effect. Mao, at that time, was still considered infallible. Attempts were made, however, to mitigate the harshness of Mao's criticism by pointing out that Mao had also said that 'achievements in the cinema, modern poetry, folk songs, fine arts and literature should not be underestimated'.[17] Yet to take single phrases from a context which was unambiguously negative was blatantly dishonest and could convince no one. This was then abandoned in favour of the argument that art and literature had, in the main, developed in a socialist direction but deviations had occurred as a result of the interference of 'Liu Shaoqi's revisionist line'.[18] Before long, however, it became no longer possible to maintain Liu Shaoqi as the universal scapegoat and arch-fiend responsible for every conceivable evil.

As we have seen, the Third Plenum of the Eleventh Central Committee, in December 1978, symbolised a dramatic shift in policy and ushered in the third period in the politics of China since the 'Gang of Four'. Implicitly, official endorsement was given to accelerating de-Maoification and Liu Shaoqi was rehabilitated in everything but name.[19] Overnight, it was discovered that Liu Shaoqi had never pursued a 'revisionist' line in art and literature at all. A responsible literary cadre, who in December 1977 had blamed the 'rightist' tendencies in literature during the 1960s on Liu's line, was in December 1978 to declare, without batting an eyelid, that such a line had never existed.[20] Understandably, some people were upset at this and sought an explanation for Mao's anger with the cultural establishment. But, with the myth of Mao's infallibility undermined, the answer was not difficult to provide. Mao, it was said, had made bad judgements because he had been misled. The accusation in 1962 that literature had been used for anti-Party purposes was apparently based on false charges concocted by 'a certain person closely connected with the Gang of Four'. This person, referred to elsewhere as the 'Gang's advisor', was the late Kang Sheng, a member of the old Central Cultural Revolution Group which had wielded so much power in 1966-9.[21] Kang, however, was not directly attacked by name, perhaps because the Third Plenum failed to reach consensus on his actions. It was also claimed that part of Mao's criticism had been based on a draft report on literary work which had been rejected by the literary leadership but which Jiang Qing had submitted to Mao as an official document.[22] In the light of all this, an article in the authoritative literary journal *Wenyibao* could only counsel people that, in the field of literature, 'certain judgements and directives, formed on the basis of incomplete, indirect and even exaggerated and falsified information, which in practice have been repeatedly proven to be one-sided and inaccurate, should...not be taken as a guide to our understanding of problems'.[23]

As the mantle of Mao began to be cast away, the new leaders found it increasingly necessary to identify themselves with Zhou Enlai. Zhou, it was claimed, had spared no pains to resuscitate the defunct policy of 'letting a hundred flowers bloom' in the aftermath of the Great Leap Forward. To this end, he had convened a series of meetings with writers and artists in the years 1961-2. Zhou's actions, however, were alleged to have provoked serious opposition from Ke Qingshi, the First Secretary of the Shanghai Municipal Party Committee and his speeches at those meetings had been denied wide publicity.[24] Of course, Ke alone had been insufficiently powerful to have obstructed Zhou's moves and one suspects that what was really crucial was Ke's influence with Mao. In any case, Ke's close association with Mao during the Great Leap Forward was well established[25] and rejection of the Great Leap could not be complete without criticising Ke. Like Kang Sheng, Ke was not officially indicted by name though reference to his exploits, before his death in 1965, disappeared from the official press. Though one cannot be sure about exactly what Ke did in the years 1961-2, the Chinese press was quite explicit about the role of Zhou and the full text of what purports to be Zhou's speech to one of the meetings at that time was published.[26] The central theme of this speech is identical to that invoked by the present Chinese leadership — an injunction that leading cadres be more tolerant of diversity and pluralism in art and literature.

The fact that Zhou's name was exploited to lend authority to the cultural policy of the current leadership should not be taken to imply that assertions about Zhou's attempts in the early-1960s to revitalise the 'hundred flowers' were fabrications or exaggerations. Hundreds of writers and artists had attended the meetings of 1961-2 and those who had heard reports of the meetings might be counted in thousands. One of these meetings, held under Zhou's aegis in Guangzhou in March 1962, ostensibly to discuss opera and drama, had been used by the late Premier to articulate, through his spokesman Chen Yi, an even more moderate version of his famous 1956 policy of enlisting the support of intellectuals.[27] This conference, which had a tremendous impact throughout intellectual circles, had come under very severe criticism in the Cultural Revolution[28] and it came as no surprise to be told that the focus of criticism had been Zhou Enlai. In my opinion, therefore, there is a great deal of truth in the assertion that much of the Cultural Revolution criticism of 'Liu Shaoqi's revisionist line in art and literature' was an oblique attack on Zhou Enlai.[29] After all, Liu did not appear to have concerned himself seriously with art and literature until 1964 when he called a meeting to reverse the liberalisation which had begun in 1961.[30]

The Rehabilitation of Writers and Artists

It was not until two years after the demise of the 'Gang of Four' that the 'revisionist line in art and literature' was declared never to have existed. The rehabilitation of writers and artists, however, began to occur before that declaration. In the period up to the reinstatement of Vice-Chairman Deng Xiaoping in early-1971, few familiar literary names reappeared. In October of that year, however, on the long list of celebrities who had turned out to commemorate National Day were the names Zhou Yang and Xia Yan. Though not entirely unexpected, the reappearance of these symbols of the entire left-wing literary movement since the 1930s, still caused some sensation. Both of these men had been Communist Party representatives in the Shanghai-based left-wing literary movement in the 1930s. Zhou Yang had played a leading role in shaping literary policy in Yan'an and both Zhou and Xia had held responsible positions in cultural departments from 1949 until 1966. Since their reappearance symbolised a positive reassessment, on the part of the Communist Party, of art and literature from the 1930s to the Cultural Revolution, one may understand the relief expressed by writers at their rehabilitation.

Yet the rehabilitation of rank-and-file writers was slower than might have been expected, so much so that an article in *Renmin Ribao* in December 1977 had to urge that the process be speeded up.[31] The reason for this tardiness was soon revealed. Apparently, the campaign to criticise the 'Gang of Four' had met with strong opposition from leading cadres in the Ministry of Culture and an entirely new Party fraction had to be set up in that ministry in December 1977 before the campaign could proceed.[32] Given the complete control which the 'Gang' had previously held in the field of culture, such a situation is hardly surprising. Discussing the reorganisation of the Party fraction in the ministry in mid-1978, the official Chinese press was to mention no names. A Hong Kong source, however, suggested that the head of the Party's Propaganda Department Zhang Pinghua had probably been behind the opposition,[33] although Zhang was not to be replaced by Hu Yaobang until later (probably at the Third Plenum in December).[34] Throughout the struggle, the Minister of Culture, Huang Zhen, managed to retain his post. This was perhaps because Huang, who had dabbled in literature before 1949, had been a diplomat ever since and thus appeared unconnected with the 'Gang of Four'.[35] Yet it would seem that Huang has not been able to give very effective leadership to the ministry and Huang's name has been eclipsed by that of Zhou Yang ever since the latter's rehabilitation. It is quite apparent that Zhou Yang enjoys enormous prestige in cultural affairs even though he has no official position in the Ministry of Culture.[36] Whatever the intricacies of the internal struggle in late-1977, the Ministry of Culture was able to report its first major victory over the 'Gang' in April 1978 when a number of writers and artists were declared rehabilitated.[37] But, as Sullivan has suggested in Chapter 1, struggles amongst the central leadership of the Party were to continue throughout 1978. These were reflected in the actions of writers and artists. In September, for example, writers and artists in Beijing were busy criticising 'a certain responsible cadre in the municipal Party Committee'[38] who insisted that a 'revisionist literary line' had existed. This was, of course, Wu De.

With the rehabilitation of writers and artists, the All China Federation of Literary and Art Circles and its various subsidiary associations could be reconstituted. Guangdong province was the first to announce that these bodies were functioning once again[39] and soon the city of Shanghai followed suit.[40] It was, however, not until May 1978 that the Federation held its first national meeting. It was announced, at that time, that the National Writers Union had been re-established and that similar unions of playwrights, musicians, artists and dancers would soon be restored.[41] No detail of the leadership of these associations is known, though scattered information has suggested that the surviving former chairmen and vice-chairmen have been given back their old titles.[42] Since so few writers and artists had remained in favour with the 'Gang', a post-'Gang' purge amongst them seemed unnecessary.

As previous chapters have noted, the Third Plenum in December 1978 did much more than rehabilitate the literary line formerly associated with Liu Shaoqi. It, in fact, implicitly repudiated the Great Leap and Cultural Revolution. As many Western scholars have pointed out, disputes over policy issues in the Cultural Revolution could be traced back to disputes during the Great Leap.[43] Thus, it came as no surprise that Wu Han, the author of *Hai Rui Dismissed from Office*, was rehabilitated[44] together with his alleged model, Peng Dehuai. But if the rehabilitation of Wu Han caused little stir, the same cannot be said for the decision, taken just before the Plenum, to rehabilitate all 'rightists' capped in 1957.[45] These 'rightists' had been victims of the Party's sudden and unexpected termination of the original 'hundred flowers' policy at a time when most intellectuals had come to believe that they would be guaranteed a greater degree of freedom. The Anti-rightist Movement of 1957, therefore, had been seen by many as the Party's most treacherous breach of faith with the intellectuals and nothing short of its complete rejection would have convinced them that the new leadership's renewed promise of intellectual freedom had been made in good faith. The decision was indeed momentous. A conference convened by the Ministry of Culture to rehabilitate writers and artists was accorded front page coverage in both *Renmin Ribao* and

Guangming Ribao[46] and there was much discussion in the whole press. Of particular interest was the positive reassessment, by *Guangming Ribao*'s 'commentator' (a pseudonym for high ranking cadres who wish to remain anonymous), of Liu Biyan's 'On the Worksite of the Bridge' and Wang Meng's 'A Newcomer to the Organisation Department.'[47] Both authors and both stories had been subjected to scathing criticism during the Anti-rightist Movement of 1957.[48]

I have already suggested that the decisions of the Third Plenum constituted an implicit de-Maoification. Has the rehabilitation of 'rightists' any implications for this de-Maoification? Here, I am inclined to support Sullivan's conclusion that cleavages amongst the Party leadership still continue. A *Renmin Ribao* editorial, announcing the rehabilitation, still spoke of the original Anti-rightist Movement in positive terms and attributed it to Mao's 'wise leadership'.[49] Yet, at the same time, a large number of rightists were declared to have been wrongly accused.[50] This was particularly the case in cultural circles where the movement was remembered for its excesses.[51] The crucial question remains: who should be held responsible for the wrongful accusations? As yet, there has been no direct reference to Mao's responsibilities. The Anti-rightist Movement amongst writers and artists was, however, directed by none other than Zhou Yang who boasted of enjoying Mao's support.[52] What then is one to make of a recent *Wenyibao* article, calling for 'self-criticism' by those who had initiated unwarranted attacks on authors and their works and who now enjoyed responsible positions in the literary hierarchy?[53] Could this be a pointed reference to Zhou Yang and his associates? It is significant that *Wenyibao*'s editors are Kong Luosun and Feng Mu, neither of whom were in the literary leadership before the Cultural Revolution. It is significant also that, although Zhou Yang was understandably very bitter about the 'Gang of Four', his comments on the Cultural Revolution have been surprisingly positive and he has spoken of Mao and his literary line with warm feelings.[54] Does the *Wenyibao* article, therefore, signify that the present struggle on the literary front is not just directed against a remnant follower of the 'Gang'? Is there, in fact, a major struggle between those who wish to depart even further from Mao's line to bring about a 'bourgeois liberalisation' and those, like Zhou Yang, who seek to go no further than to reinstitute Mao's version of a Party-controlled 'blooming and contending'? This latter possibility seems to me very likely.

'Let a Hundred Flowers Bloom': The Historical Context

Disagreements among the Chinese leadership concerning the scope of the current movement to 'let a hundred flowers bloom' must be seen in the context of earlier versions of the movement. When the original 'hundred flowers' policy was first put forward in 1956, expectations of intellectual freedom were high. In actuality, however, the policy did not promise much and was predicated upon the assumption that the political authority of the Party should never be challenged. Lu Dingyi, the first official exponent of the policy, explained that it was the binding duty of every Chinese citizen to support socialism and any who disputed this would be considered as 'enemies of the people' to whom no freedom of any kind would be granted.[55] This point was further emphasised by Mao who laid down six criteria for the movement. Authorisation would only be given to words and deeds which were beneficial to the unity of the Chinese people, to socialist transformation and construction, to the 'people's democratic dictatorship', to 'democratic centralism', to the leadership of the Party and to unity with other socialist countries and 'peace loving people' in the world.[56] Ever since that time, freedom of thought and expression has always been officially constrained by those six criteria. No one, of course, would expect a socialist state — or any state for that matter — to grant absolute freedom for its citizens to challenge the fundamental principles upon which it rested. Nevertheless, when the limits of free expression were defined so broadly, the scope for arbitrariness was also quite broad. Indeed, literary policy, since the mid-1950s, has constantly experienced the arbitrary manipulation of those limits.

To exemplify the scope for arbitrariness in literary policy, let us consider the statement by Lu Dingyi that, on matters of a 'purely artistic nature', writers might enjoy absolute freedom. Concretely, this freedom was defined as the ability not to adhere to the officially endorsed creative method — 'socialist realism'. But what was 'socialist realism'? According to the 1954 statutes of the Soviet Writers Union, 'socialist realism' was defined as 'the basic method of Soviet *belles lettres* and literary criticism' which 'demands of the artist truthful, historically concrete representation of reality in its revolutionary development'.[57] With such a vague definition, it is very difficult to know just what the freedom not to adhere to 'socialist realism' might mean. It was not even clear whether this was the definition of 'socialist realism' to which Lu Dingyi referred. According to the 1934 statutes of the Soviet Writers Union, the above definition had been qualified by the following explicitly political clause: 'at the same time, truthfulness and historical concreteness of artistic representation of reality must be combined with the task of ideologically remoulding and training the labouring people in the spirit of socialism'.[58] This qualifying clause had been done away with in the post-Stalin liberalisation in the Soviet Union of 1954 because it was felt to impose too rigid political constraints on literature, but its abolition had not been officially endorsed in China.

It would seem, therefore, that Lu's version of the 'hundred flowers' policy, which still implied a uniform political standard, might have been based upon the 1934 position. To maintain the necessity for a political standard and declare that writers were free not to adhere to the 1934 version of 'socialist realism' was at best contradictory and at worst hypocritical. But the 'hundred flowers' movement of 1957 was a time of many contradictions. With the ensuing Anti-rightist Movement, it became crystal clear that the 1934 version of 'socialist realism' was in force, and one literary critic, who supported the Soviet revision of 1954, was branded a 'rightist'.[59] During the Great Leap of 1958, 'socialist realism' was rephrased as 'the combination of revolutionary realism and revolutionary romanticism' and was established as 'the direction in which all writers and artists should aim'.[60] There was no longer any talk of freedom not to adhere to the revised formula.

The freedom, which Lu Dingyi promised on matters of a 'purely artistic nature', was also concretely defined as the ability for writers to choose their own subject matter:

> It is not right to lay down such dicta as: write only about workers, peasants and soldiers; write only about the new society; or write only about new types of people... One can write about positive people and the new society, and also about negative elements and the old.[61]

Nevertheless, when, in the 'hundred flowers' movement, writers started to discuss Party cadres corrupted by power and demoralised by the bureaucratisation of the revolution, they were accused of attacking the Party and contravening the six criteria.[62] Again, in the 1960s, when writers turned their attention to the agony and confusion of the individual peasant dislodged from the traditional way of life by the inexorable process of communisation, they were condemned for not promoting socialist transformation.[63]

A major problem was, of course, the definition of the term 'matters of a purely artistic nature'. As it turned out, even literary forms and styles, which to all appearances were 'purely artistic' and which, according to Mao, ought to be allowed to develop freely,[64] were themselves fraught with political implications. There was, for example, a protracted debate as to whether tragedy, as a literary form, should continue to exist in a socialist society. As some people saw it, tragedy implied a negative attitude towards socialism and was an implicit attack on the socialist system.[65] The crux of the matter was that, in such a highly politicised society as China, where literature was considered to be utterly subservient to politics, it was very difficult to draw a line between political and literary issues. In the final analysis, adherence to the six political criteria cannot but make nonsense of the artistic freedom which those principles are supposed to guide.

It is perhaps the case that most of the major problems in specifying the limits of intellectual freedom stem from the way the Chinese Communist Party has conceived of the nature of a socialist society and the meaning of making socialist revolution. At the core of this notion is the distinction between the 'people' and the 'enemy', which derived from the earlier idea of 'people's democratic dictatorship'. In discussing this distinction, the Party has oscillated between a substantive and a behavioural definition of these terms. Substantively, all three Chinese constitutions have echoed Mao's 1949 position that the bourgeoisie was part of the 'people'.[66] In his 1957 speech 'On the Correct Handling of Contradictions among the People', however, when Mao reiterated the position that contradictions between the bourgeoisie and the proletariat were basically non-antagonistic,[67] it was not at all clear whether he was defining the bourgeoisie substantively or behaviourally. In the same speech, Mao makes the point that, although the bourgeoisie should be given freedom to express its ideology, it must be criticised for spreading wrong ideas or 'poisonous weeds'.[68] The six criteria are supposed to be guidelines for defining 'poisonous weeds' but there is no guideline to distinguish antagonistic 'poisonous weeds' from non-antagonistic 'poisonous weeds'. This failing was immediately manifested in the confusion which attended the subsequent Anti-rightist Movement.

At that time, many 'poisonous weeds' were treated as antagonistic though a few were not. In 1958, Zhou Yang was to declare that *all* 'poisonous weeds' were antagonistic[69] and, by that time, the Party could place that label on whatever work it liked. Zhou Yang's liquidation of the 'hundred flowers' movement had been made possible by the ambiguity in the theoretical basis of that movement and by the ambiguity in the definition of class itself. What seems to have happened, since the mid-1950s, is that antagonism has been increasingly defined as a simple behavioural problem and the normal Marxist approach to class structure has been inverted. Instead of behaviour stemming from class position, class position has been defined in terms of behaviour.[70] Thus, intellectuals have been labelled 'bourgeois', not because they possessed any capital but because they were considered to think and behave in a bourgeois way. Here was the paradox. Intellectual freedom had to be denied to the 'enemy' and yet the exercise of intellectual freedom might produce that very behaviour which had come to define the 'enemy'. In such a situation, could there be any intellectual freedom?

When Zhou Enlai tried to reactivate the 'hundred flowers' policy in the wake of the Great Leap Forward, he did not confront the above paradox nor the ambiguity in the criteria for determining 'poisonous weeds'. Zhou was, after all, a practical man rather than a theoretician. All he could do was to make a personal plea that responsible cadres allow greater democracy in art and literature (*yishu minzhu*) and refrain from high-handed methods in the pursuit of conformity.[71] At the same time, Zhou sought to promote new guidelines for 'blooming and contending'. Under his auspices, the Party fraction of the Ministry of Culture drafted an eight point document on literary policy. This document did not even mention Mao's six criteria and interpreted the Leninist principle that literature should serve politics so loosely as to render it meaningless. Thus, any literature which helped towards widening people's knowledge, increasing their wisdom, providing artistic satisfaction and raising the cultural level was considered to be serving politics.[72]

Extending the Premier's 1956 discussions about intellectuals, Vice-Premier Chen Yi, speaking at the Guangzhou conference in 1962, declared that intellectuals were on a par with workers and peasants and that the stigma of 'bourgeois' ought not to be applied to them. The implication here was that vigilance against 'bourgeois ideas' was totally unnecessary and that freedom should be unconstrained. Chen even went so far as to challenge the leadership of the Party over literature and did not see why literature should be asked to perform functions which were more properly those of Party circulars. As Chen saw it, the objective of literature was merely to provide a little pleasure.[73] The efforts of Zhou Enlai and Chen Yi were, however, to come to nothing. The policy statements of 1961-2 were never authorised by the Party Central Committee and the movement towards liberalisation was again curtailed by the Tenth Plenum in the autumn of 1962.

Yet, even if the suggestions of Zhou and Chen, in the early-1960s, had been incorporated in official directives, one suspects that major problems would have remained. There was, after all, a major weakness in what Schurmann has called the policy operations dichotomy. Policy guidelines were invariably laid down in very broad terms and individual cadres were allowed a considerable amount of discretion in working out their operational implications.[74] In the control of something as elusive as ideology, this was perhaps the only possible approach. It did, however, rely to a great extent on human factors and the result could quite easily be arbitrariness on the part of cadres and scepticism on the part of writers.

No-one can blame Chinese writers for the scepticism they displayed after 1957 and again after 1962. Even after the downfall of the 'Gang of Four', this scepticism was to continue, since it was the result of an approach to ideological control initiated long before the rise of the 'Gang'. Anxious to eliminate what is called 'residual fear' (*yuji*), the present leadership has rehabilitated the victims of former arbitrariness and has constantly reaffirmed its commitment to the 'hundred flowers' policy. It has, moreover, incorporated the policy for the first time into the state Constitution. Yet the Constitution of 1978 also upholds the leading position of Marxism-Leninism-Mao Zedong Thought in all spheres of ideology and culture.[75] As Ye Jianying, the Chairman of the Standing Committee of the National People's Congress, put it:

> Under this policy, so long as the six political criteria are observed, different forms and styles in art should freely develop, different schools in science should freely contend and questions of right and wrong in the arts and sciences should be settled through free discussion in artistic and scientific circles and through practical work in these fields.[76]

This was almost an exact repetition of Mao Zedong's 'On the Correct Handling...'[77] and the position in 1978 seemed no different from that of 1957. Similarly, in a major speech on literary policy in late-1978, Zhou Yang echoed Ye Jianying's demand that intellectual freedom be predicated on political conformity.[78] Once again, it was argued that the 'blooming of a hundred flowers' only applied to academic, artistic and scientific matters and that these should not be confused with political matters. Indeed, the only concession which Zhou was prepared to make was that the rigid system of censorship needed to be modified and made more responsive to public opinion. Throughout all this, the old contradictions remained and no real attempt was made to face up to the theoretical problems outlined above. In fact, the approach of the leadership in 1978 was remarkably similar to that of Zhou Enlai in 1961. Failing to face up to the major theoretical issues, the leadership could only urge cadres to modify their behaviour and allow greater freedom. Should they fail to do so, they would be removed from their posts.[79]

It was not until after the Third Plenum of the Eleventh Central Committee in December 1978, that some people began to get to the heart of the problem. Of particular significance is a recent article in *Wenyibao* which offers a new approach to the 'hundred flowers' policy.[80]. This article warns that Mao's six criteria are quite vague and advises extreme caution in applying them. One should think carefully before one brands any work a 'poisonous weed' or declares that it is 'antagonistic'. The article argues that the essence of the 'hundred flowers' policy is to allow both 'fragrant flowers' and 'poisonous weeds' to grow. Since such is the case, the implementation of the policy cannot be subject to any political conditions. Furthermore, the 'hundred flowers' policy should apply not only to non-political matters but also to politics itself. Thus Mao's six criteria are considered to be irrelevant. It is not clear how authoritative the *Wenyibao* article is. It was written by Liu Mengxi, a new literary critic who holds no responsible position but who has written several articles articulating a more 'liberal' literary policy.[81] The fact, however, that it was carried in *Wenyibao* suggests that it was supported by some responsible literary cadres. We do not know the degree of that support but we do know that the article has caused some disquiet. An informed Chinese official, on a recent visit to Australia, informed me that the article has raised quite a few eyebrows and it is evident that opponents of the 'Gang of Four' are far from united on what is the best course to take in developing literature.

The aftermath of the Third Plenum has seen much more than a more probing discussion of literary policy. A notable trend is towards the establishment of formal institutions to guarantee freedom of thought and expression. Amidst growing concern about 'socialist legality', suggestions have been put forward that laws be formulated to guard against the conviction of people as 'counter-revolutionaries' simply on the basis of their words.[82] These suggestions seem to have borne fruit and such a law has recently been introduced.[83] But given the nature of Chinese society, the effectiveness of any institution is still dependent upon the good will of the authorities.

The Literature of the 'Wounded Generation'

Despite the theoretical problems, it would appear that the leadership's desire to restore the 'hundred flowers' policy has been put forward in good faith. This policy has already greatly enlivened the literary scene and spectacular changes have occurred in the performing arts. Gone are the days when 800 million Chinese were fed day-in and day-out on the standard fare of eight model operas. The Chinese stage now offers a wide variety of entertainment, ranging from traditional Beijing operas,[84] western-style operas, *quyi* and vernacular plays (*huaju*) with both historical and contemporary themes. The film industry has been slower in developing new productions but many pre-Cultural Revolution films have been re-released. Practically all pre-Cultural Revolution literary journals have resumed publication and some new ones (such as the Beijing-based *Shiyue* [October]) have appeared. Contributors to these journals include not only veteran writers such as Ba Jin, Ai Qing, Ai Wu and Zhou Libo but also a host of new people. In addition to short pieces which appear in journals, a number of longer works have been published, of which Yao Xueyin's voluminous novel *Li Zicheng* (still to be completed)[85] ranks amongst the best in modern Chinese fiction. But of all the literary genres, it is the short story which has been the most prolific. It is here, moreover, that one finds the most interesting trends in the current cultural 'thaw'.

Because of the comparatively short time involved in their creation, short stories easily lend themselves to the representation of topical themes. It is not surprising, therefore, that a recurrent theme in short story writing has been the fortunes of individuals during the period of the 'Gang of Four'. Though such a theme has important propagandist value, these is no doubt that its salience reflects the fact that, for many Chinese, the Cultural Revolution is still their most traumatic memory and works which deal with that subject capture the popular imagination. Significantly, some 20 out of 25 prize-winning stories in a competition sponsored by *Renmin Wenxue* (*People's Literature*) deal with the Cultural Revolution.[86] Similarly, 21 out of 26 items, in a collection of the best short stories written between 1977 and September 1978, deal with the same theme.[87] Some of these stories have been immensely popular among the Chinese people. Liu Xinwu's 'The Class Teacher' (*'Ban Zhuren'*), for instance is said to have drawn a very positive response from a wide readership. Another of his stories 'A Place of Love' (*'Aiqing de Weizhi'*) drew large crowds around radio sets in department stores when it was broadcast over the radio.[88] Yet these stories are neither technically innovative nor ideologically original and the Western reader might find the Chinese response quite strange. But is it so strange, when one considers that most Chinese are more interested in the socio-political implications of literature than its purely literary merits? 'Literature for literature's sake', it will be recalled, is not only official anathema but also a notion alien to the Chinese people. For most Chinese people, the phenomenon of the 'Gang of Four' has been very difficult to come to terms with and any opportunity to discuss that phenomenon has been welcomed. By simply talking about that painful issue, many people find emotional relief.

Although these stories have received public acclaim, it is apparent that some people have certain reservations. This is because the stories seem very close to the 'literature of exposure' which Mao condemned in his 'Yan'an Talks'.[89] It is clear that the official press supports the publication of these stories but the fact that lengthy articles have to be published in their defence[90] suggests that objections are being made in some very influential quarters (and perhaps by top Party leaders). One feels that, if we could understand the nature of those objections, we might be able to predict the fate of the current 'hundred flowers' policy. How is it that stories, considered heterodox and dissident by some, still enjoy official sanction? No general answer may be given here but, at least, it is possible to discuss a few of the more influential stories and look at some of the specific objections.

In many ways, one of the most typical of the new genre of short stories is 'The Class Teacher' written by the secondary school teacher Liu Xinwu.[91] This story portrays two secondary school students, Song Baoqi, a juvenile delinquent just released from reformatory, and Xie Huimin, the secretary of the school's branch of the Communist Youth League. The author's intention is to reveal 'the internal injury inflicted upon the younger generation by the "Gang of Four"'.[92] Thus, the story describes how, once school was closed during the Cultural Revolution, Song joined a band of thugs because there was nothing better to do and because, at that time, vandalism was synonymous with radicalism. Song, therefore, is portrayed as a typical victim of the anti-intellectualism and 'anarchism' encouraged by the 'Gang of Four'. Such a portrayal is, of course, uncontroversial. The portrayal of Xie Huimin, on the other hand, is highly controversial. According to the old canons of 'socialist realism', Xie might have been portrayed as a stereotyped paragon of virtue. In fact, she is represented as an unintelligent and unimaginative bigot and a narrow-minded philistine. Though Song and Xie might seem poles apart, they are both abominably ignorant and stupid. Take, for example, what happened when Song stole a novel about a nineteenth-century Polish revolutionary. Being unable to read the novel, Song jumped to the conclusion that it must consist of pornography because it contained illustrations of young men and women in love. Xie, however, was literate enough to read it but was horrified by the teacher's suggestion that it was readable, because she also reached the verdict that the book was depraved solely on the basis of the illustrations. Doubtless, the suggestion in the story that there is a close affinity between the young revolutionary and the young thug is most disturbing. Critics, therefore, have protested that Liu Xinwu has drawn too pessimistic a picture of the younger generation.[93] Surely Song and Xie are atypical. What, after all, has happened to the many bright and intelligent youngsters? Have they fared any better? As if to answer such questions, Liu has written another story, 'Wake up, Little Brother' (*'Xinglaiba Didi'*).[94]

Little brother is the teenage son of a high-ranking cadre. His father is the victim of several cycles of denunciation as a 'capitalist roader' and subsequent rehabilitation. Eventually the father dies a broken man and the boy is left stunned and bewildered. Becoming disillusioned and cynical, he takes to drink and seeks only the company of teenagers like himself. Finally, even the downfall of the 'Gang of Four' fails to rekindle his interest in life. Were he as unthinking as Xie Huimin, he might have found some solace in all the high sounding phrases about the Cultural Revolution. As it is, the price he pays for independent thinking is the sacrifice of his peace of mind, This, it is implied, is what has happened to many of the intelligent youngsters.

The theme of the youngster disoriented by the vicissitudes of the Cultural Revolution is echoed by Zong Pu, in her short story 'Dream on the Strings' (*'Xianshangde Meng'*).[95] Zong is the daughter of the famous philosopher, Feng Youlan, who is now in disgrace because of his connections with the 'Gang of Four'. She achieved fame in the first 'hundred flowers' movement for her sentimental love story 'Red Beans' ('*Hongdou*')[96] but this was subsequently criticised for its 'petty bourgeois sentiments',[97] though Zong herself was never capped as a 'rightist'. Her recent story 'Dream on the Strings' depicts the life of Liang Xia, the daughter of high-ranking cadres tortured to death by the endless struggle sessions of the Cultural Revolution. Ever since her parents' death, when she was only ten years old, Liang refused to accept their guilt and was thus denounced herself. Friendless and destitute, she turns to her father's sometime girl-friend who teaches her to play the cello. Though obviously talented, she develops no real interest in music and only continues to play in order to 'scrape a living'. In her relationship with boys, she is equally casual. In fact, she takes nothing seriously, jeering even at such sacrosanct ideas as love, patriotism and revolution. ('What a high-sounding word revolution is. They killed my father too in the name of revolution'.)[98] Unlike 'Wake up, Little Brother', however, 'Dream on the Strings' has not provoked any controversy, because the author has tacked on to it an orthodox ending. Liang Xia finally becomes involved in the famous Tiananmen Incident, in April 1976, in commemoration of Zhou Enlai and dies a martyr's death when the 'Gang of Four' clamps down on the demonstrators. She thus dies a cynic — turned revolutionary. Liang's final conversion, however, jars with Liang's consistent cynicism which is the main theme of the story. Once again, political considerations have been made to override artistic consistency.

Clearly Liu Xinwu is more uncompromising in his art than Zong Pu. This is not to say, however, that Liu has not been compelled to defend himself on political grounds. The secondary school teacher in 'The Class Teacher' and the Party secretary in 'Wake up, Little Brother' are both portrayed in the role of purveyors of the current political clichés who try to save the souls of 'little brother', Song Baoqi and Xie Huimin. But both stories deliberately leave it ambiguous as to whether any of them can, in fact, be saved. This is a clear violation of 'socialist realism' which demands the unequivocal victory of good over evil and the progressive over the backward. Defending himself, Liu Xinwu defiantly said that he did not think that conditions were completely ripe for the conversion of his characters.[99]

Liu Xinwu is a new amateur writer of some promise who can

handle a tragic situation without stooping to melodrama. Most other writers about the Cultural Revolution, however, are much less talented. One such writer is Lu Xinhua, a first-year student of Chinese literature at Shanghai's Fudan University. His story 'The Wound' ('*Shanghen*')[100] was at first rejected by *Renmin Wenxue* which considered it to be too depressing to have any didactic value. When, however, it was finally published in *Wenhuibao*, it touched off an animated debate and earned majority acclaim.[101] The popularity of this story was no doubt due to the fact that the portrayal of the heroine and her mother reflects the common experience of thousands of harassed cadres and their children during the Cultural Revolution. The heroine is a young girl who volunteers to leave Shanghai to settle in the countryside because she wants a complete break with her widowed mother who is suspected of having betrayed the Communist Party to the Guomindang. But, wherever she goes, she cannot escape the stigma of 'traitor's daughter' and this nearly ruins her political career and her love affair. It is only after the downfall of the 'Gang of Four' that she learns that her mother had been framed by the 'Gang' and that now she is critically ill. Hurrying back to Shanghai, she arrives to find her mother dead. Such an emotive theme was able to strike just the right chord in the hearts of the readers, for, to many, the Cultural Revolution was a most hurtful experience. Indeed some people seem to derive an almost masochistic satisfaction when that experience is probed deep. Herein lies the popularity of what one critic has called the literature of the 'wounded generation' ('*shoushangde yidai*').[102]

Such literature about deeply hurt people has perhaps been written and often acclaimed by people who have been equally hurt. These wounds are not always only emotional. Bai Shun, for example, in 'The Sacred Mission' ('*Shenshengde Shiming*')[103] is portrayed as beaten and tortured until his face is badly scarred. This occurs in one of the many ruthless power struggles between Cultural Revolutionaries and veteran cadres. Here, the former are portrayed as totally unscrupulous careerists who lie, cheat, falsely accuse the innocent and even resort to murder. The assault on Bai Shun occurs because he overhears one of the murder plots, and he is eventually sentenced to 15 years' imprisonment on a false charge. An heroic public security officer, however, suspects foul play and is killed by the criminals just as he is on the point of unmasking them. But, in the end, the crushing of the 'Gang of Four' results in the good people being rewarded and the evil-doers punished.

One might wonder why such moralistic stories should continue to provoke protest. Most of these works have not been written by conscious dissenters but supporters of the post-Mao leadership. Yet, for all their exaggeration and sensationalism, all of these works point to fundamental flaws in Chinese society. It is possible to blame the 'Gang of Four' and its followers for the deaths and suffering of thousands of innocent people. But the question still remains: if it is true that a handful of careerists could have ordered the murder, torture or imprisonment of anyone it saw fit, do not such actions make the 'dictatorship of the proletariat' into a farce? Whatever the intention of any particular author, this kind of message will be conveyed and one can understand why some people are worried about the subversive effect of the new literature. One should not be surprised, therefore, that stories like 'The Sacred Mission' and 'The Wound' have revived the perennial debate about whether tragedy should be portrayed in socialist China.

Back in the 1960s, Jiang Qing criticised people who 'created heroes only to have them die in a contrived tragic ending'.[104] By this, she could have simply meant that she did not like contrived endings. She was, however, taken to mean that there was an official taboo on all tragedy. After her demise, the taboo on tragedy disappeared. As one tragic story after another took the public by storm, it inevitably raised the uncomfortable question of how these adversities, suffered by the common people, could have squared with the reality of a supposedly superior social system. In the debate which followed, the Aristotelian and Hegelian theories, which see tragedy as the destruction of basically worthy human beings by external forces which act through flaws in their character, were rejected as 'idealist'. The theory which was accepted was that of Engels, which defines tragedy as 'a conflict between the historically necessary postulate and the practical impossibility of its realisation'.[105] But how can such a definition be applied to the contemporary Chinese situation? As some people see it, the origin of tragedy lies in the quality of the leadership. Enemies of the people such as the 'Gang of Four' are always trying to worm their way into the leadership in order to sabotage socialism and, when they succeed, they alone are responsible for the suffering of others.[106] Others feel that one has to look further than the quality of the leadership. Among the 'people' themselves there are those who are influenced by 'bureaucratism', 'commandism' and bad thinking.[107] Such people also might be the cause of tragedy. Still others feel that one has do more than consider questions of behaviour and look for structural causes. But are these structural causes remnants of the past or constantly regenerated? As some see it, the socialist system is incapable of giving rise to tragedy and can only resolve tragic conflicts.[108] Objecting to this point of view, one critic has asked where else tragedy might be rooted if not in the current social system. In his view, the injustices perpetrated by the 'Gang' were made possible by the imperfection of the socialist legal system.[109] As Sullivan has pointed out, it is possible to think of other structural explanations. Suffice it to say here that the currently dominant view accepts the position of the above critic. The official press has expressed considerable concern about socialist legality[110] and literature which does the same is tolerated and indeed encouraged.

Officially approved dissent is, of course, not dissent at all. In fact, none of the stories discussed here are really dissident. Some of the stories, however, have gone beyond officially approved criticism. Liu Xinwu's stories, for example, are far from sanguine about China's being able to resolve some of its serious social problems. Not the least of these is China's ability to bring up the younger generation to be 'revolutionary successors'. 'The Class Teacher' has, moreover, deliberately drawn attention to the fact that children from a working-class background may be intellectually dull because their parents are unable to provide any intellectual stimuli. On the other hand, the students most responsive to the current policy of upholding intellectual pursuits are themselves from an intellectual background. The author perhaps meant to do no more than present an accurate picture of the effect of Chinese education but he has in fact pointed to the class basis of the post-Mao leadership and his work might provide ammunition for those who wish to criticise that leadership for its non-proletarian inclination. Here we must face the crucial relationship between education and class, and this Price will discuss in the next chapter. It is an unresolved question which still awaits adequate theoretical treatment. In crude terms, however, it reappears constantly in China and, though criticism of non-proletarian inclination is not evident at the moment, it is not rash to anticipate it. In the meantime, the Chinese leaders are content to try to fill the cultural void left by the 'Gang'. In this, they will continue to tolerate ideological heterodoxy, provided that it is not of a fundamental nature.

Conclusion

Though the roots of current policy may be found in the past, it is safe to say that the 'hundred flowers' policy has never been given such a 'liberal' interpretation as at the moment. The literature created under the impact of this 'liberal' version of the 'hundred flowers' policy, however, though clearly different from the 'socialist realist' brand of conformist literature in vogue since the policy reversals of 1957, is not really heterodox. It serves the anti-'Gang of Four' politics very well. Yet even this basically conformist literature has been the cause of concern and has resulted in some mistrust of current literary policy. Significantly, most writers of the new literature are amateurs who have not been greatly affected by 'residual fear' because they have not experienced persecution in the past.[111] Veteran writers, on the other hand, are more worldly-wise and content themselves with the adoption of historical themes.[112]

There is still, therefore, some degree of caution and critics sympathetic to the new kind of literature have urged writers to make concessions to 'socialist realism' or what they have called the 'combination of revolutionary realism and revolutionary romanticism'.[113] Some of the new literature, therefore, has been modified by the depiction of more positive and inspiring elements, and the old didactic purpose has been preserved. We have seen how a cynic was magically transformed into a revolutionary martyr in order to convey a positive message. We have seen also a whole array of heroes who dared to 'go against the tide' to combat the evil policies of the 'Gang of Four'.[114] Why was it then that the 'Gang' was not toppled so much earlier by these armies of rebels? In short, literature is still expected to serve politics and it just happens that present politics are more 'liberal' than hitherto. Sceptics might wonder just how long the current 'liberalisation' will last.[115] But, as I suggested at the beginning of this chapter, before we attempt to answer such a question, it might not be amiss if we paused to think whether such a yardstick as 'liberalisation' has any relevance to the Chinese situation.

Notes

1. Lenin, 13 November 1905, in Lenin 1967, pp. 22-7 and 154-5.
2. Qu's essays, together with his other writings on Marxist literary criticism and his translations of Engels, Lenin and Plekhanov on literature, are collected in Qu Qiubai 1953, Vol. II. For a discussion of his contribution to Marxist literary theory, see Pickowicz 1977 (a) and Pickowicz 1977 (b).
3. Being a leader of the underground CCP, Qu could not join the League of Left-Wing Writers openly but he directed Party members working in the League and provided theoretical guidance for it. See *Wenyibao* 12, 1955, pp. 42-3; Nanjing Daxue Zhongwen Xi 1960, pp. 79-95.

4. On the League's role in Chinese politics and Chinese literature, see Hunter 1973.

5. Mao Zedong, 2 May 1942, *SW*, Vol. III, 1965, p. 69. Translation amended according to *SW*, Chinese edition, 1964, Vol. III, p. 849.

6. For Chinese left-wing comments on the Creation Society, see Qu Quibai 1953, Vol. II, pp. 988-96; Li Helin 1939, pp. 95-157. For a Western view, see Lee 1972 and 1973.

7. *Wenyibao* 1, 1979, p. 6; *RMRB* 12 November 1967, p. 6.

8. Yao Wenyuan 1967, p. 81; *Wenyibao* 1, 1979, p. 6.

9. Ansley 1971.

10. Starr 1976; Gittings 1976.

11. *RMRB* 27 February 1977, p. 2.

12. *Hongqi* 11, 1976, pp. 43-6.

13. *RMRB* 2 January 1977, p. 5; *Wenyibao* 2, 1978, pp. 20-3.

14. *RMRB* 27 February 1977, p. 2.

15. PFLP 1970, pp. 208-9.

16. Mao Zedong, 2 December 1963 and 27 June 1964, Renmin Chubanshe 1967, pp. 21-25.

17. *Hongqi* 1, 1978, p. 40.

18. *RMRB* 2 December 1977, p. 2; *RMRB* 7 December 1977, p. 2.

19. *RMRB* 24 December 1978, pp. 1-2.

20. *RMRB* 7 December 1977, p. 2; *RMRB* 19 December 1978, p. 3.

21. *Wenyibao* 1, 1979, pp. 4-7, 11-13.

22. *Renmin Wenxue* 1, 1979, p. 99.

23. *Wenyibao* 1, 1979, p. 17.

24. *Wenyibao* 2, 1979, pp. 14-18; *Renmin Wenxue* 3, 1979, pp. 3-4.

25. Solomon 1972, pp. 230 and 450; Brugger 1977, p. 175.

26. *Wenyibao* 2, 1979, pp. 2-13.

27. *SCMM* 635, pp. 17-32; *Wenyibao* 1, 1979, pp. 21-5.

28. *SCMM* 635, pp. 17-32.

29. *Renmin Wenxue* 3, 1979, p. 3.

30. Zhonggong Yanjiu Zazhishe 1970, pp. 514-19, 542-4.

31. *RMRB* 22 December 1977, p. 3.

32. *RMRB* 14 May 1978, p. 1.

33. *Dongxiang* (Hong Kong) 4, 16 January 1979, pp. 14-17, *FBIS*-CHI-79-16-N3.

34. Ibid., *FBIS*-CHI-79-16-N5.

35. A biography of Huang Zhen may be found in Klein and Clark 1971, pp. 387-90.

36. Zhou Yang is currently Deputy Director of the Chinese Academy of Social Sciences and Vice-Chairman of the All China Federation of Literary and Art Circles.

37. *RMRB* 14 May 1978, p. 1.

38. *Wenyibao* 4, 1978, p. 26.

39. *RMRB* 24 December 1977, p. 2.

40. *Wenyibao* 1, 1978, p. 28.

41. *Wenyibao* 1, 1978, p. 8.

42. E.g. Mao Dun still retains his former titles of Vice-Chairman of the All China Federation of Literary and Art Circles and Chairman of the Chinese Writers' Union. Zhou Yang also retains his former titles as Vice-Chairman of both of these organisations, *Wenyibao* 4, 1978, p. 2. Ouyang Shan retains his former title of Chairman of the Guangdong branch of the Federation.

43. Neuhauser 1967; Solomon 1972, pp. 330-509.

44. *GMRB* 29 December 1978, p. 3.

45. *RMRB* 17 November 1978, p. 1.

46. *GMRB* 20 December 1978, p. 1; *RMRB* 23 December 1978, p. 1.

47. *GMRB* 23 December 1978, p. 3.

48. Both of these authors and their works are discussed in Chan 1979.

49. *RMRB* 17 November 1978, p. 1.

50. *RMRB* 2 January 1979, p. 1; *RMRB* 13 January 1979, p. 1; *RMRB* 24 January 1979, p. 1; *RMRB* 7 March 1979, p. 4.

51. Examples of how some prominent writers and artists think of the movement may be found in: *RMRB* 13 February 1979, p. 3; *RMRB* 20 February 1979, p. 3.

52. *Renmin Wenxue* 5, 1978, pp. 6-7.

53. *Wenyibao* 1, 1979, p. 7.

54. *Wenyibao* 1, 1978, pp. 20-5.

55. Lu Dingyi, 26 May 1956, in Bowie and Fairbank (eds.) 1962, pp. 151-63.

56. Mao Zedong, 27 February 1957, *SW*, Vol. V, 1977, p. 412.

57. Swayze 1962, pp. 113-14.

58. Ibid., p. 114.

59. He Zhi (pseudonym of Qin Zhaoyang, the editor of *Renmin Wenxue*) supported it in *Renmin Wenxue* 9, 1956, pp. 1-13. He was denounced as a 'rightist' in *Renmin Wenxue* 4, 1958, pp. 103-11. See also, Goldman 1967, pp. 169-70.

60. *Hongqi* 1, 1958, p. 35.

61. Lu Dingyi, 26 May 1956, in Bowie and Fairbank (eds.) 1962, p. 157.

62. Chan 1979.

63. *Wenyibao* 8-9, 1964, pp. 3-20; *Wenyibao* 4, 1966, pp. 2-9.

64. Mao Zedong, 27 February 1957, *SW*, Vol. V, 1977, p. 408.

65. The debate dated back to 1957 and is still raging today. See *RMRB* 18 March 1957, p. 8; *GMRB* 3 November 1978, p. 3; *GMRB* 5 November 1978, p. 2; *GMRB* 16 March 1979, p. 3.

66. Mao Zedong, 30 June 1949, *SW*, Vol. IV 1961, p. 417. This was explicitly endorsed by the 1954 Constitution, Articles 5 and 10, (Renmin Chubanshe 1954, pp. 8-9), and implicitly endorsed by the 1975 Constitution, Article 14 (PFLP 1975, pp. 17-18) and the 1978 Constitution, Article 18 (PFLP 1978, pp. 143-4).

67. Mao Zedong, 27 February 1957, *SW*, Vol. V, 1977, p. 386.

68. Ibid., p. 411.

69. *Wenyibao* 17, 1958, pp. 7-11.

70. For further discussion on this point, see Kraus 1974; White 1976.

71. *Wenyibao* 2, 1979, pp. 2-13.

72. This document was classified as secret and no official text is available. Long excerpts from it, however, are quoted in Liaoning Daxue Zhongwen Xi, Wenyi Lilun Jiaoyanshi 1976, pp. 301-6.

73. *SCMM* 635, pp. 17-32.

74. Schurmann 1966, pp. 223-5.

75. PFLP 1978, pp. 141-2.

76. Ibid., pp. 211-12.

77. Mao Zedong, 27 February 1957, *SW*, Vol. V, 1977, p. 408.

78. *RMRB* 23 February 1979, p. 2; *RMRB* 24 February 1979, pp. 3-4.

79. *RMRB* 13 January 1978, p. 3.

80. *Wenyibao* 3, 1979, pp. 34-7.

81. E.g. *RMRB* 22 December 1977, p. 3; *Wenyibao* 2, 1978, pp. 35-6.

82. *RMRB* 20 February 1979, p. 3; *RMRB* 10 March 1979, p. 3; *GMRB* 16 February 1979, p. 3.

83. *New China News* Vol. XVII, No. 27, 18 July 1979, p. 7.

84. Folk art forms include ballads, story-telling, comic dialogues, 'clapper talk', 'cross talk', etc.

85. Yao Xueyin 1976 and 1977. The first volume of this novel was completed in 1963, but the second volume was not published until after the downfall of the 'Gang of Four'.

86. *Renmin Wenxue* 4, 1979, pp. 6-7.

87. Renmin Wenxue Chubanshe 1978.

88. *Wenyibao* 4, 1978, pp. 7 and 11. Both of these stories are translated in *Chinese Literature* 1, 1979, pp. 15-35 and pp. 36-57

89. *Wenyibao* 2, 1978, pp. 36-7; Mao Zedong, 2 May 1942, *SW*, Vol. III, 1965, p. 91.

90. These are too numerous to list here. The more important ones are *GMRB* 3 November 1978, p. 3; *GMRB* 4 November 1978, p. 2; *Wenyibao* 4, 1978, pp. 5-19.

91. Renmin Wenxue Chubanshe 1978, pp. 147-76.

92. *Renmin Wenxue* 9, 1978, p. 76.

93. *Qishi Niandai* 4, 1979, pp. 89-90.

94. Renmin Wenxue Chubanshe 1978, pp. 588-610.

95. *Renmin Wenxue* 12, 1978, pp. 29-44.

96. *Renmin Wenxue* 7, 1957, pp. 14-25.

97. *Renmin Wenxue* 11, 1957, pp. 121-2.

98. *Renmin Wenxue* 12, 1978, p. 34.

99. *Renmin Wenxue* 9, 1978, p. 76.

100. Renmin Wenxue Chubanshe 1978, pp. 505-19, translated in *Chinese Literature* 3, 1979, pp. 25-38.

101. *Chinese Literature* 3, 1979, pp. 103-5.

102. *Wenyibao* 4, 1978, p. 6.

103. Renmin Wenxue Chubanshe 1978, pp. 550-87.

104. PFLP 1970, p. 234.

105. *GMRB* 19 January 1979, p. 3.

106. *GMRB* 16 March 1979, p. 3.

107. *GMRB* 3 November 1978, p. 3; *GMRB* 16 March 1979, p. 3.

108. *GMRB* 19 January 1979, p. 3.

109. *GMRB* 16 March 1979, p. 3.

110. *RMRB* 15 December 1978, pp. 1 and 4; *RMRB* 31 December 1978, p. 1; *RMRB* 5 January 1979, p. 3; *RMRB* 26 January 1979, p. 3.

111. Of the 21 stories collected in Renmin Wenxue Chubanshe 1978, 18 were written by such writers.

112. Of 5 short stories on subjects other than the Cultural Revolution, collected in Renmin Wenxue Chubanshe 1978, 4 were stories about revolutionary wars, of which 3 were written by veteran writers.

113. *Renmin Wenxue* 1, 1979, pp. 95-7; *Wenyibao* 4, 1978, p. 19.

114. With the exception of 3 or 4, nearly all 21 Cultural Revolution stories in Renmin Wenxue Chubanshe 1978 have an anti-'Gang of Four' theme.

115. Such questions have indeed been asked. See, e.g., Chey 1979.

6 Education — Why a Reversal?

RONALD F. PRICE

Serious educators around the world, concerned by the failure of increased schooling since World War Two to make any impact on the inequalities of class structure and privilege, or indeed to improve significantly the level of education of large sections of the population, listened sympathetically to accounts of the reforms in education proposed in the Cultural Revolution. Aware of the problems posed by tertiary school selection examinations and the constraints these impose on the curricula of students who will never in fact sit for them, many teachers welcomed China's playing down of examinations in favour of other methods of selection. Other teachers, having experience of working with older students with work experience, responded positively to the idea of a work-break between secondary and tertiary school. Many teachers, concerned at the divorce between school and the wider society in their own countries, hoped that the experiences in 'open door' schooling and in 'combining education with productive labour' would produce results which could be generalised beyond the boundaries of China. It came, therefore, as something of a shock and certainly a disappointment when, so soon after the death of Mao, these reforms appeared to be abandoned and the focus again became 'the selection and training of talent', with priority schools and national examinations praised as the main means to achieve this.

While a wide range of educators showed sympathetic interest in developments in China, for those teachers of a radical or marxist persuasion they were of particular significance. Radicals were excited and encouraged by the promise of large-scale experiment in reducing what the Chinese referred to as 'the three great differences'[1] and by questions which dealt with the relationship between education and social class.

In this chapter, I try to show the limitations of the changes actually made during the Cultural Revolution, and perhaps more importantly, the failure to develop a marxist theory of education which could have acted as a guide to a more viable practice. By this I mean in place of the vague, undifferentiated conception of education as superstructure, 'a rich totality of many determinations and relations' of the kind about which Marx spoke in the section on 'the method of political economy' at the beginning of the *Grundrisse*.[2] I try to indicate the kinds of relations between educational and political-economic categories which need to be theorised not only if the present is to be better understood, but also if the goals set by Mao Zedong and his supporters are ever to be achieved. At the same time, I argue that recent reversals in educational policy spring from a widely held conservative view of education as vocational training, and from what is seen to be the need for the kind of specialists which traditional European style schools have demonstrated they can produce.

An Underdeveloped Theory

The twelve years of discussion (and perhaps eight years of experiment) in education which followed 1966 exhibit a poverty of theory which some sympathetic observers find hard to admit. For all the wall posters (*dazibao*), pages of newsprint, and the millions of participants in word and deed, educational theory has not been advanced beyond a small number of propositions put forward by Mao himself. The development and summing up of experience, for which Mao called, never advanced beyond the reiteration of these same propositions. All too often this was in the form of exhortation to combine theory and practice or to learn from the poor and lower-middle peasants, rather than an examination of the relations and conditions required for achieving particular outcomes. For this reason, this discussion will confine itself to Mao Zedong's formulations.

Mao, himself a trained and, if briefly, experienced schoolteacher, regrettably never wrote any extended studies of education, though large numbers of his political writings are saturated with educational precepts. He was at his best in advocating certain well-established views of education as a method of study. Such pieces as the preface to 'Rural Surveys'[3] and 'Reform Our Study'[4] illustrate this. In these he advocates making 'social investigations', seeking truth from facts, and warns that 'without investigation there is no right to speak'. Here Mao is considering education as a process, a dialectic of teaching and learning. In this he is, as Pischel shows, in the tradition of educators of the Enlightenment.[5] But while this is a necessary basis, it is insufficient. A marxist theory of education as process must explore the relations between that process and social institutions and uncover the conditions under which this or that outcome can be expected.

In a number of writings Mao deals with education as knowledge. But it is its acquisition, its relation to the 'countless phenomena of the objective external world'[6] and human practice, which particularly concerns him. He does not deal with the nature of knowledge itself, with the problems of science and ideology, or with the different stages of creation, dissemination and use, in other than the most cursory fashion. On the acquisition of knowledge, if one is really to influence the process, it is necessary to distinguish between two processes usually distinguished as socialisation and education. In the former, learning is from experience within structures which lack any intentional teaching, while in the latter some element of intention is always present. Mao, in his various references to the role of practice in education, moves from one to the other of these processes without making the distinction explicit. No doubt, like many of us, he believes that socialising experiences take precedent over the purely educational. The 'hidden curriculum', as contemporary educators outside China often put it, is more important than the classroom rhetoric. But any measure of control of the educational process requires that we distinguish clearly what is going on. Conflict and congruence of rhetoric and reality, of what is taught and what is experienced in other ways, must be theorised if it is to be used.

A related weakness of Mao's theory of the origin of human knowledge is his neglect of the role of previously held concepts in organising man's perceptions in what he refers to as the perceptual stage of knowledge.[7] True, Mao says: 'our practice proves that what is perceived cannot at once be comprehended and that only what is comprehended can be more deeply perceived.'[8] But that does not really deal with the problem. And the same essay goes on to confuse another problem by saying first that: 'whoever wants to know a thing, has no way of doing so except by coming in contact with it,'[9] and then adding that: 'one cannot have direct experience of everything; as a matter of fact, most of our knowledge comes from indirect experience'.[10] Yet surely what we need theoretical guidance on is, above all, how to break through the blinkers our preconceptions put on our thinking. We need help to make us aware of how they affect both perception and conception. We need to learn how to loosen up our preconceptions and become more receptive to new ideas. We need guidance on the relation of both direct and indirect experience to our knowledge. In addition, there is the whole problematic of the relation of knowledge to beliefs and attitudes. Neither Mao Zedong Thought nor the discussions of the Cultural Revolution take us any further in clarifying all this.[11]

Mao discusses education as structure or institution in a number of places, but always insufficiently. Again, the traditional Chinese propensity to exhortation wins over analysis. In 1933 Mao wrote: 'The raising of the political and cultural level of the people through cultural and educational work is also a most important task in the development of the economy.'[12] In the draft of 'Sixty Work Methods' in 1958 Mao wrote: 'There is no doubt whatever about the unity of politics and economics, the unity of politics and technology. This is so every year and will forever be so. This is red and expert'.[13] Here the terms 'technology', 'red' and 'expert' all imply aspects of education to which Mao refers elsewhere. In the same document, speaking of ideology and politics as 'the supreme commander and the soul', he went on to advocate that 'politicians must know some business'; this is yet another instance of education. What we need to know is what kind of business, and how its acquisition is related to the particular institutions in which the learning is done? What kind of technology goes with what politics? What experience and/or teaching induces what shades of redness and expertise? Each of these (and many more questions) requires analysis of the dialectical reciprocal relations of its parts, and not only the unity but the contradiction[14] is also important.

To theorise education within the political economic process, it is insufficient to regard it as part of the superstructure as seems to have been the case during the Cultural Revolution. Clearly, for Mao, work is an educative agent, both in the aspect of the relations of production and the productive forces. Knowledge both enters into and is shaped by the productive process, again as productive force. Mao did valuable work in drawing people's attention to aspects of the problematic. The need is to go further. Here are some examples of his formulations:

Stalin's book...[*Economic Problems of Socialism in the USSR*] says nothing about the superstructure. It is not concerned with people; it considers things, not people.[15]

The main object of study in political economy is the relations of production. But to study clearly the relations of production, it is necessary to study concomitantly the productive forces and also the positive and negative effects of the superstructure on the relations of production... If the study of the superstructure goes too far it becomes nation-state theory, class struggle theory.[16]

The bourgeoisie first changed the superstructure and took possession of the machinery of state before carrying on propaganda to gather real strength.[17]

Our revolution began with Marxist-Leninist propaganda, which served to create new public opinion in favour of the revolution. Moreover, it was possible to destroy the old relations of production only after we had overthrown a backward superstructure in the course of revolution. After the old relations of production had been destroyed new ones were created, and these cleared the way for the development of new social productive forces.[18]

The key quotations linking education with the class structure in the Cultural Revolution were vitiated by the lack of a marxist analysis of the social formation which is China today, and therefore of an accurate marxist description of its social classes. Ironically, one of the accusations against Zhang Chunqiao is that he attempted to produce a new class analysis.[19] Two much used quotations were:

In this great Cultural Revolution, the phenomenon of our schools being dominated by bourgeois intellectuals must be completely changed.[20]

While their [the students] main task is to study, they should in addition...criticise the bourgeoisie...the domination of our schools by bourgeois intellectuals should not be allowed to continue.[21]

These raise a host of educational problems and some of these will be dealt with below. On the question of class, Brugger has shown[22] how Mao's concept of class moved from the residual form, which dominated the Cultural Revolution, to a generative one at the time of the movement to study the dictatorship of the proletariat in 1975.[23] Typical of the Cultural Revolution formulations was that expressed in a long article in the *Jiefangjunbao* (*Liberation Army Daily*) in June 1966. This talked about a 'come-back' of the bourgeoisie which was clearly defined as the former property owners, imperialists, feudalists and capitalists whose reactionary ideas could not be confiscated like their property.[24] Another formulation of that period was in terms of 'degenerate' elements corrupted by 'living in peaceful surroundings'.[25] A *Renmin Ribao* editorial of the same month referred to 'some people in the Party and government organs who are degenerate'.[26] While there are hints of a generative model in this, there are also strong overtones of a Confucian moralising approach to the 'good official'. In any case, such formulations can in no way be described as educational. In application to schooling, moreover, they point backwards towards students' origins rather than forward to the effects of a highly selective school and job system and the non-rotational nature of positions of power and authority throughout government and industry.

Finally, in considering Mao Zedong Thought in its relation to marxism and education, I would like to mention a quite different question. This is the degree to which Mao (and others, of course) was influenced by the Chinese traditional philosophy so as to preclude the kind of structural exploration which I have been advocating. In particular, it would seem that he subscribed to that aspect of Confucian thought which Munro describes as 'clustering',[27] and that this accounts for much of what I previously saw only as 'repeated moral exhortation'.[28] Clustering is a belief that knowing, feeling and promptings to act are related in such a way that knowing something tends, through feelings engendered, to bring about a particular action. Munro comments: 'there is no factual knowledge that does not contain a potential association with an evaluation'.[29] But at the same time, and this is especially true of Chinese Communist practice, 'the correct feelings may not actually accompany knowing certain facts. The individual has a responsibility to ensure that such a proper accompaniment is realised.'[30] Is not this the role of group study sessions, much of the ritual reading and reciting of texts, not to mention the struggle sessions and penal processes of thought reform?

Productive Labour and the 'Open Door'

The most conspicuous changes brought about in schooling by the Cultural Revolution involved two interlinked principles: the combining of education with productive labour, and 'open door' schooling.[31] The first principle goes back to Marx's discussions of the work of Robert Owen in the first volume of *Capital*, where he speaks of 'the germ of the education of the future'.[32] Unlike developments in the USSR where, stemming rather from a document of the First International drafted by Marx, the emphasis has been on polytechnical education,[33] Chinese application seems to have been striving to realise the social implications present in two other passages by Marx:

> We consider the tendency of modern industry to make children and juvenile persons of both sexes co-operate in the great work of social production, as a progressive, sound and legitimate tendency.[34]
>
> Moreover, it is obvious that the fact of the collective working group being composed of individuals of both sexes and all ages, must necessarily, *under suitable conditions*, become a source of *humane development*.[35]

Here is the conception of a collective, working purposively and learning at the same time. Learning social skills and moral political lessons, it is envisaged that, at the same time, people will acquire the motivation to acquire technical information and skills to change and improve their lives. In such a collective, the enthusiasm and anti-conservative nature of youth will be harnessed to the social effort and not locked away behind the 'closed doors' of the conventional school. I must stress, however, the 'striving'; for, neither in the 1958-60 movement for 'schools to set up factories and farms and for the factories and agricultural co-operatives to establish schools',[36] nor in the Cultural Revolution of 1966 was the question ever clearly developed. Two much quoted passages from Mao seem to bear out my interpretation:

> On graduating from a senior high school, one should first do some practical work ... If a university course takes five years, one should work at the lower level for three years. Members of the faculty should also go along, working and teaching at the same time. Isn't it possible to teach philosophy, literature or history at the lower levels? Must they teach in tall, modern buildings?[37]
>
> The faculty of arts should take the whole society as its own workshop. Its students should contact the peasants and urban workers [in] industry and agriculture. Otherwise they are not much use on graduation.[38]

These passages were also used to justify various forms of 'open door' schooling, including sending students out of the school to work in the surrounding society, or to compile local histories, and also bringing workers and peasants into the schools to teach aspects of applied science and technology, or to give political education through relating 'past bitterness and present sweetness'. In a 1958 State Council and Central Committee Directive, it was stated that, 'there are facts to show that, provided productive labour is well led, it is of advantage ethically, intellectually, or physically to the students'.[39] Little was said, after that, about any physical advantage; rather the economic advantage to various sectors of society was stressed. I have suggested elsewhere that were these three criteria of moral-political, intellectual-cognitive and economic advantage to be combined with an analysis of the relation between the form of labour performed and its social location, we might have a theory with which to test just what are the 'suitable conditions' for a 'humane development'.[40] But no-one, inside or outside China, has so far performed such a task. The only critical discussion I have seen in Chinese sources has been about the problems of using productive processes for intellectual learning at Wuhan University[41] and a year later in Qinghua University and the Dalian Industrial Institute.[42] This is clearly a narrower question than that posed here.

Two very positive practical outcomes of the movement to combine education with productive labour have been the part-work secondary schools, and the various 'irregular' primary schools which brought schooling to villages where it had been unknown before. Agricultural high schools were set up in 1958. In the mid-1960s, the part-work principle was extended to various urban, technical high schools (*jishu zhongxue*). The 'irregular' primary schools, so-called by officials who disapproved of them, took a variety of forms. Essentially, they attempted to adjust schooling to the need of parents or farms for their pupils' labour. School vacations might be adjusted to suit the agricultural calendar. Pupils were allowed to come and go wherever necessary, or teachers might visit pupils' homes to teach. Girls were encouraged by being allowed to bring their baby siblings to school with them, to play within sight while the girl studied. In Mongol and Uighur pastoral areas teachers visited the work camps in rotation, a system described as a circulating school (*xunhui xuexiao*). In many of these schools, the curriculum emphasised those aspects of writing and calculating which could be immediately applied in the daily, adult life of the village.

_ Another positive development was the training of a variety of middle-level technical personnel to service the villages. The most famous of these were the 'bare-foot doctors'. These were medical auxiliaries trained to deal with the common ailments of the region and assist with the birth control programme. Other such personnel were veterinary auxiliaries, electricians, mechanics and even teachers. In some cases academic, senior high schools were transformed in order to train such personnel.

Unfortunately, the slogans about linking education with productive labour and open-door schooling were used to justify a number of highly negative measures. Concentration on 'the five grains' and some six types of domestic animal was accompanied, all too often, by hostility to a study of the humanities beyond the bare bones of literacy, and distaste for advanced study of the pure sciences. On account of this anti-intellectual atmosphere, and also, no doubt, on account of personal power struggles, a large number of tertiary education institutions were closed, not to reopen until after the fall of the 'Gang of Four'.[43] Many libraries were also closed, or access grossly restricted.[44] At the same time, as Chan has described, book publishing, film making, theatre production and other forms of creativity were so restricted as to cause distress to all classes and sections of society. Adding to this, physical oppression of various kinds was inflicted upon large numbers of the intelligentsia. It is thus small wonder that the fall of the 'Gang' was greeted by a good deal of genuine enthusiasm. My contention here is, not that a more developed educational theory would necessarily have decreased the anti-intellectualism or lessened the faction-fighting, but that it would have robbed the opponents of Mao's views of any shred of theoretical legitimation.

A Theory for Modernisation?

In his speech to the National People's Congress in February 1978, Hua Guofeng correctly located education as a dependent variable when he said, 'in the wake of the new upsurge in economic construction a new upsurge of construction in the cultural sphere will follow.'[45] At the same time, he narrowed the definition of education and closed discussion on those important questions about the 'three great differences' and the nature of an education which would 'serve the proletariat'. If it did not answer them, at least the Cultural Revolution had sharply posed them. Hua went on:

We must raise the scientific and cultural level of the entire Chinese nation to a much higher level so that our working people will master modern techniques of production and scientific knowledge. At the same time, we must build a vast army of working-class intellectuals. Only thus can we successfully fulfil the grand target of building a modern, powerful socialist country.[46]

Deng Xiaoping, the driving force of the new line, had already made clear his position on both revolution and education's role in that process in those documents which became known as 'the three poisonous weeds'. In one, he wrote: 'revolution is liberating the productive forces; revolution is promoting the development of the productive forces.'[47] In another, he quoted Mao Zedong on education: 'it is superfluous nonsense to talk about education or study detached from economic work'; adding: 'how wonderful these words of Chairman Mao'.[48] At the 1978 National Education Work Conference, where Deng referred to scientists and technicians as 'productive forces', he again made clear his narrow definition of education as vocational schooling:

Education, as a whole, must keep pace with the requirements of the growing national economy. Otherwise, if what the students are learning cannot meet the needs of their future profession, and if their study is completely divorced from their work, wouldn't that fundamentally violate the principle of combining education with productive labour?[49]

This definition of education focuses on the school to the neglect of other, often more significant, agents through which people acquire not only their world view (*sixiang*) but also the essential habits and behaviour patterns which go with it. It also focuses on only a limited part of the normal school curriculum. Even worse, it makes the error, fatal for the development of genuine socialism, of taking the knowledge in this area of the curriculum as neutral, or value-free. Two cadres who drafted a report on the Academy of Sciences for Deng Xiaoping said that 'one should not talk about class struggle in science and technology'.[50] More recently Mo Fei, writing in *Gongren Ribao*[51], repeated the point:

Nevertheless the advanced science, technology and management-methods of capitalism are something from which we should and must learn. These things are cats which can catch mice, and not man-eating tigers. There is nothing to be afraid of. So long as they are correctly absorbed they can be turned into tools for socialism.[52]

Along with the stress on science and technology in statements over the past two years there have, of course, been numerous references to the importance of politics. Deng, referring to 'revolutionary ideals and communist virtues', said they 'should be fostered from childhood'.[53] The force of the exhortation is indicated by the recommended action:

There is no doubt that schools should always attach primary importance to a firm and correct political orientation. This, however, does not mean devoting many classroom hours to ideological and political education.[54]

Institutions for Modernisation

The conception of value-freedom is applied not only to science and technology, but also to the school system — to the organisational pattern within which knowledge is imparted. This is in sharp contrast to the Cultural Revolution when the same kind of questions were being asked about the educational outcomes of tracking and hierarchy in the schools as have been asked by increasing numbers of Euro-American educators in recent decades. In China's present condition of poverty and scarce educational resources, inequalities in schooling are inevitable. But the measures, currently being taken, go so far beyond what in unavoidable as to indicate a strong, positive belief in the value of hierarchy and hothouse methods of 'nurturing talent' (*yang cai*). This should not be regarded as surprising since the models which have been provided traditionally, by Europe and the USSR, have all been of this nature, and neither the Great Leap Forward nor the Cultural Revolution improved upon them. In addition, a hierarchical system provides superior positions for a considerable number of teachers and students, and defines a clear path to superior jobs for successful school leavers. This lures an even wider group of parents and young people into supporting the system.

The general shape of the school system, outlined in the eight-year plan for 'reorganisation and raising of standards' which the Minister of Education, Liu Xiyao, put before the 1978 National Education Work Conference, remains basically that already developed in the early 1960s.[55] The core of the system is the full-time day (FTD) primary, secondary and tertiary schools. After three decades, in which Mao and others have urged shortening this system from the 6:6 primary-secondary model inherited from the American-influenced twenties, it now seems that the model is to be 5:5 for the cities, and 5:3 for the villages, though even this is being challenged.[56] The tertiary pattern, which was drastically curtailed in the Cultural Revolution, is being restored to a basic university course of five years, and technical courses ranging from two to five years in a variety of tertiary colleges and institutes. This variety will continue the Soviet model of tertiary schools adopted in the reform immediately following Liberation in the early 1950s. Around the core will be a range of part-work and spare-time schools on the already familiar pattern. Liu reiterated a much earlier intention to develop a 'complete system of tertiary education' in each province, municipality and autonomous region. This would mean institutions for the humanities, pure and applied science, agriculture, medicine and teacher-training. But, presumably, certain institutions would continue to recruit students on a national rather than provincial basis, while others might guarantee their students work in a certain area on graduation.[57] Such differences in the past have had significant divisive consequences and they will certainly do so in the future.

The problems posed by differences between FTD, part-work and spare-time institutions, the hierarchical links which will inevitably be forged between them and the jobs for which their graduates are eligible will be further exacerbated by the restoration of a system of *priority* schools, or *zhongdian xuexiao*.[58] These schools, referred to as 'little treasure pagoda schools' (*xiao baota xuexiao*) or 'schools for aristocrats' in the Cultural Revolution, were abolished at that time. In 1978, considerable attention in the Chinese press was given to their restoration and lists were published of schools at all three levels of education. Designation appears to be at national (under the Ministry of Education) and provincial levels, and perhaps even lower. But it is still not clear what this means as no details of financial or managerial responsibilities have been published. Statements, such as that by the Minister of Education that 'the priority schools attached to the Ministry of Education and other Ministries and Commissions should also be the priority schools under the Party Committees and educational departments of different regions',[59] hardly help here. All that is clear is that priority schools will be given preference in the allocation of resources. Where the teaching staff is considered insufficiently superior, measures, including transfers, will be taken to improve it. In tertiary priority schools the use of guest lecturers from the Academy of Sciences and other research bodies is recommended. Similarly, tertiary lecturers and other scientific and technical workers will be asked to give classes in the priority secondary and primary schools.[60] Newspaper articles have begun describing the provision of new dormitories for boarding students and measures to improve the equipment of the often already superior libraries and laboratories. Finally, but perhaps most significant, priority will be given to the selection of students by means of examinations. This will presumably result in students moving up within a system of priority schools from primary school to the highly select, national universities and institutes. It is hard to see what other implications to draw from the Minister's comment that 'during the nation's unified tertiary school enrolment, priority should guaranteed to priority schools'.[61]

There can be no doubt of the popularity of these measures among important sections of society. For huge numbers of people, priority schools are what a 'proper' school should be. Students who get in, or believe they stand a chance of so doing — and this will be at least hundreds of thousands — will have a clearly defined and assured future. Many Chinese teachers, like their counterparts abroad,[62] show a strong preference for working with selected students on a more narrowly academic curriculum. Where the Cultural Revolution failed was in concentrating criticism on the social class aspect of priority schools. It ignored the dependent nature of schools in a society. Social classes and strata are determined at the political-economic level and, therefore, Cultural Revolution proposals failed to anticipate the real and widespread support for priority schools. More importantly, discussion failed to show that there are other, better ways of raising (*tigao*) standards and producing the necessary specialists, and of just how best to *distribute* scarce resources in order to do this. Without a promising alternative, it was inevitable that responsible officials would return to the old, universally proven methods.

The restoration of the priority schools and the virtual abandonment of the work-break between secondary and tertiary schools raises another important educational question. About 1969, it seemed as if developments were leading to a distinct separation of general, basic education from advanced, vocational training. Such a distinction has been advocated by educators in different parts of the world, largely for the sake of the majority of school students who do not go on to higher studies and whose schooling is, it is claimed, impoverished by the strait-jacket of university entrance requirements. Unfortunately, the Cultural Revolution discussion, with its emphasis on 'popularisation' (*puji*), failed to theorise the question in these terms. Had it done so, it might have gone some way towards a defensible position. But it would also have had to have done a number of things. It would have had to have shown that the production of specialists was, if not improved, at least not worsened by such a division. This has always been hotly contested by certain academic specialists, especially by mathematicians, who claim that continuity of training is essential. Teaching methods in tertiary schools, notoriously backward throughout the world, would have had to be drastically improved and, at the same time, the content of tertiary syllabuses would have required adjustment. Particularly important would have been the introduction of new methods to teach 'bridging courses' between the new, general education and the particular specialised vocational subjects.[63] It is doubtful whether China, at present, has sufficient people with the will or the training to do such a massive task. It would also have been politically unacceptable to have admitted the need, as this would have been seen as giving support to those 'academic authorities' who saw worker and peasant students as, innately or otherwise, inferior.

Finally, the number of institutions and student places is important. This is particularly the case in the tertiary sector. Comparison of student places with the relevant age cohort is a measure of the competition for what is clearly seen as social advancement and, for many, the only road out of the village into a more comfortable and interesting urban life. It is also a measure of the trained manpower required for modernisation. The figures, illustrated in Table 6.1, immediately reveal one failure of the Cultural Revolution.

Table 6.1: Student Numbers in Tertiary Schools 1964-79

1964-65	700,000[a]
1965-66	900,000[a]
1971-72	200,000[b]
1975-76	500,000[b]
1977-78	600,000[b]
1978-79	850,000[c]

Sources:
a. Richman 1969, p. 164.
b. Price 1978.
c. State Statistical Bureau 27 June 1979, p. 8.

A similar shrinkage occurred in the number of tertiary institutions. This was given as 400 in 1963[64] and 663 in 1965.[65] In 1977-8, the number was officially said to be over 400.[66] To this must now be added the 55 new institutions announced in the *Guangming Ribao* in April 1978 and the 169 announced the following January,[67] which would bring the 1979 total to some 624. However, the most recent official figure, in July 1979, is only 578.[68]

Recent figures given by John S. Aird[69] suggest a single-year cohort for the tertiary school years, 18-22, to be in the order of 21 million. The 278,000 students who successfully passed the 1977 entrance examinations would comprise only 1.23 per cent of this figure. Taking the figure of 850,000 students and comparing it with estimates of 100-104 million for the total five-year age-cohort gives a figure between 0.85 per cent and 0.82 per cent. Whichever way the comparisons are made, the degree of competition is clearly very high. It is made higher still by a backlog of young people sent to the rural areas during the Cultural Revolution who feel they have missed out. These made up a substantial proportion of the 5.7 million candidates who sat the 1977 entrance examinations from which the 278,000 mentioned above were chosen. Nevertheless, while these figures can be read in terms of competition, they will also be read by a number of Chinese students as an opening up of opportunities compared with recent years. They will, moreover, endear at least the successful to the policy of the leadership which has brought this about.

Selection by Examination

'Spot, select and bring up people of talent.' This was how Minister of Education, Liu Xiyao, headed the section of his report dealing with tertiary school entrance. This was again to be by nationally organised, academic examinations. True, mention was still made of 'strict implementation of the principle of comprehensive moral, intellectual, and physical appraisal' in Liu's report and repeated in newspaper accounts of regulations.[70] But reports of practice have made it clear that it will be examination results which will dominate selection.

After a delayed enrolment in 1977, the first new national examinations were organised in the spring of 1978. Students in the humanities took papers in politics, Chinese language and literature, mathematics, history, geography and a foreign language. Science candidates were examined in politics, Chinese language and literature, mathematics, physics, chemistry and a foreign language. Special regulations catered for those students who had been unable to study a foreign language. The languages examined were English, Russian, French, German, Japanese, Spanish and Arabic.[71]

Conscious of the use made by Red Guards, in the Cultural Revolution, of Mao's attacks on examinations, a number of articles have set out to reassure their readers. According to one in *Peking Review*, 'the stress in examinations is on testing the student's basic knowledge and their ability to analyse and solve problems. The tendency to give odd or catch questions is avoided. [A reference to Mao]'.[72] To illustrate this, the article described one of the questions in the politics paper which asked: 'about Chairman Mao's theory of differentiation of the three worlds, and the candidates were asked to explain which countries or regions belong to the First World and which to the Second and Third'.[73]

Regulations provide for a majority of students to be in the 20-5 age range but, because of the desire to tap talent and because of the enormous backlog of young people sent to the rural areas during the past ten years, there are exceptions in both directions. In the 1977 examination, 92 candidates under the age of 16 passed and were admitted to the Chinese University of Science and Technology where 20 of them were placed in a special 'junior class'.[74] At the other end of the age range, allowance is made for 'those with outstanding talent in particular specialities, technical innovation, or invention'.[75] 'Unconventional means' of selection may be employed, such as 'assignment to related institutes' without taking the unified examinations. Examples of such students have been given in *Peking Review* — among them former rural teacher, Duan Yuanxing, now doing post-graduate work at the Beijing Observatory. His case is interesting as his story appeared in picture-book form in the popular *Lianhuan Huabao*.[76] He will thus join the ever-changing list of heroes held up for emulation by Chinese youth.

It is difficult to obtain any direct evidence of the reaction of young people to these changes, though the pains taken to defend them suggest that the authorities, at least, fear they may be unpopular. A 'leading member of the Ministry of Education' was quoted in *Peking Review*:

As it is not possible for our country to have universal higher education in the immediate future and only a portion of the young people will be able to study in colleges, it is quite understandable to enrol only the best.[77]

Answering the question posed by the *Review*: 'Would this method of matriculating the best of the examinees in college entrance examinations lead to the emergence of a privileged stratum?',[78] the official replied 'no'. The growth of a privileged stratum would be prevented by the 'worker-peasant origin of the majority of the candidates and the political education to which they will be subjected at college'. Furthermore, on graduation, their wages would be 'almost the same or a little higher' than that of workers with the same seniority.

A careful reading of the regulations for the examinations reveals, if not the attitude of youth to the examinations, at least their attitudes to the hierarchy of colleges and the jobs to which these lead. In 1978, students attending communist labour colleges, workers' colleges and May Seventh colleges[79] were forbidden to sit the entrance examinations, as were those youth who had returned illegally to the cities from the rural areas. But such restriction did not apply to graduates from such vocational courses who had worked for two or more years.[80]

In the advanced capitalist countries, the trend has been against examinations within tertiary schools. They have, however, remained in use for selection purposes in spite of continuing criticism from both students and a minority of teachers. It seems probable in China, with its strong tradition of examinations and reliance on rote memory to master the written language, that the opposition to examinations is less than it appeared to be during the Cultural Revolution. In addition, experience with a system based on political or character certification by a youth's workmates may have proved disappointing to large numbers of people. Certainly, the widely publicised use of influence, by Army and other officials, to get their children into university, suggests that may have been the case.[81] There is also the point that, had selection by character reference been ideally implemented when there was such a shortage of tertiary school places, strains and difficulties at the workplace would have developed. These, at the present moment in China, might be found to be intolerable. In this situation, a return to what is widely regarded as an impartial device and the normal way of doing things, would be widely welcomed. Thus, the authorities' efforts to rationalise the change of policy may not have been so necessary. What is clear, however, is that a return to competitive examinations puts the onus and the stigma of failure on the individual candidate again, and society is shielded from blame for not providing more college places and interesting jobs. An interesting admission of this stigma was published in *Guangming Ribao*:

> Candidates whose examination results are unsatisfactory must not be discriminated against or ridiculed; proper ideological work should be used to help and encourage them to continue to work hard.[82]

Finally, a more basic weakness of the Cultural Revolution policy on selection should be noted. Political or character selection was justified in moral terms. Students were expected to serve the people better and to return to the factories and farms which sent them to college. This is quite contrary to the marxist emphasis on seeking to change the social structure in order to change behaviour. Without a change in the relations of production and the whole job-class structure of society which the tertiary schools feed, it is wishful thinking to expect a changed method of selection to make any fundamental difference.

Respect the Teacher

Mao Zedong and the present leaders agree on the importance of the teacher in any reform of education.[83] But, while Mao saw progress through a growing together of teachers and non-teachers and a learning from each other, the present leadership sees progress in strengthening the professional separateness of teachers. One of the first signs of the recent changes in education was the appearance in the newspapers of the classical phrase '*zun shi*' (respect the teacher).[84] This was subsequently followed by regular announcements of the restoration of a hierarchy of ranks in the tertiary schools. In the universities, the ranks of professor (*jiaoshou*) and associate professor (*fu jiaoshou*) returned.[85] These moves were accompanied by other measures advocated in the Minister of Education's speech to the National Education Work Conference:

> It is now imperative to revive the system of periodical examination for teachers, ... the granting of academic titles and promotion to academic ranks. Titles and promotion should be by merit in work and academic level, not through seniority. The promotion of those who excel in their work can bypass the grade order irrespective of the length of schooling or teaching. Those who

have done extremely well in teaching secondary or primary schools should be granted the titles of 'Teachers of Special-Grade' ... Advanced teachers, cadres and staff members should be commended. The most outstanding among them can receive the titles of 'model teachers' or 'model educational workers' and [be granted] citations, medals or certain material rewards.[86]

It is interesting to note that the 'grade order', to which the Minister refers, is one of the things not mentioned during the Cultural Revolution, but which appears to have persisted unchanged throughout. Teachers, like their counterparts in the civil service, occupy graded posts. There are, in fact, eleven grades for the primary school and ten for the secondary.[87] One might have thought that a movement towards greater democracy would have questioned such a system.

Throughout 1977 and since, articles have appeared in the press defining the new model for teachers. In place of the scholar, turning for guidance to the workers and peasants and attempting to integrate with them, we have the single-minded pursuer of knowledge, often studying secretly and hampered by the 'Gang of Four' and its 'small handful' of supporters. In many cases, such models have not laboured alone but have helped others to learn. Mathematics teachers have been especially singled out, both at secondary and tertiary level.[88]

With the new emphasis on pure rather than applied science, it is not surprising that worker teachers are no longer heard of. They would have become more important had the concept of a general education been pursued and more serious attention been given to developing a curriculum related to the more immediate needs of the local society. Here again was a proposal which found echoes among numbers of educators in different countries, but which seems never to have been taken theoretically beyond assertions that such teachers would be a good thing. The few articles devoted to worker teachers stayed within the familiar generalisations:

worker-teachers are the most vigorous and militant revolutionary force among the ranks of the teachers ...
The school leadership helped ... worker-teachers to elevate their rich practical experience to the theoretical plane ...[89]

Lacking clear theoretical guidelines for integrating theoretical studies with practical work of different kinds, and pure with applied science, it is small wonder that the role of worker-teachers was unclear. It could not have been otherwise. There were, moreover, the practical problems of obtaining the right kind of workers and integrating them into the existing teaching staff which was itself confused and defensive after the attacks of the Cultural Revolution.

Now that goals have been reclarified and doing what training and experience have inculcated is again the correct political line, it is to be expected that most teachers will view the spate of refresher courses with sympathy and even enthusiasm.[90] These are intended to consolidate a basic grasp of key subjects and to improve teachers' ability to teach them. In addition, moves are being made to introduce courses in education and educational psychology into teacher training institutions.[91] Another of the weaknesses of the Cultural Revolution was that little or no attention was given to methods of teaching and learning. When curriculum was discussed, it was in terms of changing the context within which things like mathematical skills were taught. Problems were set in terms of American airmen shot down over Vietnam or the degree of exploitation suffered by poor peasants before liberation. The intrinsic difficulties of the mathematical process were ignored. It is doubtful, however, whether the present hurried and, apparently, uncritical look at foreign methods of training teachers will produce much improvement. The problems are particularly complex and evidence supporting different approaches is conflicting. Thus, attempts at cultural borrowing, should they be made, are particularly hazardous.

One other aspect of the whole movement to 'respect the teacher' and restore hierarchy in education which must not be forgotten is that it represents a backlash against the excesses by youth, and against the non-excessive moves by youth to gain more power, by the older members of Chinese society. No different from most parts of the world, the older and socially more powerful are loath to share their power and they found the experiences which followed 1966 hard to take. But it seems unlikely that the clock can ever be put back completely, though the forms in which youth will seek to expand their power again are at present indiscernible.

A Cultural Restoration

As Chan has noted, it was one of the ironies of 1966-9 that a movement claiming to be a cultural revolution produced a cultural desert. People were reduced to seeing 'four good operas', two ballets and hearing one cantata, while those bookshops which remained open had to turn their books facewise on the shelves to give a semblance of stock. At the level of theory, there was little more than a repetition of Mao's 'Yan'an Talks' and denunciations of various works. In the early stages, 'black films' were shown with sheets of instructions on how to denounce them. The genuine problem of creating viable art forms, which would really 'serve the workers and peasants', or the cause of moving towards a more communist society, were hardly formulated, much less solved. Small wonder, therefore, that the recent revival of what must accurately be described as 'bourgeois' — if, as with much of the opera and circus, it is not 'feudal' — has met with considerable enthusiasm from the entertainment-starved 'masses'.

In the arts, the cultural restoration has involved all fields. Local and Beijing operas have been revived to play to packed houses. In the theatres, a growing repertoire of new plays includes for the first time the portrayal of Party and government leaders such as Mao Zedong, Zhou Enlai, Zhu De and Mao's second wife, Yang Kaihui.[92] Foreign films, in bewildering variety, have been screened in the major cities and on television. Youth have been seen learning ballroom dancing in the parks from Kunming to Beijing, and foreign guests have again been invited to such events. Publishing has burgeoned on a wide front, from science texts to novels, and dozens of new periodicals span the arts and sciences. The publication of some of these works, like the edition of the encyclopedia, *Cihai*, has been held up since as long ago as 1965!

On another level, the Academy of Science and the Scientific and Technical Association have sprung into new life. In 1977 the latter, which has numerous scientific societies affiliated to it, organised meetings for young people to hear scientists talk about their work, and also held a forum on how best to run the Association and its affiliates.[93] In August 1977, a separate Academy of Social Sciences was established. Its Institutes (*yanjiusuo*) include Archaeology, Economics, Anthropology, History and Foreign Literature. The Institute for World Religions of this Academy held its first big meeting in April 1978, attended by some 110 academics including Zhou Yang.[94] In December 1978, in Shanghai, a Society for Research into the History of Chinese Peasant Rebellions was established. This was followed in Guangzhou by a Society for the Study of the Revolution of 1911, and later still by another in Shanghai devoted to the Study of the Taiping Regime.[95] Of more direct interest for education was the setting-up, in Beijing, of the Education Institute (*Beijing Jiaoyu Xueyuan*). Replacing two institutions scrapped during the Cultural Revolution, this institute will give advanced training to teachers and other education cadres, produce teaching materials and audio-visual aids and conduct research in educational theory.[96]

Another aspect of this cultural restoration has been the sudden increase in contacts with other countries. Foreign language institutes and departments in tertiary institutions have again been recruiting foreign staff on a big scale. Foreign specialists have been invited to give guest lectures at tertiary institutions.[97] More than 480 students and academics from different institutions in China have gone abroad to study. Recipient countries have ranged from Belgium and Bangladesh to the United States and Yugoslavia — a total of 28 countries in all.[98]

Foreign contacts have always been a sensitive issue in the People's Republic, and the Chinese Communist Party, like other such parties elsewhere, has always felt it necessary to limit them. A recent comment by Deng Xiaoping is another instance of such an attempt and a warning that restrictions are likely to continue.[99] From the point of view of the questions raised in this chapter, the result of increased foreign contact would seem likely to be a strengthening of the high technology, urban-style tendencies in education characteristic of the 'four modernisations' programme in general. It is unlikely to further any of the tendencies put forward by the Cultural Revolution. Of course, it is possible that really widespread and free contact could expose China to the discussions of European-American marxists and radical educators. But such people are few and at present relatively uninfluential. They, therefore, pose little threat to present Chinese policies were such unlikely exposure to take place.

Political Education

The Cultural Revolution must be considered the longest and the most powerful, so far, of a series of movements (*yundong*) typifying Mao's style of political education.[100] It continued and developed forms which had already been used in previous movements. Study groups pored over Central Committee directives, *Renmin Ribao* and *Hongqi* editorials, or passages from the marxist classics and the works of Mao. The newly distributed 'little red book' of quotations rapidly became the prime symbol of a cult which rose to startling emotional heights and removed most 'study' from the realm of the intellectual to that of ritual and faith. Red Guards were urged to emulate new heroes such as young members of the PLA, following in the footsteps of Lei Feng and Wang Jie whose exploits had been published in 1963 and 1965 respectively. As the movement developed through 1966-8, young people formed groups, or went their individual ways, with a freedom previously unknown, and unlikely, probably, to return for some time to come. They travelled widely and learnt firsthand about the diversity of their country. Many of them worked for a time far from home on their own initiative. Others, who had been forced to leave the urban areas to work in the countryside before 1966, returned to the cities to make trouble. In the course of 'struggle against and overthrow(ing) those persons in authority who (were) taking the capitalist road',[101] many people engaged in violence unknown since land reform. Wall posters, leaflets and other publications denounced, informed and argued in a new-found, if ultimately limited, freedom. The lessons which many learnt from this are becoming apparent in the revelations and changes which began after the arrest of the 'Gang of Four'. But one must remember that the pressures to conform to central authority continue and that one hears little about minority, non-conformist opinions. The Cultural Revolution was a very complex movement and much still remains to be revealed.[102]

Movements like the Anti-Confucius Campaign of 1974, or that directed against certain interpretations of the *Water Margin*, in 1975, present other problems. They clearly were, and were seen to be, largely battles between different groups within the leadership of the Party. Much of the writing was so obscure as to be unintelligible to all but the initiated. But much must have reinforced that traditional Chinese view of politics as faction-fighting and thus something which should be carefully evaluated in order that one might survive by, at least, outward compliance with the winning side. One example of this second reaction is described in the book *Red Guard*. Commenting on this elsewhere, Bennett speaks of Red Guard students' 'temporarily uncomfortable feeling of being adrift',[103] when the familiar certainties of where power lay were removed.

If one aim of Mao Zedong was to move Chinese society towards the marxist goal of a grass-roots democratic community, the major techniques and forms used would seem to contradict it. Traditional Chinese emphasis on the personal moral-political attitudes of individuals in authority[104] was combined with the use of scapegoats much in the way the Soviet Communist Party uses them. Thus, attention was focused on individuals rather than on policies and the structures within which individuals act. Such methods reinforce tyranny and encourage petty spite rather than educating people in the problems of and possibilities for change. In such conditions, the slogan, 'never forget class struggle', becomes an un-marxist encouragement to selfish strife.

It remains to be seen how different things will be from now on. Speaking to the National Education Work Conference, Deng Xiaoping said:

> There is no doubt that schools should always attach primary importance to a firm and correct political orientation. This, however, does not mean devoting many classroom hours to ideological and political education.[105]

But this is to ignore the question as to where and how one's 'political orientation' is obtained. If, as I have suggested, it is experience of social-political situations rather than simply the rhetoric which is important, there are contradictory trends to be noticed.[106] On the one hand, there has been a surprising explosion of information, on issues wider than domestic and foreign scientific and technical matters. On the other, the campaign against the 'Gang of Four' and its supporters has been conducted according to the familiar 'plot pattern' in which demonstration of loyalty to the Party and denunciation of the victim (target or *bazi*) preclude serious examination of the issues which are at stake.[107] On the one hand, in addition to new heroes who are devotees to academic study and the natural sciences, Lei Feng and his Boy Scout-type exploits are again the model for youth. Here the Confucian and the bourgeois blend rather than it being anything one might associate with the marxist vision. On the other, at the adult level, there are the demands for the rule of law. One wonders whether this will weaken the pattern of struggle meetings and thought reform which characterise both inner-Party life and prison reform.[108] Will this simply encourage an apolitical pursuit of a private career, or will it be the necessary basis for a political education leading to a different, socialist society? The increasing variety of experiences to which Chinese are becoming exposed can only complicate the picture.

Conclusion

In this chapter, I have tried to show that a major weakness of the

Cultural Revolution was its failure to theorise on education, to show the interrelations of education as knowledge, process and structure with the political-economic structures of society at large. Thus, while it was able to ask important questions about the role of schools in producing an urban élite cut off from the realities of the vast rural areas of China, the Cultural Revolution failed to understand the constraints on solving this problem. Recognising the need to integrate youth with the world of work, it remained without a theory which would show clearly how and why particular policies should be pursued. The question is not that of producing a formula which will ensure that children are schooled for communism, or drilled into 'giving their hearts to the Party',[109] but of having that 'rich totality of many determinations and relations'[110] which will enable educators of all kinds, school-teachers, Party officials, factory technicians or parents, to understand what is happening and be able, therefore, really to influence it. The Cultural Revolution put such a need on the agenda and we should understand how and why it failed to satisfy it.

There would appear to be at least three reasons why no such theory of education was forthcoming. Firstly, there is a paucity of detailed, structural analysis of problems in the Chinese Communist Party. This is perhaps related to traditional ways of thinking and has certainly been reinforced by contact with the Soviet Communist Party. Secondly, there is the way in which political movements operate and the penalities attached to defending 'wrong' ideas. This makes a majority of people very cautious about going beyond the ideas expressed already by Party leaders, *Renmin Ribao* editorials and the like. Thirdly, the terms in which goals were set suggested certain concrete steps which must to many have appeared unproblematic. In this chapter, I have suggested two main reasons for the recent reversal of policies. Firstly, for most Chinese, from the leaders of the Party to the poor peasantry, education is still regarded as a ladder to particular types of jobs. Thus a 'good school' is one, like the selective academic high schools (priority schools), which give access to the best (priority) universities. Of course, a majority of people, being realistic, aspire only to second-best vocational paths. But this does not alter their inability to conceive of education differently. Secondly, given the present leadership's economic goals and perceived need for specialists, it is not surprising that they turn to methods of training which have demonstrated this effectiveness in China and abroad. As with so many institutions around the world, education structures are self-perpetuating and governments are generally composed of, and certainly advised by, the successful products of the existing system. In China, recent events have amply demonstrated the support of the intelligentsia for those measures of the leadership which have restored its power and privilege. The Cultural Revolution has shown once again how difficult it is to change them.

Judging both from previous Chinese experience and from that of other countries which operate a selective, specialist-orientated school system, the problems posed in the Cultural Revolution will return to plague future Chinese leaders. Doctors will continue to prefer prestige surgery in comfortable Shanghai theatres to tending sick peasant families in the village. Youth in schools which 'lead nowhere' will refuse to learn what is offered and threaten delinquency of the kind which torments the secondary schools of urban Europe and North America. In the present euphoria over burgeoning cultural freedom and expanding school enrolments, it is hard to see whence the initiative will come to answer these problems or along what lines those answers might be. Marxists will, however, expect no lasting solutions which are not 'revolutionising practice'[111] and which do not include educational changes within changes in the wider society.

Notes

1. Between urban and rural areas; between industry and agriculture; and between mental and manual-labour.
2. Marx 1857-8, p. 100.
3. Mao Zedong, 17 March 1941, *SW*, Vol. III, pp. 11-13.
4. Mao Zedong, May 1941, *SW*, Vol. III, pp. 17-25.
5. Pischel 1977.
6. Mao Zedong, May 1963, Mao Zedong 1966, p. 134.
7. Mao Zedong, July 1937, Mao Zedong 1966, p. 4 and *SW*, Vol, I, p. 297. See also Price 1970, p. 13.
8. Mao Zedong, July 1937, Mao Zedong 1966, p. 4 and *SW*, Vol. I, p. 299.
9. Ibid., p. 7 and p. 299.
10. Ibid., p. 8 and p. 300.
11. A classic in this field, influenced by both Marx and Freud, is Adorno *et al.* 1969.
12. Mao Zedong, 20 August 1933, *SW*, Vol. I, p. 135.
13. Mao Zedong, 19 February 1958, *CB*, 892, p. 6
14. Lenin (1915, *Collected Works*, Vol. XXXVIII p. 360) asserts that while unity is conditional and temporary, struggle is absolute.
15. Mao Zedong c 1959, *JPRS* 1974, p. 191 and Mao Zedong 1977, p. 135 (quote from this).

16. Mao Zedong 1960 (or 1961-2), *JPRS* 1974, p. 280 and Mao Zedong 1977, p. 82 (quote from this). Translation amended for reasons of style.

17. Ibid., *JPRS* 1974, p. 269 and Mao Zedong 1977, p. 66 (quote from this).

18. Ibid., *JPRS* 1974, p. 259 and Mao Zedong 1977, p. 51 (quote from this). Translation amended for reasons of style.

19. *PR* 7, 11 February, 1977, p. 10.

20. CCP.CC, 8 August 1966, 'Decision Concerning the Great Proletarian Cultural Revolution', *PR* 33, 12 August 1966, p. 10.

21. Mao Zedong, 7 May 1966, 'Letter to Comrade Lin Biao', *CB* 888, p. 17.

22. Brugger (ed.), 1978, pp. 25-7.

23. Kraus seems to suggest Mao chose to remain within the former 'safely classic definition of class' for tactical reasons. Kraus 1977, p. 64.

24. *Jiefangjunbao* 6 June 1966, in PFLP 1966, Vol. V, p. 11.

25. Ibid., p. 12.

26. *RMRB* 4 June 1966, PFLP 1966, Vol. IV, p. 37, also *PR* 24, 10 June 1966, p. 13.

27. Munro 1977, pp. 26-56.

28. Price 1970, p. 17.

29. Munro 1977, p. 25.

30. Ibid., p. 43.

31. A Ministry of Education official recently made the link in *PR* 15, 14 April 1978, p. 14.

32. Marx 1867, p. 614.

33. Price 1974.

34. Marx, August 1866, p. 79.

35. Marx 1867, p. 621; first emphasis added. See Price 1977, pp. 70-2.

36. State Council and CCP.CC directive, 19 September 1958, Fraser 1971, pp. 558-66.

37. Mao Zedong, 21 December 1965, CB 888, p. 16. Translation amended for stylistic reasons.

38. Mao Zedong, 1964, *CB* 891, p. 47.

39. State Council and CCP.CC directive, 19 September 1958, Fraser 1971, p. 558.

40. Price 1977, pp. 184-219.

41. *RMRB* 27 June 1971, SCMP 4935, pp. 56-66.

42. *Hongqi* 9, 1972, pp. 36-45.

43. *GMRB* 26 April 1978, p. 2.

44. Some restrictions in reading had, of course, existed before the Cultural Revolution. See Price 1977, pp. 241 and 244.

45. *PR* 10, 10 March 1978, p. 27.

46. Ibid.

47. Deng Xiaoping, 7 October 1975, Chi Hsin 1977, p. 226.

48. Ibid., p. 225. Deng makes use of a large number of quotations from Mao referring to the importance of education for the economy. See ibid., p. 225, 228 and Deng Xiaoping, 2 September 1975, Chi Hsin 1977, p. 268. See also Mao Zedong, 20 August 1933, *SW*, Vol. I, p. 135; Mao Zedong 19 February 1958; *CB* 892, p. 6 (point 22 of the 'Sixty Work Methods'). There is no doubt that Mao believed in economic growth for China, as all marxists must in conditions of such poverty. But the question remains whether Mao was unable to make clear in his utterances, or was himself insufficiently clear in his own mind, about the distinctive political-educational line he was trying to make in the Cultural Revolution.

49. Deng Xiaoping, 22 April 1978, *PR* 18, 5 May 1978, p. 10.

50. Domes 1977, p. 481.

51. Mo Fei, *Gongren Ribao* 3 February 1979, *SWB* FE/6041/B11/9-11.

52. *China Aktuell,* March 1979, p. 179. Different translation in *SWB* FE/6041/B11/10.

53. Deng Xiaoping, 22 April 1978, PR 18, 5 May 1978, p. 9.

54. Ibid., p. 7.

55. Price 1970, pp. 108-220.

56. *GMRB* 26 April 1979, p. 4; *GMRB* 10 May 1979, p. 4.

57. Chan and Price (1978, p. 246) report that the Beijing Engineering University and Beijing Teachers' Training College both promised graduates employment in Beijing in 1977.

58. The translation 'key schools' used by PFLP does not convey the flavour of being given preference and ignores current (British) English usage; it thus creates confusion.

59. Liu Xiyao, *GMRB* 11 June 1978, p. 1, translated in Price 1978, pp. 40-50.

60. Ibid., p. 44.

61. Ibid.

62. In British grammar schools, French *lyceés,* etc.

63. Vocational is here taken to include those liberal arts/humanities subjects which are not normally seen as vocational, though in the full sense they clearly are.

64. *China Reconstructs* 2, 1963, pp. 8-10.

65. *Zuguo Yuekan* 11 and 12, 1965, pp. 22-30 and 30-4.

66. Price 1978, p. 112.

67. *GMRB* 10 January 1979, p. 1.

68. Of the new institutions announced, it was reported that 13 of the first and 16 of the second group were restorations of institutions closed during the Cultural Revolution. See also State Statistical Bureau 27 June 1979, p. 8 and *GMRB* 28 June 1979, p. 2.

69. Aird 1978, pp. 470-1.

70. *GMRB* 14 June 1978, p. 1, translated in Price 1978, pp. 61-3.

71. *GMRB* 14 June 1978, p. 1.

72. *PR* 31, 4 August 1978, p. 5.

73. Ibid.

74. *PR* 15, 14 April 1978, p. 15.

75. *GMRB* 14 June 1978, p. 1.

76. *Lianhuan Huabao* 4, 1978, pp. 14-16. This is a 'comic' magazine for young people.

77. *PR* 15, 14 April 1978, p. 14.

78. Ibid., p. 13.

79. This is a strange reference since the May 7th colleges were cadre schools.

80. *GMRB* 14 June 1978, p. 1.

81. *RMRB* 18 January 1974, reported in *CQ* 58, April/May 1974, pp. 414-15.

82. *GMRB* 14 June 1978, p. 1.

83. Mao Zedong, 5 July 1964, CB 888, p. 14.

84. I first noticed this in *GMRB* 19 March 1977, p. 1.

85. E.g. *GMRB* 12 April 1978, p. 1; *GMRB* 11 May 1978, p. 2; *GMRB* 5 June 1978, p. 3; *GMRB* 26 June 1978, p. 1.

86. Liu Xiyao, *GMRB* 11 June 1978, p. 1, translated in Price 1978, p. 47.

87. *PR* 21, 26 May 1978, p. 24.

88. *GMRB* 20 August 1977, p. 2; *GMRB* 18 August 1977, p. 3; *GMRB* 27 August 1978, p. 2.

89. Seybolt 1973, p. 159 and pp. 160-1. This is one of the few articles to give any details of practice.

90. E.g. *GMRB* 6 November 1977, p. 2; *GMRB* 12 November 1977, p. 2; *GMRB* 30 April 1978, p. 2.

91. *GMRB* 31 May 1978, p. 2; *GMRB* 21 December 1978, p. 4.

92. *China Pictorial* 5, 1979, pp. 1-4.

93. *China Aktuell*, June 1978, p. 321.

94. Ibid.

95. *China Aktuell*, January 1979, pp. 17-18.

96. *GMRB* 22 May 1978, p. 1.

97. *BR* 5, 2 February 1979, p. 30 gave a figure of some 100 from 12 countries who were invited to China for a one to three month lecture tour in 1978.

98. *China Aktuell*, January 1979, p. 17.

99. *China Aktuell*, March 1979, p. 180.

100. This must not be taken, of course, to imply that Mao either foresaw, controlled or approved all that was done during this movement.

101. CCP.CC, 8 August 1966, *PR* 33, 12 August 1966, p. 6.

102. Problems of political education exist at the level of exposure to an idea; understanding what one is exposed to; and conceiving an idea as possible in practice. It is still not well established just what ideas Chinese have been exposed to. Such studies as there are have largely concentrated on what can be counted and the use of certain key names and phrases. I am currently trying to go beyond this in a study of politics textbooks used in some of the schools during the seventies.

103. Bennett 1976, p. 93.

104. The idea of 'self-cultivation' in Liu Shaoqi's book translated into English as *How To Be a Good Communist*, and the phenomenon of 'clustering' mentioned above.

105. Deng Xiaoping, 22 April 1978, *PR* 18, 5 May 1978, p. 7.

106. A major experience for all Chinese is the CCP. While I accept what Pfeffer says about a tutelary, revolutionary vanguard and the possible alternatives, I am less optimistic about its ability to 'raise the consciousness of the masses' than he is. See Pfeffer 1972, pp. 620-21.

107. For the model study of this process, see Ragvald 1978.

108. It is time the subject of thought reform was taken up by writers on the political left instead of being left to writers like Lifton 1967, Bao Ruowang 1976 and Leys 1978.

109. A campaign in March 1958. See Prybla 1970, p. 258.

110. Marx 1857-8, p. 100.

111. Marx's third thesis on Feuerbach. See Marx 1845, pp. 13-14.

7 China's Foreign Relations: The Reintegration of China into the World Economy

GREG O'LEARY

The course of Chinese foreign policy since 1949 has, it seems, come full circle. The Sino-Soviet alliance and Sino-American hostility of the 1950s have almost been replaced by their opposites in the 1970s. During the intervening decade, China was hostile to both super-powers as well as to most of the major Western powers. Even within each of these 3 ten year periods there have been subtler reformulations of China's view of the world which have also had significant policy implications. Few countries, if any, have found cause for such decisive realignments during the same period. Nevertheless, of all the changes that have occurred in the period since liberation, it will be argued in this chapter that foreign policy developments since the fall of the 'Gang of Four' have been so dramatic and far-reaching in their consequences as to constitute a decisive break with China's previous international role.

Some indication of the significance of the developments concerned is gained by enumerating the more notable events. At the beginning of 1979, China and the United States established formal diplomatic relations. More importantly, during the preceding period, China reached an effective accommodation with US strategic and economic policy in most parts of the world. In the post-Mao era, three of the major reference points in China's interpretation of international reality — Vietnam, Albania and Yugoslavia — were invested with a new political meaning. In February 1979, China invaded Vietnam with whom she had enjoyed a relationship 'as close as lips and teeth' in the 1960s and the first half of the 1970s. From being the very archetype of how United States imperialism ought to be opposed, Vietnam had become 'the cat's-paw of Soviet imperialism'. Albania, which had been presented as the most outstanding example outside China of how 'revisionism' should be combated and with whom China had closest political affinity, has experienced the summary withdrawal of Chinese aid and technicians as well as a rupture in the relations between the Albanian Party of Labour and the Chinese Communist Party. In the case of Yugoslavia, designated in the 1960s as the country in which 'revisionism' had developed first and progressed furthest, it was now claimed that 'persistent revolutionary struggle over the decades... (had) ...won continuous victories in the cause of socialism'.[1]

In spite of these reversals in policy towards specific countries, China's relations with the super-powers appears, at least superficially, to have altered only marginally. Prior to Mao Zedong's death, the Soviet Union had come to place increasing emphasis on him as a personal barrier to improved Sino-Soviet relations at both Party and State levels. It was not surprising, therefore, that in the period immediately after Mao's death, protracted overtures were made to the new Chinese leadership in an attempt to construct a less hostile relationship. Anti-Chinese polemics in the Soviet press were suspended and American sources suggested that there was a tendency within the new Chinese leadership which sought a *rapprochement* with the Soviet government.[2] The Soviet Union countered that the US government was fearful of a rejuvenated Sino-Soviet alliance and was reacting predictably by offering carrots to China and sticks to the Soviet Union.[3] Whatever the truth behind these allegations and counter-allegations, it is probable that there were divisions within the Chinese and American governments at least as to how relations between the 'super-powers' and China could be reconstituted in the post-Mao era. It is also probable, when one considers previous American attempts to manipulate the Sino-Soviet relation in a direction favourable to its own perceived interests, that the United States did exert political pressure to ensure the consolidation of Sino-Soviet hostilities and Sino-American *rapprochement*. For example, after former US Defence Secretary, James Schlesinger, had suggested, in September 1976, that Chinese weaponry was inadequate to deter a Soviet threat to Xinjiang and Inner Mongolia — areas which he considered the Soviets could detach and defend from Chinese counter-attack — Kissinger warned that a massive attack on China 'would not be taken lightly'. Kissinger's statements were also apparently in response to the Soviet journalist Victor Louis' comments that China should 'find a common language' with the Soviet Union or face 'an irreversible decision'.[4]

What is certain is that the new Chinese leadership did not respond in kind to the lessening of Soviet polemics, in spite of divisions within the previous leadership about appropriate policies towards the Soviet Union.[5] Rather it intensified its anti-Soviet polemics, particularly in relation to Soviet international activities in Africa, South East Asia, the Middle East and in the development of *détente* with the United States.

These same trilateral tensions, between the US, the USSR and China, emerged in sharper focus during the period immediately prior to the exchange of diplomatic recognition by China and the US. By this time, the direction of Deng Xiaoping's domestic policies had become apparent and had posed a dilemma for American policy-makers which diplomatic recognition was, it seems, intended to resolve. While Deng's policies had laid the ground-work for fulfilling American hopes for reintegrating China into the world economy, they nevertheless eroded much of the objective basis for China's ideological disagreements with the Soviet Union.[6] In this context, the immediate price — severing diplomatic relations with Taiwan — was considered less than the potential bene-fit — diminishing the possibility of a rejuvenated Sino-Soviet alliance and incorporating China into a strategy of international capitalist revival.[7]

These manoeuvres attracted widespread comment in the major capitalist countries, being intelligible within the conceptual paradigm of 'power politics'. Nevertheless, the relationships of China with the 'super-powers' have undergone minimal alteration at this level of understanding. All that has happened is that the Soviet Union has been criticised more extensively than in the Mao era while the ties with the United States — substantially developed since 1971 — were formalised at the beginning of 1979.

Given the apparently marginal character of such developments, how is it then that a decisive break has been made in China's inter-national relations? The answer to this question exposes the limita-tions, if not the deliberate evasiveness, of the conceptual framework alluded to above, namely the attempts to analyse China's inter-national relations in terms of diplomatic considerations which exclude reference to major economic developments.

The International Environment in the Post-war Era

To establish a more realistic framework for understanding China's foreign relations, it is necessary to situate them within the context of the international political economy of the post World War II era. Fundamental to this context was the establishment by the United States, in concert with its Western allies, of a series of international agreements designed to ensure Western prosperity in the post-war period. The attention paid to reconstructing a viable international economic system was fuelled by widespread fears of a relapse, in the post-war period, into further depression — from which the West had only been rescued by government war expenditures. In the new order, the United States was ensured of pre-eminence as a result of the economic and military power with which it emerged from the war, and the new financial institutions which formalised this position. The restrictive spheres of influence of the inter-war period were replaced by an 'open door' policy providing the investment opportunities, raw materials and markets which the American economy required. The dollar alone was made directly convertible into gold to facilitate these developments.

The imposition of this system was constrained by a number of political factors — notably the reluctance of the allied powers, especially Britain, to agree with it, the gains in domestic power which the Communist-led left in the West had attained during the war, the threat of a reconsolidated Soviet economy and the potential victory of Communist guerrilla movements in post-colonial Asia.

The economic and military power of the United States enabled most of these difficulties to be overcome expeditiously. The state of the British post-war economy was no match for the independent aspirations of its leaders so that, within a few years, Anglo-American competition over Southern Europe and over oil reserves in the Middle East gave way to reluctant acceptance of American economic dominance. The left-oriented resistance movements were excluded from post-war governments, by force if necessary as in Greece where they controlled most of the country, and frequently with the compliance of the Soviet Union which was fearful of American military might as well as successful left movements not under Soviet control. The Soviet Union, however, was not overcome in Eastern Europe where the United States sought, among other things, 'the protection and furtherance of legitimate American economic rights, existing or potential'.[8] Nor was access gained to the raw materials and markets of the Soviet Union itself — upon which the receipt of American aid and the Marshall plan were made contingent.

The West was unable to exclude Asian Communists from government in Vietnam — though in the north it spent nine years trying and in the south, thirty. It was unsuccessful also in North Korea and in China, but elsewhere, especially Malaya, concerted efforts were necessary to ensure that governments remained in power which endorsed the global objectives of the new order. In most parts of the Third World, the United States was entrusted with the role of policing the new empire and it was frequently found necessary to employ methods ranging from subversion to invasion.

The incompatibility of Western economic goals with those of the emerging Soviet bloc — of which China became part after 1949 — gave rise to the ideological phenomenon of the Cold War in the 1950s which was manipulated domestically to suppress socialist tendencies and internationally to keep the Third World particularly within the designs of the new order.

Economically, the post-war arrangements were an unprecedented success and resulted in the phenomenon of the 'long boom'. The major capitalist countries exhibited substantial growth rates, averaging in the industrialised capitalist countries nearly 5 per cent per annum and in some, such as Japan, reaching double that figure. The industrial growth rate was even higher, and throughout the 1960s averaged 5.7 per cent in the industrialised countries and 10.9 per cent in Japan. Foreign trade also expanded more rapidly than economic growth, while unemployment (commonly between 1 per cent and 2 per cent) and inflation were at historically low levels. The oscillations in the business cycle were of a low amplitude and proved amenable to Keynesian demand management techniques.

In the 1970s, this picture changed rapidly, the industrialised capitalist countries averaging a growth rate between 1970 and 1976 of 3.2 per cent and the US 2.5 per cent. The average rate of industrial growth slowed markedly to 3.2 per cent in the 1970s, with the US average being only 0.9 per cent. The impasse which had been reached in the capital accumulation process was dramatically illustrated in the slowdown of gross domestic investment which declined from an average rate of increase of 5.7 per cent between 1960 and 1970 to only 0.7 per cent between 1970 and 1976, with the US figure declining from 4.8 per cent to -0.3 per cent per annum. The inflation rate had increased from the 1960s' average of 4.2 per cent to 9.3 per cent with half of the major countries concerned having rates above 10 per cent. Unemployment reached the stage where 6-8 per cent levels were common.[9]

While the causes of the 'long boom' need no elaboration for the purposes of this discussion, one feature central, paradoxically, to both the success and the collapse of the boom warrants mention. The stability of the post-war economic system, orchestrated at the end of World War II, as well as the pre-eminence of the US within that system, was predicated on the revival and continued growth of the Western European and Japanese economies. It was to them that the bulk of the US investment flowed and with them that the US conducted most of its trade. This was facilitated, in both cases, by the unique position enjoyed by the dollar within the financial structures established at Bretton Woods in 1944 and by the rapid growth of American transnational corporations. Without an expanding Europe and Japan, such developments would scarcely have been possible. These measures were, in fact, so successful that, by the end of the 1960s, Europe and Japan were presenting major challenges to the US in foreign markets which it formerly dominated as well as in the US itself. They had also attained levels of productivity which increased the reluctance of their central banks to hold inflated American dollars — eventually resulting in devaluation of the dollar and a breakdown of the Bretton Woods agreement.[10]

The 1970s have, so far, witnessed no decisive elimination of the forces which generated this situation. By 1974-5, the recession was, for the first time in the post-war period, synchronised in the advanced capitalist states, compounding the seriousness of the problem and the difficulty of recovery.

What is of most interest here is the character of the major capitalist powers' response to this crisis in the accumulation of capital. Apart from the general deflationary policies pursued domestically in order to make investment more profitable and the abandonment of much of Keynesian orthodoxy in managing the business cycle, at the international level there has been a marked shift in the destination of foreign investment generated in the major capitalist powers away from each others' economies and towards selected Third World countries. Western trade showed a similar tendency. While only a few Third World countries benefited from this change in direction — notably the Republic of Korea, Taiwan, Hong Kong, Brazil and Mexico — it resulted in greatly expanded growth rates for those concerned and the phenomenon of export-led development in them, particularly in the area of labour-intensive manufactured products.[11]

The logic of this change in investment patterns is understandable — even if its long-term prospect for success is dubious. The cheap, and generally docile, labour available in Third World countries had always made them an attractive investment proposition. The technology, organisation and communications potential of contemporary transnational corporations now made a globally integrated production strategy possible. What had also changed was the diminished possibility of profitable investment in the West as well as rapidly declining market opportunities.

The highly concentrated 'development' which has taken place in specific Third World countries — designated by the OECD as the 'Newly Industrialising Countries' — has left the development prospects of the vast majority of Third World countries unchanged, with the exception of the oil-exporting countries whose cheap product had contributed to the success of the 'long boom' and who have now managed to reverse the terms of trade under which they had been disadvantaged. The Newly Industrialising Countries are generally those in which the minimal infra-structural requirements, necessary for the forms of labour-intensive production which have developed, were already in existence. In the particular countries concerned, this had frequently been acquired because of their strategic/military interest to the West in its conduct of the Cold War.

It is within this broad context, which has resulted in realignments, as yet far from stabilised, in the character of global political and economic structures and relationships, that an explanation of the fundamental changes in China's foreign relations must be sought and indeed can be found.

Prior to exploring these changes, however, it is instructive to review the partial reintegration of the Soviet Union into Western economic strategies since the early-1960s, as in many ways the method used constitutes the model adopted by the United States in dealing with China in the 1970s. By the end of the 1950s, the Soviet Union had firmly adopted a policy of *détente* with the West rather than one of confrontation. The policy adopted by the Soviet Union was inseparable from domestic changes which the Chinese were to characterise as 'capitalist-oriented'. The Chinese interpreted such developments as an acceptance, by Khrushchev, of the international constraints imposed by the possibility of nuclear warfare and the domestic tendency towards 'revisionism'. The American response to these developments — one of cautious compliance — was predicated, not upon any softening towards socialism or the need to contain it internationally, but on a political recognition of the possibility of isolating China. In addition, it promoted those political tendencies within the Soviet leadership whose antagonism towards capitalism, both domestically and internationally, was less firm. Moreover, the threat to the operation of capitalism internationally no longer seemed to come from the possibility of a major confrontation with the Soviet Union but from fragmented assaults by liberation movements in Third World countries, to which China offered vocal support but to which the Soviet Union counselled caution lest they disturb the delicate balance of *détente*. Thus, contacts of a cultural, scientific and, to a lesser extent, economic kind with the Soviet Union were countenanced by the United States while its Cold War rhetoric was retargeted towards China. The 'containment' of China became the cornerstone of US foreign policy, partly in an effort to consolidate the Sino-Soviet dispute and partly in recognition of the fact that Soviet policy represented the lesser threat to US economic and political interests. When the recession struck in the West at the end of the 1960s, a new factor entered the Soviet-American relationship. The Soviet Union became the object of increased US trade and investment activity in order to offset the reduced opportunities in the West, even though this meant that the embargo on the export of 'strategic' goods had to be relaxed.

It is the essence of the argument of this chapter that these major changes in the international environment have been of decisive significance in determining China's relations with the world. The requirements of the international order of the post-war period, which have been sketched above, dictated United States policies and, to the extent that US influence dominated the perspectives of its allies, the policies of the West generally towards China. In the 1950s and 1960s, China was not part, in a direct economic sense, of the strategy for capitalist revival and stability. Rather, in the 1950s, it formed a subsidiary target and, in the 1960s, was the central focus of US military and strategic antagonism. This antagonism was one of the means whereby the imperatives of the economic order were impressed upon Western Europe, Japan and Third World governments. These latter consequently became the recipients of US military bases and troops in addition to investment and expanded trade. The very exclusion of China from the new order thus became a stimulus to its consolidation. The policy of the Chinese government of self-reliance in international economic terms may have been a rational response to its development potential and available resources, given a socialist orientation, but it was not a matter in which it exercised freedom of choice.

With the collapse of that order at the end of the 1960s, the rationale for China's exclusion from the capitalist economic system could no longer be sustained, since markets and investment opportunities outside the old post-war order were deemed essential to its revival. Consequently, the application of Cold War ideology to China had, also, to be jettisoned. This change was made all the more imperative by events surrounding the Vietnam war. As a number of both US government spokesmen and critical commentators made clear, the balance of payments crisis which America was experiencing was compounded by its overseas military expenditures, considerable amounts of which were rationalised by the need to contain China. As the US Treasury Secretary Connally, reputedly the architect of Nixon's 'New Economic Policy', claimed:

> I find it an impressive fact, and a depressing fact, that the persistent underlying balance of payments deficit which causes such concern is more than covered, year in and year out, by our net military expenses abroad, over and above amounts received from foreign military purchases in the United States.[12]

The Tet Offensive in 1968 made it clear that the United States would have to increase substantially its commitment to the Vietnam War in order to retain the initiative. Although this was counselled by General Westmoreland and the Joint Chiefs of Staff, a turning point in the war was reached as it became apparent that, even with the massive increase in commitment called for by the military, victory could not be guaranteed.

The critical situation facing the dollar in Europe compounded the poignancy of the choice faced by the American administration. The relative decline in the 1960s of both US industrial capacity and technological innovation, *vis-à-vis* Europe and Japan, was producing unrest over the dollar's inflated value on the Eurodollar markets. A further major military expansion in Asia, which would again be financed by letting other countries acquire increasingly unwanted dollars, would introduce uncontainable stresses into the international financial system. Johnson opted for retreat even though, as his personal military advisor General Maxwell Taylor clearly saw at the time, this would ultimately mean defeat.[13] West-moreland was recalled to Washington and his request for a further 200,000 troops was denied. In March, a major reduction in bombing was announced and Johnson stated his intention not to nominate for a further presidential term. Nixon continued the policy and announced, shortly after his assumption of office, that troop with-drawals would commence the following May. In mid-1969, the 'Nixon Doctrine' emerged as a formula for coping with America's decreased capacity to afford the kind of military support for the post-war order which had been customary. In 1968, the impending dollar crisis was staved off, 'by the willingness of European central banks to hold and accumulate paper dollars. But, in 1971, the day of reckoning arrived.'[14]

By this time, the long-standing United States surplus in its trade balance had shrunk from $6.8 billion (1964) to a deficit of $2.7 billion. The outflow of dollars had, however, continued — the balance on current account and long-term capital having become a deficit four times larger than that recorded in 1965-7. Since 1965, US imports had risen at a rate nearly double its GNP, whereas in the previous 15 years they had risen at a rate slightly lower than its GNP. The disproportionate rise after 1964 was accounted for by increases in the import of manufactured products, particularly capital and durable consumer goods from Japan, West Germany and Canada. Manufactured products had accounted for 17 per cent of total US imports in 1964 but, by 1971, had risen to 37 per cent.[15] Moreover, the prices of US exports had risen faster than those of its rivals during the period. By early-1971, these pressures produced heavy speculative attacks on the dollar and, by August, they could no longer be contained. An end to the direct convertibility of the dollar into gold was announced. World money markets closed for a week to reopen with a mixture of fixed and floating exchange rates. A wage freeze and tax surcharges on imports were implemented in the US and, by December, the 'Group of Ten' major capitalist powers had agreed on a realignment of currencies including a devaluation of the dollar.

In light of the profound influence these events had on the political and economic position of the United States in terms of its entire international relations, it would seem most unrealistic to interpret the sudden American interest in reaching an accommodation with China as in some way divorced from them. Most commentators on the subject have, however, chosen to do so and it is for this reason that the changes taking place in the international environment have been spelled out at such length. It is no doubt true that the timing of America's approach was influenced by Nixon's assessment that it would boost his re-election chances and Kissinger's assessment that it would do his global trouble-shooting image no harm, and such motivations for the commencement of the normalisation process have received widespread academic and press attention. But such an initiative would not have been possible without the international conditions, alluded to above, which provided the climate in which such personal ambitions could be realised. It is symptomatic of the poverty of the vast bulk of literature of China's foreign relations that such personal motivations receive attention almost to the exclusion of the fundamental factors which constrain or promote them.

China's Response

In so far as the American initiative in creating a post-Cold War international political economy was related to China, its success required Chinese compliance with the initiative. This, as it transpired, was not readily forthcoming since Chinese foreign policy is, like that of any other country, a function of domestic as well as international developments. Though the Chinese government responded to the diplomatic olive branches appropriately — resulting in the Shanghai communiqué in 1972 — domestic policies were not then in force which allowed for the reintegration of China into the world economy as the US sought. Even the approval of diplomatic normalisation with the United States was, it seems, resisted by the group surrounding Lin Biao who did not accept that the position of the United States had fundamentally altered.[16] But with this obstacle overcome, agreement was reached, by the time of the Tenth Party Congress in September 1973, on a basic formulation of China's conception of the international balance of class forces. By this time also, there had been considerable discussion of the critical question of trade with the West, particularly the import of modern technology and whole (turnkey) plants. The political tendency, the leadership of which was to become isolated and purged as the 'Gang of Four', advocated a far more cautious introduction of such imports than that which prevailed.

In the years after the Tenth Congress, until its dismissal in October 1976, the political tendency associated with the 'Gang of Four' exercised considerable influence in domestic policy. Its influence on foreign policy, however, would appear to have been minor, with the exception of two areas. In opposing the tendency of which Deng Xiaoping was to re-emerge as leader, parallels were drawn between the policies of Deng and the domestic policies of the Soviet Union. Consequently, the 'Gang of Four' was vocal in its opposition to the 'revisionism' of the Soviet Union. The 'Gang's' intentions were thus less concerned with foreign policy than its domestic implications. This was also the case in the other area — foreign trade — where those associated with the 'Gang of Four' held an identifiable position.

The question of foreign imports has had a significant history in the development of Chinese economic policy. The effects of importing Soviet technology and whole plants, during the First Five Year Plan, gave immense impetus to the need for 'self-reliance' and independence in economic planning and development, after Soviet aid and technicians were summarily withdrawn in 1960. In the years from 1962-5, however, there was for the first time an inflow of technology, industrial products and to some extent whole plants from Western Europe. At a time when Deng Xiaoping was influential in domestic economic decision-making and in international policies, a number of western European countries were attempting to construct trading patterns outside the American-imposed Cold War constraints. The domestic climate, which made these developments possible, changed with the Cultural Revolution when the fortunes of Deng and the policies he advocated went into recess.

As the Cultural Revolution subsided and, with it, the isolationism which had steadily reduced foreign trade from the level attained in 1966, the debate was once more taken up in earnest between those advocating domestic policies which were centred on economic development and the imports deemed necessary to fuel such development, and on the other hand, those whose orientation centred on the political question of ensuring that a basically self-reliant socialism remained the focus of any development efforts.

By 1973, Deng Xiaoping had been rehabilitated and was instrumental in formulating a policy of greatly expanded imports from the West. The radical opposition presented a number of arguments to show that such imports, of the kind and in the quantities proposed, reduced self-reliance and put China at the mercy of economic conditions in the exporting countries. It pointed out that technological imports embodied the (non-socialist) relations of production of their countries of origin and would deform China's socialist orientation. China's ability to develop its own technology, moreover, would be impaired by making modern technology from the West freely available. Imports, on the scale proposed by Deng, would serve the one interest the West had in supplying them and that was to bale it out of its economic crisis. The influence of this radical tendency on economic decisions was, however, so weak that it was unable completely to redress the growth in trade with the West begun in 1971.[17]

Deng, and those who argued along similar lines, frequently used aspects of the arguments presented by the 'radicals' and by Mao Zedong in support of their case. The import of advanced technology was not a matter of 'trailing behind others' or 'slavishly copying them'. The technology acquired would be incorporated 'in a planned and appropriate way' and the 'good things of foreign countries' had to be studied. The arguments were similar but the stress was entirely different. For Deng, such imports were regarded as indispensible to rapid development which was the centre-piece of his economic programme. 'It is', he claimed, 'by the adoption of the most advanced technologies that the industrially backward countries catch up with the industrially advanced countries in the world. We must also do the same.'[18] It was also envisaged that such an approach would entail modification of China's 'conservative' commercial practice. Deng argued, for instance, that:

We must develop production as quickly as possible and increase our exports as much as possible... The external market is very important and we must not neglect it.

In order to hasten the exploration of our coal and petroleum, it is possible that on the condition of equality and mutual benefit, and in accordance with the practices of international trade such as deferred and instalment payments, we may sign long-term contracts with foreign countries and fix several production sites where they will supply complete sets of modern equipment required by us, and we will pay for them with coal and oil we produce.[19]

In other statements, Deng's enthusiasm was less restrained. In August 1975, he was reported as having said:

We must adopt new technology. There is a problem of export policy here. We must use more things to exchange for the latest and the best equipment from foreign countries ... To import, we must develop oil production as far as possible and export as much oil as we can ... Let's export something and obtain in return some high, precise and top-notch things to accelerate the technical transformation of industry and raise labor productivity. As I have heard, with our geological prospecting techniques, we can only find poor mines. The foreigners, using comprehensive techniques, can find rich deposits. Why shouldn't we import such equipment?[20]

After Deng's removal in 1976, his policies were trenchantly attacked in the publications where the 'radicals' had the most influence. Deng's programme of 'twenty points' was seen as 'an effort to link the fate of our industry to the moods of foreign capitalists'[21] and its implementation 'would cause China to sink back into the abyss of semi-colonialism and semi-feudalism'.[22] Whether as a result of radical influence, the Western recession or generalised concern at the level of the trading deficit in 1974 (nearly $US 1 billion) and the smaller deficit in 1975, the growth of imports was curtailed in 1976. This, according to some sources, was by as much as one quarter.[23] As one commentator notes, however, the timing was remarkable:

Within six months of the time that Deng was replaced, Chinese imports began to show significant reductions of precisely the kind so keenly criticised by the radicals in the anti-Deng campaign.[24]

In the case of Japan, the most prolific supplier of technology, the value of contracts signed in 1976 for whole plants 'amounted to only about one-half of the US$ 405.6 million worth purchased in 1975'.[25]

But, with the demise of the 'Gang of Four' in October 1976, statements critical of foreign trade, of the kind which they had generated, virtually ceased. The usual reminders about 'self-reliance' and 'independence', however, were retained. With Deng Xiaoping's second rehabilitation in July 1977, the importance of foreign trade once again assumed prominence as his 'twenty points' became 'fragrant flowers' rather than the 'poisonous weeds' they had been a year before. At the same time, in fact, as his rehabilitation was being formalised at the Third Plenum of the Tenth Central Committee, the relevant sections of Beijing's administration were being urged, at a foreign trade conference, to excel in 'importing advanced technology and equipment' so as to 'increase greatly the country's foreign trade'.[26] As the political tendency personified by Deng Xiaoping has consolidated its position since that time, such policies have been reflected in China's trading statistics. Gu Ming, the Vice-Minister in charge of the State Planning Commission, reported recently that the import of technology in 1978 was 'twice the total for the five years from 1973 through 1977'.[27] In spite of the scaling down of economic plans in early-1979 and the restrictions placed on the growth of heavy industry in particular, Yu Qiuli, the Minister in charge of the State Planning Commission, reported, at the Second Session of the Fifth National People's Congress, that imports of technology and complete sets of equipment would cost ¥4,730 million ($US 2,870 million), an increase of 220 per cent over the 1978 figure.[28] While the growth in overall imports in 1978 (41 per cent)[29] was unprecedented and the projected growth for 1979 (32.4 per cent)[30] is of comparable proportions, it is apparent that the fastest growing component of imports is of a technological kind, particularly complete plants.

There have also been theoretical departures of some novelty within Marxist literature on the subject. By June 1979 it was being stated forthrightly that 'science and technology have no class nature and belong to the realm of productive forces'.[31] Presumably, by way of explanation for the hiring of Western management consultants to enhance the modernisation campaign, it was asserted that 'their (capitalist countries') ways and means of managing enterprises (such as efficiency, few managerial personnel, less overlapping labour, socialised services and rapid application of scientific research results to production)' were 'among their strong points' and 'worth studying'. 'These', it was claimed, 'belong to the science of management which has developed out of the rational organisation of productive forces in large-scale socialised production'.[32]

Although the general direction of the change since Deng's second rehabilitation has remained unaltered, there has been some inconsistency in its development. In early-1977, it was asserted that:

> We do not allow foreign capital to exploit China's resources nor do we run joint enterprises with foreign countries, still less beg them for loans. It is common knowledge that China is free from both foreign and domestic debts.[33]

By mid-1979, however, the Second Session of the Fifth National People's Congress had produced a code for the conduct of foreign investors in China in their joint ventures with Chinese investment. The code, which does not make specifications in a number of important areas — no upper limit, for example, is set to the level of foreign equity — in large part only formalises arrangements which have been in operation for some time. Most previous arrangements have been expressed in the form of compensation trading agreements, many of which, according to the Director of Hong Kong's General Chamber of Commerce, will now be convertible to equity agreements.[34]

By mid-1979, the new code constitutes the formal pinnacle of China's new preparedness to accept foreign investment. It reflects the consistent emphasis placed by Deng Xiaoping on the importance of 'truly advanced' technology. Though ill-defined at this stage, it is this advanced technology which will benefit particularly from the new legislation. Article seven allows for tax reductions or exemption for the first two or three profit-making years if 'up-to-date technology by world standards' has been supplied. More importantly, the code encourages joint ventures primarily to develop exports, though access to the Chinese market is also made possible. This provision should accommodate an increasing tendency on the part of transnational corporations to rely heavily on their global distribution and marketing networks and to become less involved in the actual production process — a trend evident throughout Asia, particularly in manufacturing production in Free Trade Zones, as a recent UNCTAD report notes.[35] Though the vagueness of the code, at present, may not reflect its final operational form, as one commentator has observed, the possibility of the foreign partner charging to the joint venture his promotion and marketing in retail outlets in the West is not ruled out. There is a 25 per cent minimum limit on the share of foreign equity and, while some Chinese sources[36] and commercial pundits have suggested the unlikelihood of China accepting more than 49 per cent foreign equity, there is nothing in the provisions at present to rule out 100 per cent foreign ownership. Other provisions include: income tax restitution for profits re-invested by the foreign partner in the venture; the right to remit profits and wages abroad and to borrow from foreign banks; the receipt of 'encouragement' (presumably preferential interest rates) for depositing foreign exchange earnings with the Bank of China; and the establishment of 'affiliated agencies outside China'.[37]

The Chairman of the board of directors, which such corporations will have, is to be appointed by the Chinese, but it is difficult to foresee how the code, as it stands, will avoid many of the disadvantages which accrue to Third World countries in joint venture arrangements. There are no provisions, for example, for monitoring transfer-pricing arrangements orchestrated by the foreign partner with its affiliates in the West[38] and no mention is made of how China will limit the widespread and institutionalised collusive practices in tendering and market allocation.[39] The dependence of such export-led development on fluctuation in Western economies has already become apparent in Asia. In the generalised recession in the West in 1975, the export economies of South Korea, Taiwan and Hong Kong were dramatically slowed down as Western production capacities provided for a larger proportion of their own requirements. China will clearly become subject to the same contradiction — receiving the foreign investment because of the recession in the West but also being reliant on an upturn in Western economies for the successful marketing of its products. There is little in the Chinese literature, moreover, which would inspire confidence that the Chinese leaders have come to terms with the major contemporary symptom of this problem, the protectionism of Western countries unable quickly to restructure their domestic economies. A rapidly expanded Chinese export structure will undoubtedly exacerbate this problem.

The extent of Chinese developments in foreign trade, in terms of both quantity and variety, are worth sketching to illustrate the dimensions of the changes which have so far taken place in the 1970s, even if they are to be overshadowed by developments which the joint venture code now make possible.

Throughout the 1960s, China's trade (import and exports) had varied between $US 2.7 billion in 1962 and $4.2 billion in the peak year of 1966. For the 1970s, the growth of trade is illustrated in Table 7.1.

As Table 7.1 indicates, China's total trade in the 1970s has grown, in current dollar terms, by nearly 450 per cent and, if the 1979 estimate is approximately correct, then it will have grown by nearly 750 per cent, almost all of the growth having taken place after 1972. If long-term trade agreements which have been signed in the two years prior to 1979 are honoured, the expansion could be even more rapid in the next six years. Agreements were signed with the Japanese for $20 billion-worth of trade over the eight years, 1978-85;[40] with Britain for $14 billion between 1979 and 1985 (two-way trade totalled $400 million in 1978);[41] with the French for total bilateral trade over the seven years ending in 1985, for $13.6 billion (about eight times the present trade volume);[42] and with a number of other countries. Negotiations have begun with the EEC and Beijing seeks imports

Table 7.1: Chinese Trade, 1970-9
$US millions, current prices

Year	Exports		Imports		Total Turnover	
1970[a]	2,050		2,240		4,290	
1971[a]	2,415		2,305		4,720	
1972[a]	3,085		2,835		5,920	
1973[a]	4,960		5,130		10,090	
1974[a]	6,515		7,490		14,005	
1975[a]	6,930		7,385		14,320	
1976[b]	7,245		6,010		13,255	
1977[b]	7,840		6,450		14,290	
1978[c]	10,114	(10,175)[d]	9,675	(11,375)[d]	18,620	(21,515)[d]
1979[d]		(11,640)[e]		(15,030)[e]		(36,670)[e]

Sources:
a. Central Intelligence Agency 1976.
b. Based on figures of Japan External Trade Organisation, quoted in *CQ* 75, September 1978, p. 704.
c. Based on figures given by Yu Qiuli at Second Session of Fifth National People's Congress, 21 June 1979, *BR* 26, 29 June 1979, p. 8 and the Ministry of Foreign Trade, quoted in *CQ* 78, June 1979, p. 425.
d. *BR* 27, 6 July 1979, p. 40 (For d. and e. below an exchange rate of $US 1.00 = RMB ¥ 1.65 has been used.)
e. *BR* 29, 20 July 1979, p. 13.

The apparent precision of the trade figures of most countries does not apply to China which publishes no comprehensive figures of its own. Various estimates may be derived from countries trading with China. These figures are generally lower than the occasional figures given by Chinese sources (see the various editions of *FEER*, *Asia Yearbook*). The trends indicated by the set of figures provided are more accurate than the figures themselves and are common to the various statistical series.

from the area of between $25 and $30 billion annually, compared to the 1978 figure of $2.7 billion.[43] The signing of the Sino-American trade pact in July 1979 is expected to increase trade from $800 million — $1 billion in 1978 (three times the 1977 figure)[44] to $5 billion in 1985.[45] It is not yet clear what effect, if any, the downward revision of growth targets, announced in April 1979, and the redirection of investment away from heavy industry in favour of light industry and agriculture, announced at the Second Session of the Fifth National People's Congress in June 1979, will have on these trade projections. Deng Xiaoping, however, assured the US Secretary of Commerce, in May 1979, that they would be unaffected.[46]

Apart from the sheer magnitude of the growth which has taken place and of that projected to 1985, the method of financing the increased trading levels has also changed dramatically. The traditional barter arrangements have given way to an acceptance of export credits, foreign loans from both governments and private sources (though as late as June 1977 Chinese officials were insisting that they would not borrow from the West)[47] and a variety of other means. Over the next five years, it is expected that China's external borrowing will be of the order of $20 billion,[48] in addition to the $20 billion already available to it as tied credits.[49] Trade with the industrialised capitalist countries rose from 46.8 per cent in 1966 to nearly 64 per cent in 1975 as a proportion of total trade. In subsequent years (to 1985), it will undoubtedly increase to a much higher proportion if current plans are fulfilled. The products traded have also expanded to include the sale of armaments to China, and those with an anti-Soviet potential, such as the British Harrier jump-jets, have given rise to strong Soviet diplomatic pressure on the countries of origin. West Germany, France and Japan have also discussed arms sales. The United States has finally committed itself to a position which neither approves nor opposes allied arms sales to China, though Washington does not sell arms to China or the Soviet Union. Secretary of State, Cyrus Vance, has announced that, 'as far as other nations are concerned, this is a matter which each of them must decide for itself'.[50]

In light of all these developments, it is realistic to situate the remarkable changes in China's economic relations within the context of the strategies adopted by Western capitalism to meet the changed circumstances of the 1970s. Although the ideological barriers built up over the previous twenty years were not broken without difficulty, they have been surmounted with remarkable rapidity and to an extent unthinkable ten years ago. The various domestic obstacles to the process have been removed even though it required the dismantling of a good deal of Chinese political orthodoxy, much of which was closely associated with Mao Zedong. As the patterns of foreign trade and its financing make clear, the possibility of China assuming its prescribed role in the new international order was dependent on the removal of the Cultural Revolutionary rump, personified by the 'Gang of Four'. The interest of the latter in foreign policy was confined to the two issues which were critical to tensions established in domestic economic structures by the demands of the new order on China — 'revisionism' and foreign trade. In both areas, the tendency associated with the 'Gang' sought, in 1975 and 1976, to redress the process already initiated during Deng Xiaoping's first rehabilitation. Its success in opposing 'revisionist' tendencies has been evaluated elsewhere in this book. Its partial success in the foreign trade area is quantified in the statistics supplied above. With the consolidation of Deng's position and views after the 'Gang's' demise, the warnings that the policies to which it was opposed would merely serve the contemporary needs of capitalism in crisis[51] have been disregarded.

Yugoslavia

While the issues surrounding the reversals in China's relations with Yugoslavia, Vietnam and Albania cannot be dealt with at length here, the above analysis does provide the basis for understanding them. In the case of Yugoslavia, it is worth recalling the basis of China's objections to that country's domestic system and international policy in the 1960s. Internationally, it was claimed, Yugoslavia, 'has become a market for imperialist dumping ... an outlet for imperialist investment ... a base from which imperialism extracts raw materials ... (and) the industrial enterprises of Yugoslavia have become assembly shops for Western monopoly capitalist companies'.[52] In summary, it was concluded that Yugoslavia had become 'an integral part of the world market of Western monopoly capital. In the financial and economic spheres it is tightly bound to the capitalist world market and has degenerated into a dependency of imperialism, particularly of US imperialism.'[53] At the domestic level, it was argued that Yugoslavia was no longer socialist — in spite of Khrushchev's insistence that it was.[54]

By 1978, however, Tito had been warmly received in China and Hua Guofeng in Yugoslavia. Party-to-Party relations had been re-established and, most importantly, the social system and international relations of Yugoslavia had been reassessed, not merely in the contemporary period but in terms which embraced the entire post-war era. The Yugoslav League of Communists, the Chinese Communist Party Central Committee claimed, 'has applied the universal truths of Marxism-Leninism to the concrete practice of Yugoslavia, ... has established a socialist self-management system suited to the conditions at home, roused the socialist initiative of the working class and other working people, and promoted the rapid development of the economy'. Internationally, it was claimed that the League 'immensely treasures and gallantly defends Yugoslavia's independence and sovereignty ... (and) resolutely combats imperialism and hegemonism'.[55] Beyond these formal reclassifications, educational, cultural and aid programmes have been established, a trade agreement signed to double bilateral trade in 1979 and considerable Chinese interest has been shown in the 'Yugoslav model' of socialism.[56]

The change which has taken place has thus been complete. While the many implications this has for the future course of Chinese policy cannot be explored here, its fundamental meaning in the context of China's changed relationships with the capitalist world are apparent. Yugoslavia has led the way, among countries formerly designated by China as the 'socialist bloc', in adjusting to the requirements of international capitalism in terms of trade and investment as well as in accommodating domestic economic structures to its needs. In pursuing similar goals at a much later stage, the current Chinese leadership is being no more than consistent in its concerted attempts to 'learn from the Yugoslav experience', even if the difficulties of rationalising the new stand in light of previous perspectives would seem insuperable.

Vietnam

China's changed attitude towards Vietnam is most obviously a function of its hostility towards the Soviet Union. In view of the new role the Chinese leadership was constructing for itself in international relations and the increased emphasis placed throughout the 1970s on opposing the Soviet Union, the Vietnamese were under intense pressure, after the American retreat, to choose either the Soviet Union or China as an ally. Neither of these countries was prepared to tolerate a mutual ally with equanimity. The Vietnamese chose the Soviet Union. Apart from the ideological tensions involved, there were perhaps sufficient reasons, even on a geopolitical level, for the Vietnamese choice. The possibility of undue influence from a neighbouring ally would have been much greater than the distant one they chose. In the interests of independence, which the Vietnamese were unlikely to abandon, and the absolute necessity for economic assistance, which the West refused to supply, the Soviet Union was the more logical of the two potential allies. The Vietnamese have subsequently supplied an ideological explanation for their differences with the Chinese Communist Party relating to inter-party differences which have a considerable history. It would be surprising, however, if the Vietnamese could not do the same with the Soviet Party were the circumstances different.

The choice of allies having been made, the inevitable tensions developed and the ethnic Chinese in Vietnam provided the flashpoint. The Chinese allege that the Vietnamese authorities engaged in persecuting the ethnic Chinese under the guise of attacking the class enemy with which there happened to be a close ethnic correlation. The Vietnamese allege that the pressure on the common border from ethnic Chinese fleeing Vietnam was inspired by Chinese fifth columnists and propaganda rumours of ethnic persecution. It is likely that both are correct. The Vietnamese invasion of Kampuchea provided the Chinese with the necessary occasion for invading Vietnam, ostensibly for reasons relating only to border security but clearly also involving their support for the Pol Pot regime. This latter support, it would seem, was predicated far less on the character of Pol Pot's domestic policies than its role as an anti-Soviet beachhead in Indochina.

Other factors were also involved. In relation to the United States, China sought to demonstrate that Soviet influence could effectively be confronted, that the Soviet Union 'feared the strong' and that the United States should assume its 'responsibility' in resisting Soviet expansion — by force if necessary. In relation to ASEAN states, the Chinese may well have intended to demonstrate that China was not prepared to tolerate Soviet-inspired expansion in their area. The net result of China's involvement in Indochina so far, with the eventual outcome still uncertain, can scarcely be comforting to the Chinese, for, though it was presumably not their intention to increase Vietnamese dependence on the Soviet Union, they have in fact done so.

Albania and the Formulation of China's World-view

The changes which have taken place in China's policy towards Albania illustrate not only the Chinese realignment, within the perspectives of international political economy, but also the articulation of an international stance which has been extensively undertaken in response to Albanian criticism. As argued in this book's precursor, comprehensive analyses of the international order have consistently been presented by successive Chinese leaders as the justification for changes in China's international behaviour. These analyses, it was argued, provide an invaluable insight into Chinese

foreign policy. In the period since October 1976, it is a quite outstanding feature of foreign policy statements that no wide-ranging
disputes, analysing such international changes, have occurred which
are comparable to those of former periods.

The conceptualisation of the international order which has
spanned the period under review is that enunciated by Deng
Xiaoping at the United Nations in 1974.[57] In Deng's formulation,
there was a tripartite division of the world. The First World was
constituted by the two super-powers — the United States and the
Soviet Union. The features which they were considered to have in
common included their attempts to seek world hegemony, to bring
'the developing countries of Asia, Africa and Latin America under
their control' and 'to bully the developed countries'. Together, they
were regarded as the 'biggest international exploiters and oppressors
of today' and, as such, constituted 'the source of a new world war'.
The political, military and economic oppression conducted by both
countries was said to be grounded in a common cause — the monopoly capitalism which was the basis of their social systems. Thus, the
more limited behavioural definition of super-powers, provided in
earlier formulations, was given a class content. Subsequent Chinese
elaborations of the class basis of Soviet international behaviour have
claimed that Lenin's criteria for distinguishing capitalist countries,
which have attained the highest stage of monopoly capitalism or
imperialism, all apply to the Soviet Union. The Soviet Union was
singled out for attention as being 'especially vicious', not honouring
its words, being 'perfidious', 'self-seeking' and 'unscrupulous'.

The developed countries of both the Eastern and Western blocs
constituted the Second World. Their position was such that they
were 'in varying degrees, controlled, threatened or bullied by the one
super-power or the other', while, on the other hand, some of them
still retain colonialist relations of one form or another with Third
World countries'. Such countries were urged to recognise their
common interests with the Third World in opposing the super-
powers. In the conduct of their relations with Western 'Second
World' countries, it was apparent that the Chinese displayed a
preference for dealing with the leaders of conservative parties rather
than those of social democratic ones. These latter parties were
considered to be no less bourgeois in their class allegiances but were
less reliable in their opposition to the Soviet Union and in their
recognition of the need for defence preparations. The consolidation
of Western European economic and military unity, through the EEC

and NATO, has been given particular prominence as a means of withstanding super-power hegemony.

The Third World was not subject to geographic redefinition in Deng's formulation save for the inclusion of China in a more definitive way than previously. It was, however, argued that this collection of states, with its wide range of social systems, constituted 'a revolutionary motive force propelling the wheel of world history' and 'the main force combating colonialism, imperialism, and particularly the super-powers'. The origins of such progressive characteristics clearly did not reside in the character of the classes which were dominant in Third World states. Rather, the historical experiences of these countries — as the victims of colonialism and imperialism — were identified as the objective basis of their leadership in opposing imperialism. 'Having suffered the heaviest oppression', it was argued, 'they have the strongest desire to oppose oppression and seek liberation and development'. The economic power, accruing to Third World countries as a result of their raw materials, is also seen as a source of their unified opposition to the super-powers. Economic independence as well as political independence was advocated for Third World countries but Deng's comments, on how this might be achieved, underlined the novelty — at least in Marxist terms — of the new formulation. After a number of generalised statements about matching the meaning of independence and self-reliance to the prevailing conditions in each country, Deng stated that:

> At the present stage, a developing country that wants to develop its national economy must first of all keep its natural resources in its own hands and gradually shake off the control of foreign capital.[58]

He further argued that a 'step-by-step' resolution of the difficulties faced by many developing countries would be possible if they 'took in their own hands the production, use, sale, storage and transport of raw materials' and were able to arrange improved terms of trade for their products in relation to imports needed for their industrial and agricultural production.

Apart from the endorsement given to gradualist processes of social change in these statements, the more fundamental strategy for change which is implied is noteworthy. While an attempt was made to identify common class forces at work in generating the international behaviour of the super-powers, in the case of Third World countries there was no attempt to disguise the fact that they range from various forms of socialist societies to various forms of capitalist societies and that, in many of them, a 'comprador bourgeoisie' is the dominant class. The social change, envisaged in Deng's formulation, would seem to be the 'gradual', 'step-by-step' replacement of a comprador class by a national bourgeois one.

Only minor alterations have been made to this formulation since that time, even during the time of Deng Xiaoping's removal — a fact which reflects the lack of influence of the 'Gang of Four' over foreign policy issues. A number of criticisms of the above formulation have, however, been made by the Albanians in the context of strains introduced into the Sino-Albanian relationship after the Cultural Revolution by China's *rapprochement* with the United States, its tactical endorsement of NATO, the European Economic Community and the governments of numerous Second and Third World countries.

Domestic Albanian developments also contributed to the divorce of its world view from that of China. A series of differences occurred within the Albanian Party of Labour concerning, among other issues, the virtues of guerrilla warfare as opposed to the development of a professionally trained and highly equipped army, the extent of cultural diversity considered appropriate and the desirability of trade with the West. These issues were all resolved in a manner which consolidated the political power of the group within the leadership headed by Enver Hoxha. Most importantly, they were resolved in a way more akin to that of the 'Gang of Four' than that of Hua Guofeng or Deng Xiaoping. Guerrilla warfare was supported, cultural diversity limited and trade with the West reduced after a period of dramatic expansion up to 1975. Hoxha's political opponents were removed from office in 1975 and 1976.[59]

Thus, the issues debated corresponded in time, and to some extent in substance, with those which were in contention in China. What differed was the outcome. Once this outcome was clarified in both countries, the muted criticism, made by Albania of China's foreign policy after the announcement of Nixon's visit in 1971, was suddenly stepped up.

Geopolitical factors compound the ideological divisions between China and Albania. The situation faced by Albania in Eastern Europe is one of increasing American economic influence, not one of increasing Soviet military influence as in the global pattern of super-power development depicted by China. Relations were also strained by China's courting of Yugoslavia — Albania's arch protagonist.

The Chinese have been insistent that their world view delineates the major political tendencies operating internationally. Their perception, moreover, does coincide with their own situation in Asia where the position of the United States is far less secure than at any other time since World War II and where the expansion of a Soviet military presence is observable. In Albania, which has refused to enter into normalisation negotiations with the United States, China's world view corresponds far less neatly.

Such factors as the above cannot be considered independently of ideological differences, nor as their ultimate determinants. Nevertheless, it is clear that Albania's geopolitical position and its recent political history scarcely incline it towards an acceptance of China's view of the world.

The critique made by Albanian spokesmen, including Enver Hoxha himself,[60] charges the 'three worlds' theorists with undermining the world's revolutionary forces, lessening the opposition to imperialism — particularly the imperialism of the United States — and with disloyalty to the Marxist-Leninist movement and its ideological tradition. Hoxha has further charged that the Chinese have themselves become social-imperialists, seeking to dominate Asia and Oceania in concert with Japan.[61]

In general terms, it is argued that the Chinese formulation obscures the class character of contemporary political forces — the fundamental differences in principle between socialism and capitalism. While the Chinese were not mentioned by name until July 1978 — much in the manner of the earlier Sino-Soviet polemics — 'three worlds' theorists are reminded that the socioeconomic order of different countries forms the basis of any Marxist-Leninist classification. The division between socialist states and capitalist states is reaffirmed as fundamental to any international categorisation, so that the Chinese formulation, being premised on the dissolution of the socialist camp, is by definition, heterodox.

The Albanians are opposed to what they regard as a Chinese tendency to 'rely on one imperialist bloc or another', and to brand the Soviet Union as the 'main enemy'. For them, the two super-powers are equally dangerous. While accepting China's categorisation of the Soviet Union as 'social-imperialist' they do not accept that it is any more aggressive or dangerous than United States imperialism. Nor do they accept that the 'imperialist camp' has disintegrated as a result of Western European and Japanese rivalry with the United States and the rise of the Soviet Union as an imperialist power. That rivalries exist, they argue, does not mean that the character of the imperialist social system has changed.

In relation to the Third World, China's position is said, first, to deny the internal class structure of Third World states, and hence to promote class collaboration. Secondly, it is said to deny the imperialist exploitation of Third World states particularly by the Second World. Thirdly, it is said to promote schemes of co-operation such as the New International Economic Order which may be acceptable to imperialism because of their potential in further integrating the Third World countries into imperialist designs.

The Chinese have responded to the Albanian accusations,[62] placing great emphasis on the likelihood or inevitability of war. If, as the Chinese assert, 'the Second World countries are faced with the super-powers' growing threat of war', then it follows logically, from the position adopted by the Chinese Communist Party during the struggle for liberation and from the position of the Soviet Union in World War II, that 'it is necessary for them to strengthen unity among themselves and their unity with the Third World and other possible allies, so as to advance in the struggle against the common enemy'.[63] Since, moreover, the Soviet Union is regarded as 'the most dangerous source of world war', it is against that super-power that alliances must primarily be constructed. While the Chinese spokesmen do not acknowledge the critical importance which the 'inevitability of war' thesis has in the logic of their argument, it is clearly central to their refutations of Albania's position.

The Chinese response hinges on their perception of the Soviet Union. While they claim continued adherence to a class analysis of international politics, they argue that this should, at present, be tactically subordinated to the formation of a united front of Second and Third World states directed primarily against the most dangerous source of war, the Soviet Union. Inter-imperialist rivalries between the First and Second Worlds are so advanced, they consider, that the Second World may be 'won over' to such an anti-super-power alliance.

The differences between the Albanians and the Chinese have resulted in the withdrawal of aid and technicians by China and the recall by Albania of students training in China. In the Sino-Vietnamese conflict, the Albanians supported the Vietnamese. As a result of these disagreements with China, Albania has been the object of conciliatory approaches by the Soviet Union, but these it has rejected.

Conclusion

The 1970s have witnessed an almost universal impasse in the accumulation of capital. Declining rates of growth in the industrialised capitalist countries have accelerated their domestic and international competition for expanded markets and viable investment opportunities. The Soviet Union and its more or less willing allies have sought wider participation in and modification of the prevailing international division of labour and the pattern of world trade. Peripheral capitalist countries of the Third World have, through a variety of means, ranging from revolutionary to reactionary, sought access to the material benefits denied them at least since the colonial era. Viewed from this perspective, Chinese leaders (although a change in personnel was necessary), decided that the solution to what was perceived as domestic stagnation was to be found in an increased participation in world trade and greater access to the technology of the advanced capitalist countries.

It has been argued in this chapter that initiatives taken by capitalist powers in the West, particularly the United States, to reintegrate China into the world economy, as the long post-war boom collapsed, have by and large been successful. While the Chinese domestic political economy in the early-1970s was relatively unresponsive to these Western pressures, in the post-Mao period policies were adopted which enabled the process to be begun in earnest. This necessitated the acceptance of an economic involvement with the capitalist world system which had hitherto been deemed politically undesirable, if not unthinkable, and a restructuring of its traditional alliance patterns and international policies to an extent that they now bear little more than rhetorical resemblance to those operative in the 1950s and 1960s.

In the early-1970s, the tendency associated with the 'Gang of Four' resisted, with some success, China's incorporation into the new designs of Western capitalism. With its demise, however, new trading and investment relationships, new political alliances under the banner of opposition to social-imperialism and the severance of political ties which remained hostile to the perspectives being developed in the West, led to the institutionalisation of policies which have decisively altered China's international relations.

The implications of this development are indeed considerable, not only for China itself, where the pattern of economic development is being altered in dramatic fashion, but for the character of future development in East and South East Asia as well as the way in which these countries will, in future, relate to the developed economies of the West.

The fact that Chinese political structures were capable of responding to these external pressures with such rapidity would also seem to pose questions for the China scholar, for which no ready answers are available. How was it that a society, so vast and apparently dedicated to the construction of socialism, could so rapidly reorient its political goals in a way that seemed to imply the abandonment of many of its former views? It may be argued that there has always been a political tendency within China which sought economic development by adjusting to the requirements of capitalist growth in the West. It has been argued in this chapter that, in the 1970s, Western capitalism required China's incorporation into the world economy rather than its exclusion in order to help salvage the West's flagging fortunes. What then can be learnt about the character of Chinese politics from the fact that such a tendency could become dominant within China so quickly, when the international environment favoured it for the first time? The answers to these questions may well leave little conventional orthodoxy on the subject intact.

In terms of China's relations with the Third World, its image as a country which provided leadership for radical governments and revolutionary movements opposed to imperialism has suffered as a result of its international realignments. In Latin America, China's endorsement of the Pinochet junta in Chile, albeit limited to more or less 'correct' government-to-government relations, has decimated its credibility with the groups it purported to foster, if not lead.[64] In Africa, its new alignments have involved opposing any Soviet initiatives even though this has frequently given the appearance of supporting United States policy. In Asia, these issues are of greater substance and it is here that the most far-reaching questions about China's leadership role in the Third World are raised. Is China's leadership role in the Third World based on anti-imperialism giving way to leadership of those countries in the area which have moved furthest to integrate their economic development with that of the West? The outcome of the delicate *rapprochement* already begun with Taiwan, the complex economic relations with Hong Kong and the subtle economic relations being fashioned with other states in the region may well provide the answer in the near future.

Notes

1. *PR* 25, 23 June 1978, p. 3.
2. E.g. Senator Mansfield, following a visit to China, counselled speedy normalisation of Sino-American relations to prevent 'greater comity with the Soviet Union even at the expense of US relations'. The *Guardian* 23 November 1976, quoted in *CQ* 69, March 1977, p. 219.
3. *Pravda* 27 October 1976, quoted in *CQ* 69, March 1977, p. 210.
4. *The Times* 29 and 30 September 1976, quoted in *CQ* 68, December 1976, p. 906; *Daily Telegraph* 20 October 1976, quoted in *CQ* 69, March 1977, p. 220.
5. See Lieberthal 1977; O'Leary 1978.
6. For an interesting discussion of these issues, see Zorza, *The Guardian* 4 February 1979, p. 7.
7. China did, in fact, ease its terms on Taiwan. See Levine 1978, p. 441. US arms sales and military assistance to Taiwan increased. See Whiting 1977, p. 1034.
8. E. Stettinus, US Secretary of State, quoted in Kolko 1968, p. 167. This work and its sequel (Kolko 1972) are invaluable sources on the establishment of the new post-war order.
9. All figures from World Bank 1978, p. 77.
10. Useful studies of these developments include Block 1977; Mandel 1975; Mandel 1978; Spero 1978; Magdoff and Sweezy 1977; Schurmann 1974.
11. See McEachern and O'Leary 1979.
12. W. Connally, *US News and World Report*, 14 June 1971, p. 52.
13. See *New York Times* (ed.) 1971, p. 600.
14. Barraclough 1974, p. 17.
15. Bank for International Settlements, *42nd Annual Report*, June 1972, quoted in Robinson 1974, p. 415.
16. See O'Leary 1978.
17. See Table 7.1
18. *SPRCM* 926, pp. 22-3.
19. Ibid., pp. 23-4.
20. Ibid., pp. 29-30.
21. *Xuexi yu Pipan* 4, 1976, p. 30.
22. Gong Xiaowen, *Xuexi yu Pipan* 6, 1976, p. 17.
23. General Agreement on Tariffs and Trade 1978, p. 154.
24. Morrison 1978, p. 698. In the original, the name 'Teng' was used.
25. Ibid.
26. *Dagongbao* 4 August 1977, quoted in ibid., p. 702.
27. *BR* 30, 27 July 1979, p. 9.
28. *BR* 29, 20 July 1979, p. 13.
29. *BR* 27, 6 July 1979, p. 40.
30. *BR* 29, 20 July 1979, p. 13.
31. *BR* 22, 1 June 1979, p. 9.
32. Ibid.
33. *PR* 9, 25 February 1977, p. 18.
34. *Asiaweek* 20 July 1979, p. 69.
35. UNCTAD 1978.
36. *BR* 17, 27 April 1979, p. 19, in a 'special feature' on the role of foreign trade

in China's economy. An interview with the Minister of Foreign Trade, Li Qiang, is included.
37. *FEER* 20 July 1979, pp. 50-1.
38. UNCTAD 1977.
39. Newfarmer 1978, chapters III and IV.
40. *CQ* 76, December 1978, p. 950.
41. *FEER* 16 March 1979, p. 108.
42. *CQ* 77, March 1979, p. 183.
43. *FEER* 16 March 1979, p. 108.
44. *BR* 21, 25 May 1979, p. 6.
45. *FEER* 20 July 1979, p. 52.
46. *BR* 21, 5 May 1979, p. 6. There are some indications of a slowdown in new contracts. See *FEER* 16 March 1979, p. 106.
47. *CQ* 75, September 1978, p. 704.
48. *FEER* 6 July 1979, pp. 40-1.
49. Ibid., p. 42.
50. *CQ* 77, March 1979, p. 185.
51. E.g. in 1976, they argued: 'If (this great policy) was allowed to continue, would not our country become a market where the imperialists could dump their goods, a source for their raw materials, a repair and assembly facility for (their use) and somewhere they could invest? Would not our workers then become nothing more than hired labourers for foreign capitalists?' *Xuexi yu Pipan* 4, 1976, p. 30.
52. CCP.CC, 26 September 1963, PFLP 1965, pp. 164-5.
53. Ibid., p. 166.
54. Ibid., p. 145 ff.
55. *PR* 25, 23 June 1978, p. 3.
56. *CQ* 76, December 1978, p. 968. A further irony warrants mention in this context. Early in 1978, Beijing officials delegated greater responsibility to provincial and sub-provincial officials to deal with foreign businesses and simultaneously doubled foreign exchange allocations to local production units for the purchase of foreign equipment, (*FEER, Asia Yearbook 1979*, p. 174). Such decentralisation of foreign trading contact had been bitterly denounced in China's earlier criticism of Yugoslavia. Yugoslavia was said to have complied with 'Western monopoly capitalism's demand' to penetrate it. See CCP.CC, 26 September 1963, PFLP 1965, p. 163.
57. Deng Xiaoping, 10 April 1974, *PR* 15 (special supplement), 12 April 1974.
58. Ibid., p. 4.
59. For accounts of Albania's domestic developments during this period, see Pano, *FEER* 26 August 1977, pp. 34 and 39; Pano 1977 (a); Pano 1977 (b); Prifti 1977.
60. Hoxha 1976, especially pp. 158-211.
61. Hoxha 1979, pp. 38-50.
62. *PR* 45, 4 November 1977, pp. 10-41.
63. Ibid., p. 33.
64. E.g. of the hostility engendered, see Revolutionary Communist Party of Chile, 1978.

Bibliography

Adorno, T. *et al. The Authoritarian Personality*, New York, Norton, 1969

Aird, J. 'Population Growth in the People's Republic of China', in US Congress, Joint Economic Committee, 1978, pp. 439-75

Andors, S. 'The Dynamics of Mass Campaigns in Chinese History. Initiators, Leaders and Participants,in the Great Leap Forward, the Cultural Revolution and the Campaign to Criticise Lin Biao and Confucius', *Bulletin of Concerned Asian Scholars*, Vol. VIII, No. 3, October-December 1976, pp. 37-46

Ansley, C. *The Heresy of Wu Han*, Toronto, University of Toronto Press, 1971

Axilrod, E. *The Political Economy of the Chinese Revolution*, Hong Kong, Union Research Institute, 1972

Bao Ruowang (Jean Pasqualini) and Chelminski, R. *Prisoner of Mao*, Harmondsworth, Penguin Books, 1976

Barmé, G. 'Flowers or More Weeds? — Culture in China Since the Fall of the Gang of Four', *The Australian Journal of Chinese Affairs* 1, 1979, pp. 125-31

Barraclough, G. 'The End of an Era', *New York Review of Books*, Vol. XXI, No. 11, 27 June 1974, pp. 14-20

Beijing Renmin Chubanshe, *Banhao Shehuizhuyi Qiye — Pipan Xiuzhengzhuyi Ban Qiye Luxian*, (*Run Socialist Enterprises Well — Denounce the Revisionist Line on Running Enterprises*), Beijing, 1974

_____*Xue Yidian Zhengzhi Jingjixue*, (*Study Some Political Economy*), Beijing, 1976

Bennett, G. *Yundong: Mass Campaigns in Chinese Communist Leadership*, Berkeley, California, University of California, Center for Chinese Studies, *China Research Monographs*, No. 12, 1976

Berliner, J. *Factory and Manager in the USSR*, Cambridge Massachusetts, Harvard University Press, 1957

Bernstein, T. 'Urban Youth in the Countryside: Problems of Adaptation and Remedies', *CQ* 69, March 1977, pp. 75-108

Bettelheim, C. and Burton, N. *China Since Mao*, New York, Monthly Review Press, 1978

Block, F. *The Origins of International Economic Disorder: A Study of US International Monetary Policy from World War II to the Present*, Berkeley, California, University of California Press, 1977

Bonavia, D. 'The Fate of the "New Born Things" of China's Cultural Revolution' *Pacific Affairs*, Vol. LI, No. 2, Summer 1978, pp. 178-93

Bowie, R. and Fairbank, J.K. *Communist China 1955-1959: Policy Documents with Analysis*, Cambridge Mass., Harvard University Press, 1962

Breth, R. *Mao's China: A Study of Socialist Economic Development*, Melbourne, Longman Cheshire, 1977

Brugger, B. *Contemporary China*, London, Croom Helm, 1977

——(ed.) *China: the Impact of the Cultural Revolution*, London, Croom Helm, 1978

——'Forces of Production, Relations of Production and the Logic of Industrialism', in Sawer (ed.), 1979

Central Intelligence Agency, *Research Aid, People's Republic of China: International Trade Handbook*, Washington D.C., October 1976

Chan, S. 'The Image of a "Capitalist Roader" — Some Dissident Short Stories in the Hundred Flowers Period', *The Australian Journal of Chinese Affairs* 2, 1979, pp. 77-102

Chan S. and Price, R. 'Teacher Training in China: A Case Study of the Foreign Languages Department of Peking Teachers' Training College', *Comparative Education*, Vol. XIV, No. 3, October 1978, pp. 243-51

Chang, P. 'The Anti Lin Piao and Confucius Campaign. Its Meaning and Purposes', *Asian Survey*, Vol. XIV, No. 10, October 1974, pp. 871-86

——'The Passing of the Maoist Era', *Asian Survey*, Vol. XVI, No. 11, November 1976, pp. 997-1011

——'Constraints on China's "New Economic Policy" ', *The World Today*, Vol XXXIII, No. 8, August 1977, pp. 312-20

Chao Kang, 'The Production and Application of Chemical Fertilizers in China', *CQ* 64, 1975, pp. 712-29

Cheng, J. 'Strategy for Economic Development', in Brugger (ed.), 1978, pp. 126-52

Chey, J. 'Chinese Cultural Policy — Liberalization?', *The Australian Journal of Chinese Affairs* 1, 1979, pp. 107-12

Chi Hsin, *The Case of the Gang of Four*, Hong Kong, Cosmos Books, 1978

Chin, S. *The Gang of Four. First Essays After the Fall*, Hong Kong University, Centre of Asian Studies, 1977

Cocks, P. 'The Role of the Party Control Committee in Communist China', Harvard University, *Papers on China*, Vol. XXII B, 1969, pp. 49-96

Commoner, B. 'How Poverty Breeds Overpopulation (and Not the Other Way Round)', *Ramparts*, August/September 1975, in Mack, Plant and Doyle (eds.) 1979. pp. 301-14

Croll, E. (a) 'A Recent Movement to Redefine the Role and Status of Women', *CQ* 71, September 1977, pp. 591-7

_____(b) 'Chiang Village: A Household Survey', *CQ* 72, December 1977, pp. 786-814

Cutler, A. Hindess B., Hirst P. and Hussain A., *Marx's Capital and Capitalism Today*, Vol. I, London, Routledge and Kegan Paul, 1977

Dernberger, R. 'The Program for Agricultural Transformation in Mainland China', *Issues and Studies*, Vol. XIV, No. 10, October 1978, pp. 59-97

Dittmer, L. 'The Succession Drama in China', *Problems of Communism*, Vol. XXVI, No. 1, January/February 1977, pp. 57-63

_____'Bases of Power in Chinese Politics: A Theory and an Analysis of the Fall of the "Gang of Four" ', *World Politics*, Vol. XXI, No. 1, October 1978, pp. 26-60

Domes, J. 'The "Gang of Four" and Hua Kuo-feng: Analysis of Political Events in 1975-76', *CQ* 71, September 1977, pp. 473-97

_____'China in 1977: Reversal of Verdicts', *Asian Survey*, Vol. XIX, No. 1, 1978, pp. 1-16

Eckstein, A. *China's Economic Revolution*, Cambridge University Press, 1977

Engels, F. 'On Authority', 1872-73, in Marx and Engels 1970, Vol. II, pp. 376-9

Erisman, A. 'China: Agriculture in the 1970s', in US Congress, Joint Economic Committee, 1975, pp. 324-49

_____'PRC: 1977 Crop Output and Its Impact on China's Agricultural Trade', *Current Scene*, Vol. XVI, Nos. 6/7, June/July 1978, pp. 20-9

Esherick, J. 'On the "Restoration of Capitalism"': Mao and Marxist Theory', *Modern China*, Vol. V, No. 1, January 1979, pp. 41-77

Esmein, J. *The Chinese Cultural Revolution*, Garden City, New York, Doubleday, 1973; Anchor Books, 1973

Evans, L. *China After Mao*, New York, Monad Press, 1978

FEER, *Asia Yearbook, 1976 and 1979*, Hong Kong, 1976 and 1979

Field, R. 'Civilian Industrial Production in the People's Republic of China: 1949-74', in US Congress, Joint Economic Committee, 1975, pp. 146-74

——Lardy, N. and Emerson, J. 'Industrial Output by Province in China, 1949-73', *CQ* 63, September 1975, pp. 409-34

Fitzgerald, S. *China and the World*, Canberra, ANU Press, 1978

Fraser, J. 'And the Walls Came Tumbling Down', *The Christian Science Monitor*, 18 June 1979, p. 11

Fraser, S. *Education and Communism in China*, London, Pall Mall Press, 1971

Friedman, E. 'The Politics of Local Models, Social Transformation and State Power in the People's Republic of China; Tachai and Teng Hsiao-p'ing', *CQ* 76, December 1978, pp. 873-90

——and Selden, M. *America's Asia: Dissenting Essays on Asian-American Relations*, New York, Vintage Books, 1971

Frolic, B. 'Reflections on the Chinese Model of Development', *Social Forces*, Vol. LVII, No. 2, December 1978, pp. 384-418

Gartman, D. 'Marx and the Labour Process: An Interpretation', *The Insurgent Sociologist*, Vol. VIII, No. 2/3, Fall, 1978, pp.97-108

General Agreement on Tariffs and Trade, *International Trade 1977/78*, Geneva, 1978

Gittings, J. 'New Material on Teng Hsiao-p'ing', *CQ* 67, September 1976, pp. 489-93

Goldman, M. *Literary Dissent in Communist China*, Cambridge, Mass., Harvard University Press, 1967

——'China's Anti-Confucius Campaign 1973-74', *CQ* 63, September 1975, pp. 435-62

——(ed.), *Modern Chinese Literature in the May Fourth Era*, Cambridge Mass., Harvard University Press, 1977

Goodman, D. 'China: The Politics of Succession', *The World Today*, Vol. XXXIII, No. 4, April 1977, pp. 131-40

Goodstadt, L. *Mao Tse-tung: The Search for Plenty*, Hong Kong, Longman, 1972

Gray, J. 'The Two Roads: Alternative Strategies of Social Change and Economic Growth in China', in Schram (ed.), 1973, pp. 109-57

Guangzhou Gongren Daibiao Dahui Zhengzhibu, *Ziliao Zhuanji (Special Edition of Materials)*, No. 3, November 1968

Gurley, J. 'Capitalist and Maoist Economic Development', in Friedman and Selden (eds.), 1971, pp. 324-56

____*China's Economy and the Maoist Strategy*, New York, Monthly Review Press, 1976

Han Suyin, *Wind in the Tower: Mao Tsetung and the Chinese Revolution, 1949-76*, Frogmore, St. Albans, Triad/Panther Books, 1978

Harding, H. 'China After Mao', *Problems of Communism*, Vol. XXVI, No. 2, March/April 1977, pp. 1-18

____'China: The First Year Without Mao', *Contemporary China*, Vol. II, No. 1, 1978, pp. 81-98

Howe, C. and Walker, K. 'The Economist', in Wilson (ed.), 1977, pp. 174-222

Hoxha, E. *Report Submitted to the 7th Congress of the Party of Labour of Albania*, 1 November 1976, Tirana, The 8 Nëntori Publishing House, 1976

____*Imperialism and the Revolution*, Tirana, The 8 Nëntori Publishing House, 1979

Hunter, N. *The Chinese League of Left-Wing Writers, Shanghai 1930-1936*, Unpublished Ph.D Thesis, Canberra, The Australian National University, 1973

JPRS, *Miscellany of Mao Tse-tung Thought (1949-1968)*, 2 vols: (JPRS 61269-1 and 2), Arlington, Virginia, 20th February 1974

Jao, Y.C. 'Trends in Economic Thinking in China', in Kirby (ed.), 1968, pp. 42-57

Kirby, E. (ed.), *Contemporary China*, Vol. VI, 1962-64, Hong Kong University Press, 1968

Klein, D. and Clark, A. *Biographic Dictionary of Chinese Communism, 1921-1965*, Cambridge Mass., Harvard University Press, 1971

Kolko, G. *The Politics of War: The World and United States Foreign Policy 1943-5*, New York, Random House, 1968

____and J. *The Limits of Power*, New York, Harper and Row, 1972

Kraus, R. *The Evolving Concept of Class in Post-liberation China*, Unpublished Ph.D dissertation, New York, Columbia University, 1974

_____'Class Conflict and the Vocabulary of Social Analysis in China', *CQ* 69, March 1977, pp. 54-74

Kuo, W. 'Hua Kuo-feng's Uncertain Future', *Issues and Studies*, Vol. XIV, No. 5, May 1978, pp. 1-24

Lee, G.W. 'Current Debate on Profits and Value in Mainland China', *Australian Economic Papers*, Vol. IV, No. 1/2, June-December 1965, pp. 72-8

Lee, H.Y. 'The Politics of Cadre Rehabilitation Since the Cultural Revolution', *Asian Survey*, Vol. XVIII, No. 9, 1978, pp. 934-55

Lee, L.O. 'The Romantic Temper of the May Fourth Period', in Schwartz (ed.) 1972, pp. 69-84

_____*The Romantic Generation of Modern Chinese Writers*, Cambridge Mass., Harvard University Press, 1973

Lenin, V. *Collected Works*, Moscow Foreign Languages Publishing House, 1961, Vol. XXXVIII, *Philosophical Notebooks*

_____*Selected Works*, Moscow, Progress Publishers, 1970, 3 vols

_____*On Literature and Art*, Moscow, Progress Publishers, 1967

_____'The State and Revolution', 1917, *SW*, Vol. II, pp. 283-376

Levine, S. 'China Policy During Carter's Year One', *Asian Survey*, Vol. XVIII, No. 5, May 1978, pp. 437-47

Levy, R. 'New Light on Mao: His Views on the Soviet Union's "Political Economy" ', *CQ* 61, March 1975, pp. 95-117

Leys, S. 'The Myth of Mao', *Dissent*, Vol. XXIV, No. 1, Winter 1977, pp. 13-21

_____'Human Rights in China', *Quadrant*, Vol. XXII, No. 11 (136), November 1978, pp. 70-6

Li Helin, *Jin Ershi Nian Zhongguo Wenyi Sichao Lun*, (*On Trends in Literature and Art in China in the Past Twenty Years*), Chongqing, Guilin, Shanghai, Hong Kong, etc. Shenghuo Shudian, 1939

Liao, K.S. 'Factional Politics After the Cultural Revolution: the Gang of Four and "Old Revolutionaries" ', in Chin (ed.) 1977, pp. 123-40

Liaoning Daxue Zhongwen Xi, Wenyi Lilun Jiaoyanshi, *Wenyi Sixiang Zhanxian Sanshi Nian*, (*Thirty Years on the Ideological Battlefront of Literature and Art*), 2nd edition, Shenyang, 1976

Lieberthal, K. 'The Foreign Policy Debate in Peking as Seen Through Allegorical Articles, 1973-76', *CQ* 71, September 1977, pp. 528-54

_____(a) *Central Documents and Politburo Politics in China*, Ann

Arbor, University of Michigan, Center for Chinese Studies, *Michigan Papers in Chinese Studies*, No. 33, 1978

____(b) 'The Politics of Modernization in the PRC', *Problems of Communism*, Vol. XXVII, No. 3, May/June 1978, pp. 1-17

Lifton, R. *Thought Reform and the Psychology of Totalism*, Harmondsworth, Penguin Books, 1967

MacDougall, C. 'The Chinese Economy in 1976', *CQ* 70, 1977, pp. 355-70

McEachern, D. and O'Leary, G. 'Capitalist Recession and Industrialisation in the Third World: The Warren Thesis', Unpublished mimeo, Adelaide, Flinders University, Sociology Discipline, July 1979

Mack, A., Plant, D. and Doyle, U. (eds.), *Imperialism, Intervention and Development*, London, Croom Helm, 1979

Magdoff, H. and Sweezy, P. *The End of Prosperity*, New York, Monthly Review Press, 1977

Mandel, E. *Late Capitalism*, London, New Left Books, 1975

____*The Second Slump*, London, New Left Books, 1978

Mao Zedong, *Selected Works*, Beijing, PFLP: Vols. I-III, 1965; Vol. IV, 1961; Vol. V, 1977; Chinese edition, Vol. III, 1964

____*Miscellany of Mao Tse-tung Thought (1949-1968)*; see *JPRS* 1974

____*Four Essays on Philosophy*, Beijing, PFLP, 1966

____*A Critique of Soviet Economics*, (trans. by M. Roberts with introduction by J. Peck), New York, Monthly Review Press, 1977. This is a translation of the same material in JPRS 1974

Marx, K. 'Theses on Feuerbach', 1845, in Marx and Engels 1970, Vol. I, pp. 13-14

____*Grundrisse*, 1857-58, Harmondsworth, Penguin Books, 1973

____'Instructions for the Delegates of the Provisional General Council. The Different Questions', August 1866, in Marx and Engels 1970, Vol. II, pp. 77-85

____*Capital*, Vol. I, 1867, Harmondsworth, Penguin Books, 1976

____'Critique of the Gotha Programme', 1875, in Marx and Engels 1970, Vol. III, pp. 9-30

____and Engels, F. *Selected Works*, 3 vols., Moscow, Progress Publishers, 1970

Miliband, R. and Saville, J. (eds.), *The Socialist Register, 1973*, London, Merlin Press, 1974

Moody, P. 'The Fall of the Gang of Four: Background Notes on the

Chinese Counter-revolution', *Asian Survey*, Vol. XVII, No. 8, August 1977, pp. 711-23

Morehouse, W. 'Notes on the Hua-tung Commune', *CQ* 67, September 1976, pp. 582-96

Morrison, K. 'Domestic Politics and Industrialization in China: The Foreign Trade Factor', *Asian Survey*, Vol. XVIII, No. 7, July 1978, pp. 687-705

Munro, D. *The Concept of Man in Contemporary China*, Ann Arbor, University of Michigan Press, 1977 and 1979

Nanjing Daxue, Zhongwen Xi, *Zuolian Shiqi Wuchanjieji Geming Wenxue*, (*Literature of Proletarian Revolution in the Period of the League of Left-wing Writers*), Nanjing, Jiangsu Wenyi Chubanshe, 1960

Nathan, A. 'Continuity and Change in Chinese Policy', *Contemporary China* Vol. II, No. 1, 1978, pp. 99-115

Neuhauser, C. 'The Chinese Communist Party in the 1960s: Prelude to the Cultural Revolution', *CQ* 32, 1967, pp. 3-36

New York Times (ed.) *The Pentagon Papers*, New York, Bantam Books, 1971

Newfarmer, R. *The International Market Power of Transnational Corporations*, Geneva, UNCTAD, 1978, ST/MD/13

Nolan, P. 'China After Mao', *Australian Left Review*, 63, March 1978, pp. 29-40

Oksenberg, M. 'The Political Leader', in Wilson (ed.) 1977, pp. 70-116

O'Leary, G. 'Chinese Foreign Policy — From "Anti-imperialism" to "Anti-hegemonism" ', in Brugger (ed.) 1978. pp. 203-52

Onate, A. 'Hua Kuo-feng and the Arrest of the "Gang of Four" ', *CQ* 75, September 1978, pp. 540-65

Pano, N. (a) 'Albania in the Era of Brezhnev and Kosygin', in Simmonds (ed.) 1977, pp. 474-94

Pano, N. (b) 'Albania in the 1970s', *Problems of Communism*, Vol. XXVI, No. 6, November/December 1977, pp. 33-43

PFLP *The Polemic on the General Line of the International Communist Movement*, Beijing, 1965

____*The Great Socialist Cultural Revolution in China*, Vols. IV and V, Beijing, 1966

____*Important Documents on the Great Proletarian Cultural Revolution in China*, Beijing, 1970

____*The Seeds and Other Stories*, Beijing, 1972

____(a)*The Tenth National Congress of the Communist Party of*

China (*Documents*), Beijing, 1973

_____(b) *Three Major Struggles on China's Philosophical Front*, (*1949-64*), Beijing, 1973

_____*Documents of the First Session of the Fourth National People's Congress of the People's Republic of China*, Beijing, 1975

_____*Documents of the First Session of the Fifth National People's Congress of the People's Republic of China*, Beijing, 1978

Perkins, D. 'Constraints Influencing China's Agricultural Performance' in US Congress, Joint Economic Committee 1975, pp. 350-65

_____'A Conference on Agriculture', *CQ* 67, September 1976, pp. 596-610

Pfeffer, R. 'Serving the People and Continuing the Revolution', *CQ* 52, October/December 1972, pp. 620-53

Pickowicz, P. (a) 'Ch'ü Ch'iu-pai and the Chinese Marxist Conception of Revolutionary Popular Literature and Art', *CQ* 70, June 1977, pp. 296-314

_____(b) 'Qu Qiubai's Critique of the May Fourth Generation: Early Marxist Literary Criticism', in Goldman (ed.) 1977, pp. 351-84

Pien Hsi, 'The Story of Tachai', in PFLP 1972, pp. 166-93

Pischel, E. 'The Teacher', in Wilson (ed.) 1977, pp. 144-73

Price, R. *Education in Communist China*, London, Routledge and Kegan Paul, 1970 and 1975, 3rd edition 1979, title changed to *Education in Modern China*

_____'Labour and Education in Russia and China', *Comparative Education*, Vol. X, No. 1, March 1974, pp. 13-23

_____*Marx and Education in Russia and China*, London, Croom Helm, 1977

_____(ed.), *The Anti-Confucius Campaign in China*, Melbourne, La Trobe University, Centre for Comparative and International Studies in Education, *Asia Studies Papers, China Series*, No. 1, 1977

_____(ed.), *Education After Mao*, Melbourne, La Trobe University, Centre for Comparative and International Studies in Education, 1978

Prifti, P. 'The Dismissal of General Begir Balluku, Albania's Minister of Defense: An Analysis', in Simmonds (ed.) 1977, pp. 495-502

Prybla, J. *The Political Economy of Communist China*, Scranton Pa., International Textbook Co., 1970

_____'Some Economic Strengths and Weaknesses of the People's

Republic of China, *Asian Survey*, Vol. XVII, No. 12, December 1977, pp. 1119-42

____'Changes in the Chinese Economy: An Interpretation', *Asian Survey*, Vol. XIX, No. 5, May 1979, pp. 409-35

Qu Qiubai, *Qu Qiubai Wenji* (*Collected Works of Qu Qiubai*), Beijing, Renmin Wenxue Chubanshe, 1953 (Vols. I-III) and 1954 (Vol. IV)

Ragvald, L. *Yao Wenyuan as a Literary Critic and Theorist: The Emergence of Chinese Zhdanovism*, Unpublished dissertation for the doctors degree in humanities, University of Stockholm, 1978

Rawski, T. 'Recent Trends in the Chinese Economy', *CQ* 53, January/March 1973, pp. 1-33

Renmin Chubanshe, *Zhonghua Renmin Gongheguo Xianfa* (*Constitution of the People's Republic of China*), Beijing, 1954

____(ed.), *Mao Zhuxi Guanyu Wenxue Yishu de Wuge Wenjian* (*Five Documents on Literature and Art by Chairman Mao*), Beijing, 1967

Renmin Wenxue Chubanshe, *Duanpian Xiaoshuo Xuan, 1977-1978.9* (*Selected Short Stories*, 1977-September 1978), Beijing, 1978

Revolutionary Communist Party of Chile, *Open Letter to the Communist Party of China*, Toronto, Norman Bethune Institute, 1978

Richman, B. *A First-hand Study of Industrial Management in Communist China*, Los Angeles, University of California, Graduate School of Business, Division of Research, 1967

____*Industrial Society in Communist China*, New York, Random House, 1969

Robinson, H. 'The Downfall of the Dollar', in Miliband and Saville (eds.) 1974, pp. 397-450

Sawer, M. (ed.), *Socialism and Participation*, Adelaide, Australasian Political Science Association, 1979

Schram, S. 'Mao Tse-tung and the Theory of Permanent Revolution', CQ 46, April/June 1971, pp. 221-44

____*Authority, Participation and Cultural Change in China*, Cambridge University Press, 1973

Schurmann, H.F. *Ideology and Organization in Communist China*, Berkeley California, University of California Press, 1966

____*The Logic of World Power*, New York, Pantheon Books, 1974

Schwartz, B. (ed.), *Reflections on the May Fourth Movement*,

Cambridge Mass., Harvard University, East Asian Research Center, 1972

Seybolt, P. *Revolutionary Education in China: Documents and Commentary*, White Plains N.J. International Arts and Sciences Press, 1973

Shehuizhuyi Zhengzhi Jingji xue Bianxie Xiaozu, *Shehuizhuyi Zhengzhi Jingji xue* (draft, 2nd printing), Shanghai, Renmin Chubanshe, June 1975

Sigurdson, J. 'Rural Industrialization in China', in US Congress, Joint Economic Committee, 1975, pp. 411-35

Simmonds, G. (ed.), *Nationalism and the USSR and Eastern Europe in the Era of Brezhnev and Kosygin*, Detroit University Press, 1977

Skinner, G. 'Vegetable Supply and Marketing in Chinese Cities', *CQ* 76, December 1978, pp. 733-93

Smil, V. 'Food in China', *Current History*, Vol. LXXII, No. 439, September 1978, pp. 69-72, 82-4

Smith, B. *Mao's Last Battle: The Next Stage*, London, China Policy Study Group, n.p.d

Solomon, R. *Mao's Revolution and the Chinese Political Culture*, Berkeley California, University of California Press, 1972

Spero, J. *The Politics of International Economic Relations*, London, George Allen and Unwin, 1978

Starr, J. 'Conceptual Foundations of Mao Tse-tung's Theory of Continuous Revolution', *Asian Survey*, Vol. XI, No. 6, June 1971, pp. 610-28

_____ 'From the Tenth Party Congress to the Premiership of Hua Kuo-feng: The Significance of the Colour of the Cat', *CQ* 67, September 1976, pp. 457-88

State Statistical Bureau, *Ten Great Years: Statistics of the Economic and Cultural Achievements of the People's Republic of China*, Beijing, PFLP, 1960

_____*Communique on Fulfilment of China's 1978 National Economic Plan*, 27th June 1979, Beijing, NCNA, 27 June 1979

Stavis, B. 'A Preliminary Model for Grain Production in China', *CQ* 65, March 1976, pp. 82-96

Swayze, H. *Political Control of Literature in the USSR, 1946-1959*, Cambridge Mass., Harvard University Press, 1962

Teiwes, F. *Politics and Purges in China: Rectification and the Decline of Party Norms 1950-1965*, White Plains NY, M.E. Sharpe, 1979

Terrill, R. *The Future of China After Mao*, Sydney, Rigby, 1978

Ting Wang, 'A Concise Biography of Hua Kuo-feng', *Chinese Law and Government*, Vol. XI, No. 1, Spring 1978

Tsou Tang, 'Mao Tse-tung Thought, the Last Struggle for Succession and the Post-Mao Era', *CQ* 71, September 1977, pp. 498-527

UNCTAD *Dominant Positions of Transnational Corporations: Use of the Transfer Pricing Mechanism*, Geneva, 1977, ST/MD/6/Rev 1

____*Transnational Corporations and the Expansion of Trade in Manufactures and Semi-manufactures*, Geneva, 1978, TD/B/C.2/197

US Congress, Joint Economic Committee, *China: A Reassessment of the Economy*, Washington D.C., US Government Printing Office, 10 July 1975

____*Chinese Economy: Post Mao*, Washington DC, US Government Printing Office, 9 November 1978

Walker, K. *Planning in Chinese Agriculture: Socialisation and the Private Sector 1956-1962*, London, Frank Cass, 1965

Watson, A. 'Industrial Management — Experiments in Mass Participation', in Brugger (ed.), 1978, pp. 171-202

____'Worker Self-management and Political Participation in China', in Sawer (ed.), 1979

Wayne, E. 'The Politics of Restaffing China's Provinces: 1976-77' *Contemporary China*, Vol. II, No. 1, 1978, pp. 116-65

Wheelwright, E. and McFarlane, B. *The Chinese Road to Socialism*, New York, Monthly Review Press, 1970

Whiting, A. 'China After Mao', *Asian Survey*, Vol. XVII, No. 11, November 1977, pp. 1028-35

Wilson, D. (ed.) *Mao Tse-tung in the Scales of History*, Cambridge University Press, 1977

Wong, C. 'Nutrient Supplies in the PRC: An Assessment of the Small-scale Phosphorus Fertilizer Industry', *Current Scene*, Vol. XVI, No. 6/7, June/July 1978, pp. 1-20

Woodward, D. 'Political Power and Gun Barrels — the Role of the PLA', in Brugger (ed.) 1978. pp. 71-94

World Bank (International Bank for Reconstruction and Development), *Development Report, 1978*, Washington DC, August 1978

Yao Wenyuan, *On the Counter-Revolutionary Double Dealer, Chou Yang*, PFLP, 1967

Yao Xueyin, *Li Zicheng*, Beijing, Zhongguo Qingnian Chubanshe; Vol. I, Pts. 1 and 2 (revised edn.) 1977; Vol. II, Pts. 1, 2 and 3,

1976

Young, G. 'Party Building and the Search for Unity', in Brugger (ed.) 1978, pp. 35-70

_____and Woodward, D. 'From Contradictions Among the People to Class Struggle: The Theories of Uninterrupted and Continuous Revolution', *Asian Survey*, Vol. XVIII, No. 9, September 1978, pp. 912-33

Zhonggong Yanjiu Zazhi she, *Liu Shaoqi Wenti Ziliao Zhuanji* (*A Special Collection of Materials on Liu Shaoqi*), Taibei, 1970

Zhongguo Caizheng Jingji Chubanshe, *Qiye Guanli Liangtiao Luxian de Douzheng* (*The Two Line Struggle in Enterprise Management*), Beijing, 1976

Zweig, D. (a) 'The Peita Debate on Education and the Fall of Teng Hsiao-p'ing', *CQ* 73, March 1978, pp. 140-59

_____(b) 'A Second Cultural Revolution: Why and Why Not?', *Contemporary China*, Vol. II, No. 2, 1978, pp. 81-91

Contributors

Bill Brugger is Reader in Politics at the Flinders University of South Australia. He formerly worked at the Beijing Second Foreign Languages Institute (1964-66) and the Contemporary China Institute, School of Oriental and African Studies, University of London (1968-71). He is the author of *Democracy and Organisation in the Chinese Industrial Enterprise: 1948-53* (1976), *Contemporary China* (1977) and a number of articles. He is the editor of the precursor of this book, *China: The Impact of the Cultural Revolution* (1978). He last visited China in 1976.

Sylvia Chan is Senior Lecturer in Chinese at the Centre for Asian Studies, Adelaide University. She lived in Beijing from 1951-72. She formerly worked at Beijing Teachers' College (1961-72). She has translated a number of English language works into Chinese and has worked on a dictionary and several English language text books published in China. Since taking up residence in Australia, she has written articles on education, literature and politics in China. She is a contributor to *China: The Impact of the Cultural Revolution*. She last visited China in 1979.

Greg O'Leary is Lecturer in Sociology at Adelaide College of the Arts and Education. He formerly worked at Adelaide University where he completed a PhD on Chinese foreign policy. A revised version of this thesis is to be published in 1980. He has written several articles on Chinese foreign policy and problems of political economy. He is also a contributor to *China: The Impact of the Cultural Revolution*. He last visited China in 1979.

Ronald F.Price is Senior Lecturer in Education at La Trobe University, Melbourne. He has worked in England, Bulgaria, Ghana and also at the Beijing Second Foreign Languages Institute (1965-67). He is the author of *Education in Communist China* (1970/79) [third edition 1979, title changed to *Education in Modern China*], *Marx and Education in Russia and China* (1977) and a number of articles on

Chinese education. He has also edited several collections of articles and primary materials on Chinese education and politics. He last visited China in 1978.

Michael Sullivan is a post-graduate student in politics at the Flinders University of South Australia. His thesis deals with the politics of 'continuous revolution' in China. He visited China in 1979.

Andrew Watson is Senior Lecturer in Chinese at the Centre for Asian Studies, Adelaide University. He formerly worked at the Xi'an Foreign Languages Institute (1965-67) and Glasgow University (1968-74). He is the author of *Living in China* (1975) and a number of articles. He has edited and translated *Transport in Transition: The Evolution of Traditional Shipping in China* (1972) and *Mao Zedong and the Political Economy of the Border Region* (1980). He is a contributor to *China: The Impact of the Cultural Revolution*. He last visited China in 1979.

Graham Young is Research Fellow in the Contemporary China Centre, Australian National University, Canberra. He formerly worked at the Flinders University of South Australia where he completed a PhD on the reconstruction of the Chinese Communist Party after the Cultural Revolution. He is a contributor to *China: The Impact of the Cultural Revolution* and the author of a number of articles on Chinese politics. He visited China in 1975.

INDEX

accounting, level of agricultural 152 – 8, *see also* economic management
Africa 233, 253, 259
agriculture *see* rural policy
Ai Qing 191
Ai Wu 191
Albania 231, 252 – 8
'anarchism' 31, 67, 69 – 70
Anhui 61
Anshan Charter 101
Anti-rightist Movement 39, 183 – 4, 186 – 8, 190
Aristotle 196
art and literature 18, 174 – 98, 208, 210, 221 – 2; All China Federation of Literary and Art Circles 183
ASEAN 252

Bai Shun 195
Ba Jin 191
Bangladesh 223
Bank of China 246
'bare-foot doctors' 149, 210
Belgium 223
Bennett, G. 224
birth control 149
'bourgeois right' 24 – 9, 42, 88, 91 – 2, 136 – 7, 157, 159 – 60, 166 – 7
Brazil 236
Bretton Woods 236
Britain 234, 247, 249
'bureaucratism' 13, 62 – 5, 196

cadres: and class struggle 25; criticism of 30 – 1, 34 – 6, 39, 44, 57, 59 – 84; dismissal of 60 – 5, 72 – 81; literary and artistic 181 – 91; new and old 29 – 30, 71 – 81; participation in manual labour 26, 135 – 6, 148 – 9
Canada 240
capitalism, international crisis of 14, 235 – 41
Changjiang (Yangtze) 144

Changzhou 'dragon' 119 – 22
Chen Xilian 33, 43
Chen Yi 181
Chen Yonggui 43, 77, 158, 167
Chen Yun 32, 38 – 40, 43, 62, 66, 135, 138, 167
Chile 259
China Reconstructs 33
China Youth News (Zhongguo Qingnianbao) 148
Chinese Agricultural Bank 142
Cihai 222
class: comprador 255; generative view of 24 – 5, 36, 136 – 7; struggle 21 – 32, 36, 38, 40 – 1, 51 – 4, 56, 64, 66, 71, 101, 135 – 7
Cold War 234 – 42
'commandism' 67, 136, 164, 167
Communist Party of China: and cadres 71 – 81; and ideological leadership 54 – 9; and masses 67 – 71; and revolution 51 – 4; commissions for inspecting discipline 61 – 3; congresses: 8th 41, 9th 95, 10th 20, 22 – 3, 27, 241, 11th 34, 52, 60 – 2, 65, 12th 44; organisation 59 – 66; Third Plenum 39 – 44, 51, 53, 56, 58, 62, 65 – 6, 84, 137 – 8, 141, 143, 155 – 7, 165, 179, 182 – 3, 190, 244
Confucius 23, 29, 41, 96, 146, 175, 177, 207, 224 – 5
Connally, J. 239
'continuous revolution' 20 – 2, 25, 36, 44 – 5, 52, 54
Creation Society 176

Dalian Car Plant 35
Dalian Industrial Institute 209
Daqing 37, 99, 101, 102, 106, 178
Dazhai 28, 33, 37, 102, 106, 135 – 6, 141, 149, 158, 160, 167
'democratic centralism' 62, 65, 68, 185
Deng Xiaoping 23 *passim*
Deng Yingchao 62

277

'dialectics' 14
'dictatorship of the proletariat' 18, 20 – 2, 24 – 7, 29, 51, 53, 57, 92, 196
Duan Yuanxing 217

Eastern Europe 234, 255
economic management: accounting 95, 102 – 4; centralisation and decentralisation 18, 26, 40, 43, 98 – 9, 105 – 6, 114 – 15, 117, 138, 142, 144 – 5, 151 – 8, 161 – 2; 'command economy' 112; contracts 109, 113, 115, 118; cooperation 99, 115, 118 – 22; growth 89 – 90, 103, 127 – 30; 'market socialism' 16 – 17, 40, 104, 106 – 7, 110 – 11, 115, 123, 127, 137, 157, 167; ownership 91 – 3, 152 – 8; planning 37, 39, 89 – 90, 99, 103 – 4, 107 – 10, 112 – 14; readjustment 40, 102; role of banks 40, 104, 110 – 11, 115 – 17, 142
economic theory 88 – 95, 102, 127 – 8, 130
education: and class structure 202 – 7, 214, 219; and modernisation 210 – 16, 223; 'combining education with productive labour' 202, 207 – 10; Deng Xiaoping on 211 – 12, 225; full-time day schools 213; Hua on 210 – 11; Mao's theory of 203 – 11, 219, 224 – 5; 'open door' schooling 202, 207 – 10; part-work 213; political 202 – 7, 223 – 5; priority schools 213 – 14, 226; 'respect the teacher' 219 – 21; selection by examination 202, 216 – 19; spare-time 213; specialisation 214 – 15, 226; tertiary 202, 208 – 10, 213 – 23, 226; worker-teachers 221
Emerson, J. 129
Engels, F. 92, 196
European Economic Community 247 – 8, 253, 255

factions: 'cover-up' 79; 'earthquake' 78 – 9; 'practice' 39, 43, 45; 'whatever' 39, 45; 'wind' 78
'February Adverse Current' 41
Feng Mu 184
Feng Youlan 194
Field, R. 129
five-year plans: 1st 89, 110, 125, 128 – 9, 242; 2nd 125; 3rd 128; 4th 128; 5th 26

foreign credit 28, 245, 249
foreign policy: *détente* 233, 237 – 8; foreign investment 245 – 7, 250 – 1; isolationism 241 – 2; self-reliance 239, 241 – 2, 244; trade 235 – 51; tripartite division of world 252 – 8
'four modernisations' 24 *passim*
'fragrant flowers' and 'poisonous weeds' 28, 34, 185 – 91, 211, 244
France 247, 249

'Gang of Five' 34
Gansu 35
Gao Gang 63, 176
Germany 240, 249
Gongren Ribao 211
Great Leap Forward 15 – 16, 32, 37 – 8, 40 – 1, 89, 104, 120, 127 – 8, 135, 137 – 8, 140, 145, 151, 159, 161, 176, 180, 183, 186, 188, 212
Greece 234
Grundrisse 203
Guangming Ribao 104, 109, 115, 184, 216, 219
Guangzhou 33, 181, 188, 222
guerrilla warfare 234, 255
Gu Ming 245
Guomindang 32, 195

Hai Rui 40 – 1, 176, 183
Haixia 177 – 8
Hegel, G. 196
Heilongjiang 35, 156
Hong Kong 14 – 15, 39, 182, 236, 246 – 7, 259
Hongqi (*Red Flag*) 33, 223
Hoxha, E. 255 – 6
Hua Guofeng 16, 20, 28 – 30, 32 – 9, 43 – 5, 51 – 2, 60, 66, 89, 102 – 4, 106, 135, 138, 156, 167, 177, 210 – 11, 250, 255
Huai River 139, 144
Huang Kecheng 62
Huang Zhen 182
Hubei 35
Hu Feng 63
Hunan 165
'hundred flowers' policy 16, 18, 90, 180, 185 – 91, 197 – 8
Hu Qiaomu 37 – 8, 43, 108 – 9, 115
Hu Yaobang 43, 56 – 7, 62, 182

industrial policy: discipline 95 – 8, 101; enterprise management 100 – 1, 105, 110 – 11, 113; 'five fixes' and

'five guarantees' 105, 123; incentives 96, 100, 104, 109, 121, 123 – 6; investment 99 – 100, 116 – 17, 121; losses due to disruption 31, 88 – 9, 93, 95, 98, 100; 'one man management' 124; participatory industrial democracy 17, 96, 122; productivity 88, 97, 106, 119, 124; profits 93 – 4, 102, 105, 109 – 11, 113, 122 – 5; quality control 98, 103; relationship with agriculture 99, 106; representative industrial democracy 17, 124; responsibility at work post 95, 98, 101, 105, 124; 'seventy points' 123, 126; specialisation 118 – 22; 'storming' 113; targets 95, 98, 103, 105, 109 – 10, 113, 122, 125; 'thirty points' 105 – 6, 109, 114, 123; trusts 18, 109, 118 – 19; 'walking on two legs' 122; waste 107 – 8, 111
Inner Mongolia 232

Japan 43, 235 – 6, 238 – 40, 244, 247, 249, 256 – 7
Jiang Qing 21, 27, 32, 167, 176, 179 – 80, 196
Ji Dengkui 43
Jiefangjunbao (*Liberation Army Daily*) 78 – 9, 207
Jilin 154 – 5
Jinan 35
Jingji Guanli (*Economic Management*) 94
Jingji Yanjiu (*Economic Research*) 109
Johnson, L. 240

Kampuchea 252
Kang Sheng 41, 180 – 1
Ke Qingshi 180 – 1
Keynes, J. 235 – 6
Khrushchev, N. 21, 42, 237, 250
Kissinger, H. 232, 241
Kong Luosun 184
Korea, Democratic People's Republic of 235
Korea, Republic of 236
kuaikuai guan 114
Kunming 222

Lardy, N. 129
Latin America 253, 259
League of Left-wing Writers 175
Legalism 177
Lei Feng 224 – 5

Lenin, V. 17, 155, 175, 188, 253
Liang Xia 194
Lianhuan Huabao 217
Lin Biao 22 – 4, 28 – 9, 34 – 6, 41, 56 – 7, 88, 92, 95, 102, 128, 140, 146, 148, 165, 241
Li Si 23
Liu Biyan 184
Liu Shaoqi 32, 36, 41, 95, 137, 161, 174, 176, 178 – 81, 183
Liu Xinwu 192 – 4, 197
Liu Xiyao 212 – 14, 216
Liu Zhidan 176
Li Xiannian 106 – 7, 150
Louis, V. 233
Luda 35
Lu Dingyi 40, 185 – 6
Lu Xinhua 195

Malaya 235
Mao Zedong: five criteria for 'revolutionary successors' 75; 'On Contradiction' 38; 'On Democratic Centralism' 65; 'On Practice' 38; 'On the Correct Handling of Contradictions among the People' 36, 187, 189 – 90; 'On the Ten Major Relationships' 28, 34, 101, 103 – 4, 106, 111; 'Reform our Study' 203; 'Rural Surveys' 203; *Selected Works* 34, 77; 'Sixty Work Methods' 205; 'Talks at the Yan'an Forum' 174 – 5; Thought 22, 36, 38 – 9, 43, 54 – 7, 59, 105, 189, 205, 207
Marshall Plan 235
Marx, K. 94, 203, 208
Mass Line 27, 64, 67 – 71, 83, 127, 166 – 7
May Fourth Movement 176
Mexico 142, 236
Middle East 233 – 4
Ming Dynasty 15, 29, 41
Mo Fei 211
Munro, D. 207

National Conferences: Army Political Work Conference 39, 60; Education Work 39, 211 – 13, 219 – 20, 225; Finance and Trade 39, 106 – 8; Learning from Dazhai in Agriculture: (1975), 28 – 9, 135 – 6, 149, (1976), 33 – 4; Science 39, 52
National People's Congress: 4th 24, 29, 44, 97, 102; 5th 20, 35, 37, 89,

102 – 3, 105 – 6, 129, 159, 245, 248
National Programme for Agricultural Development (NPAD) 135, 139 – 40
Natiònal Writers Union 183
NATO 254 – 5
'Newly Industralising Countries' 237
Nie Rongzhen 65
Nixon, R. 239 – 41, 255
Ni Zhifu 43
North China Plain 144

Oceania 256
OECD 237
Owen, R. 208

Peking Review 33, 217 – 18
Peng Dehuai 15, 32 – 3, 41, 151, 176, 183
Peng Zhen 41 – 2, 176
People's Bank of China 117
'people's democratic dictatorship' 185
People's Liberation Army 24, 79, 96, 224
'people's war' 26, *see also* guerrilla warfare
Philippines 142
Pinochet, A. 259
Pioneers 177 – 8
Pischel, E. 204
Pol Pot 252
'post-war long boom' 235 – 7, 258
'productive forces' 13, 25 – 6, 37 – 8, 52 – 3, 91 – 5, 126, 138, 156
production teams 40, 152 – 62

Qin, First Emperor of 15, 23, 41
Qinghai 139
Qu Qiubai 175

Rao Shushi 63
'red' and 'expert' 52, 130, 205
Red Guards 217, 224
relations of production: and economic base 90 – 2; and superstructure 90 – 2; capitalist 94; socialist 20, 24 – 5, 37, 53, 90 – 4
Renmin Ribao 57, 63 – 4, 101, 110, 182 – 4, 207, 223, 226
Renmin Wenxue (Peoples Literature) 191, 195
'revisionism' 13 – 14, 22, 25, 27, 29 – 30, 36, 57, 67, 112, 137, 160
'revolutionary committees' 26
rightists *see* Anti-rightist Movement

rural policy: cash crops 137, 140; centralisation 138 – 51; 'centralised policy and dispersed operations' 138; collective sector 152 – 3, 156 – 7, 164 – 5; decentralisation 152 – 65; 'Decisions on Accelerating Agricultural Development' 138, 143; fertiliser 143 – 4; fish 140; forestry 140; grain output 138 – 40; 'green revolution' 142 – 3; incomes 141, 154 – 66; investment 141 – 2; industries 143 – 4; irrigation 144 – 6; labour force 145 – 7, 149, 157, 159; livestock 163; markets 165; methods of remuneration 158 – 62; prices 141, 165; private sector 152 – 3, 162 – 5; research 142 – 3; responsibility system 161; 'sixty articles' 138, 151; specialisation 140 – 1; state farm sector 152, 156; tax 158 – 9; tractors 149 – 51; vegetables 163; yields 138 – 9
rusticated youth 147 – 9, 160, *see also* agriculture, Dazhai

Schlesinger, J. 232
Schurmann, F. 26, 40, 114, 137 – 8, 189
science 24, 37, 52, 89, 93 – 5, 211 – 13, 221 – 2, 225
Sciences, Academy of *see* Universities
Scientific and Technical Association 222
self-reliance 17, 26, 37, 97, 100, 137, 140 – 1, 151, 158, 166, 239, 241 – 2, 244
'seventies recession' 235 – 6, 259
Shanghai 88, 93, 119, 149, 154 – 6, 163, 180, 182, 195, 222, 227, 241
Shuihuzhuan (The Water Margin) 29, 177, 224
Sichuan 165
socialism: 'market socialism' *see* economic management; Socialist Education Movement 30 – 1, 136; 'socialist new things' 26, 148; 'socialist realism' 185 – 7, 193, 198
Social Sciences, Academy of *see* Universities
Society for Research into the History of Chinese Peasant Rebellions 222
Society for the Study of the Revolution of 1911 222
Society for the Study of the Taiping Régime 222

Song Baoqi 192 – 3
Song dynasty 29
Song Jiang 29
South East Asia 233, 235 – 6, 239 – 40, 247, 251 – 2, 258 – 9
Soviet Union 14, 21, 63, 108, 137, 185 – 6, 208, 212 – 13, 224, 226, 231 – 5, 237 – 8, 242, 249 – 53, 256 – 8; Communist Party of 63, 224, 226; Writers Union of 185 – 6
Stalin, J. 13, 42, 116, 186, 205
State Council 28 – 9, 32 – 3, 43, 103, 108, 142, 178, 209
State Planning Commission 101, 245

Taiwan 233, 236, 247, 259
'taking the capitalist road' 21, 25, 29, 72
Tangshan 31
Tao Zhu 161
Taylor, M. 239
Taylor system 18, 93
technology, importation of 28, 37, 40, 43, 93, 150, 242 – 6, 249
Teiwes, F. 59
Tet Offensive 239
Third World 235 – 8, 253 – 4, 256 – 9
'Three Family Village' 41
'three great differences' 24, 29, 202
Tiananmen Incident 30 – 1, 41, 194
Tianjin 35, 165
tiaotiao guan 114
Tito, J. 250
totalitarianism 13
trade unions 68, 124
Trotsky, L. 13, 63

'ultra-leftism' 13, 28, 40, 56, 96, 140, 167, 178
UNCTAD 246
'uninterrupted revolution' 20 – 2, 25, 36 – 9, 41, 44 – 5
United States 43, 223, 231 – 42, 248 – 51, 253, 257 – 8
Universities: Academy of Sciences 222; Academy of Social Sciences 222; Chinese University of Science and Technology 217; Fudan 195; Qinghua 209; Wuhan 209

value, law of 38, 106 – 10
Vance, C. 249
Vietnam 231, 235, 239 – 40, 251 – 2, 258

wage system *see* industrial policy and rural policy
Wang Dongxing 32 – 3, 39, 43
Wang Guangmei 41
Wang Haibo 93
Wang Hongwen 21 – 3, 27, 32
Wang Jie 224
Wang Meng 184
Water Margin see *Shuihuzhuan*
Weber, M. 13
Wei Guoqing 36
Weihuibao 195
Wenyibao 180, 184, 190
Westmoreland, W. 239
Women's Federation 68
World War II 234
'Wounded Generation' 191 – 7
Wu De 33, 35, 43, 183
Wu Han 41, 176, 183
Wu Jinglian 93

Xiaojinzhuang 167
Xia Yan 181 – 2
Xie Huimin 192 – 4
Xinjiang Autonomous Region 156, 232
Xu Shiyu 36

Yan'an 138, 174 – 6, 182, 192, 222; '*Defending ___*' 176
Yang Kaihui 222
Yao Wenyuan 21, 24, 32, 51, 127, 136, 176
Yao Xueyin 191
Ye Jianying 33, 60, 62, 65, 189
Yellow River (Huanghe) 139, 144
Youth League 68, 70, 192
Yugoslavia 17, 156, 223, 231, 250 – 1, 256
Yu Qiuli 43, 60, 101 – 3, 106, 245

Zhang Chunqiao 21, 24, 31, 51, 127, 136, 155, 167, 176, 206
Zhang Pinghua 30, 43, 182
Zhejiang 35
Zhou, Duke of 23
Zhou Enlai 15, 20, 22 – 4, 28 – 32, 97, 177 – 81, 188, 194, 222
Zhou Libo 191
Zhou Shulian 93
Zhou Yang 181 – 2, 184, 187, 222
Zhu De 31, 222
Zhuzhou 165
Zong Pu 193 – 4
Zunyi Conference 51

DATE DUE

GAYLORD
PRINTED IN U.S.A.